In the Way
of Nature

In the Way of Nature

Ecology and Westward Expansion in the Poetry of Anne Bradstreet, Elizabeth Bishop and Amy Clampitt

ROBERT BOSCHMAN

McFarland & Company, Inc., Publishers
Jefferson, North Carolina, and London

"The Fish," "At the Fishhouses," "Arrival at Santos" and "Santarém" and excerpts from "Sandpiper," "Filling Station," "Over 2,000 Illustrations and a Complete Concordance," "Pink Dog," "Florida," "The Map," "North Haven," "The Moose," "Brazil, January 1, 1502," "Questions of Travel," "End of March," "Crusoe in England," "The Unbeliever," "The Riverman" from *The Complete Poems 1927–1979* by Elizabeth Bishop. Copyright 1979, 1983 by Alice Helen Methfessel. Reprinted by permission of Farrar, Straus and Giroux, LLC.

Quotations from poems by Amy Clampitt from *The Collected Poems of Amy Clampitt* by Amy Clampitt, copyright 1997 by the Estate of Amy Clampitt. Introduction copyright 1997 by Mary Jo Salter. Used by permission of Alfred A. Knopf, a division of Random House, Inc.

LIBRARY OF CONGRESS CATALOGUING-IN-PUBLICATION DATA

Boschman, Robert, 1961–
    In the way of nature : ecology and westward expansion in the
poetry of Anne Bradstreet, Elizabeth Bishop and Amy Clampitt /
Robert Boschman
       p.   cm.
    Includes bibliographical references and index.

    ISBN 978-0-7864-3356-8
    softcover : 50# alkaline paper ∞

    1. American poetry — Women authors — History and criticism.
2. Ecology in literature. 3. Travel in literature. 4. Geography
in literature. 5. Nature in literature. 6. Bradstreet, Anne,
1612?–1672 — Criticism and interpretation. 7. Bishop, Elizabeth,
1911–1979 — Criticism and interpretation. 8. Clampitt, Amy —
Criticism and interpretation. I. Title.
PS147.B67   2009
811.009'9287 — dc22   2009000686

British Library cataloguing data are available

On the cover: grass background ©2009 Clipart; gold trim ©2009 Shutterstock

Manufactured in the United States of America

McFarland & Company, Inc., Publishers
  Box 611, Jefferson, North Carolina 28640
    www.mcfarlandpub.com

To my family:
My wife and visionary best friend, Sari MacPherson,
and my beloved daughters, Nina and Christy.
With you, I am at home.

Acknowledgments

This project began with an essay on Anne Bradstreet and Elizabeth Bishop written for Dr. Jeffery Donaldson's graduate studies seminar on American Literature at McMaster University. I am indebted to Dr. Donaldson for his friendship, patience, and encouragement, as well as for his inviting me to present a revised version of that initial paper at his *Telling It Slant* conference, where I met the keynote speaker, Amy Clampitt, who also encouraged me by her enthusiastic response to my ideas. A revised version of that paper thereafter appeared in Cambridge University's *Journal of American Studies*. I am grateful to *JAS* for permission to reprint revised portions of that article in chapters five and six. My research evolved from there, eventually taking into account not only Bradstreet and Bishop but also Amy Clampitt herself. A doctoral dissertation was completed with multi-year funding from the Social Sciences and Humanities Research Council of Canada (SSHRCC Doctoral Awards). To my careful, distinguished readers during this time — especially Jeffery Donaldson, Richard Morton, Joe Adamson, and John Reibetanz (University of Toronto) — I offer my appreciation and thanks.

My colleagues in English at Mount Royal have been incredibly supportive of this project. Their culture of writing, research, teaching, and collegiality has nurtured me for a decade. Two English chairs, Sabrina Reed and Lee Easton, have supported me through this project. Clifford Werier, Jerre Paquette, and Sam McKegney have provided constant feedback and advice. Without them, and without the release from teaching duties made possible by my Dean, Manuel Mertin, and the Office of Research Services at Mount Royal, this book could not have been completed. Trevor Davis and Susan Isherwood of the latter office, along with the members of the Committee for Internal Funding, have provided solid financial support and guidance. Finally, I also need to thank Robin Fisher, Mount Royal's V.P. Academic, who stepped forward with support at a critical juncture late in this project.

Contents

Preface

In Western culture, with its grounding in Judeo-Christian thinking, the Word (*Logos*) comes first. Although we must keep in mind that the *Genesis* story is itself heavily revised to fit a patriarchal ideology, the mythic moral moment when Eve, the Mother of all Living, talks Adam into eating from the Tree of the Knowledge of Good and Evil is simultaneously the point at which, in the terms of the narrative, humanity is irreversibly estranged from nature (Graves *fn.* 257). Entropic, death-loving nature swallows up the original couple whose estrangement from the world is typified by the Pauline angst of being in it but not of it. A culture that embraces this as its originary myth will naturally see pilgrimage or questing as fundamental, as it seeks to reclaim materially what it believes it once had. (Indeed, such is the thesis of Carolyn Merchant in *Reinventing Eden* [2003].) At the same time, the Word stands over against a natural order that stakes no moral claim and from which no morality can be derived. So Western culture necessarily has embraced *Logos* and rejected nature partly because nature, it is assumed, will never say, "Thou Shalt Not Kill." Outside nature, the Western person with the putatively immortal soul is, must be, alienated, guilty, yearning for the path, the road, the straight line through time that will take him or her back to God, the Source. It is easy to see how such a perspective on being in the world would need a Messiah, the One who comes to "save" the trapped and tormented individual and restore the world to its Omega point. It is also understandable that North American aboriginal cultures encountering this kind of thinking would regard it as strange. In an interview in 1991, Vine Deloria, for one, caustically observes the Puritan settlers' "determination to make the world appear to be what they believe it is. And no other group deludes themselves to this extent. You're dealing with a very aggressive people with a single thought: settle the continent" (Kirby). Comparing

1

the transatlantic vision of John Winthrop with the transcontinental vision of the Puritan generations that followed, Sacvan Bercovitch, in *The Rites of Assent: Transformations in the Symbolic Construction of America* (1993), writes:

> Having been left alone with America, the second- and third-generation Puritans felt free to incorporate Renaissance geo-mythology ... into their own vision. Explicitly and implicitly, they adapted the European images of America (land of gold, second paradise, utopia, primitivism as moral regeneration) to fit the Protestant view of progress. And having thus taken possession of the rhetoric of America, they proceeded one crucial step further. Reorienting their vision from a transatlantic to a transcontinental direction, they situated the Protestant apocalypse — or what amounted to the same thing, the Protestant road to the apocalypse — in the New World. We can hardly overestimate the importance of that astonishing Westward leap of the imagination [*Rites* 75–76].

Chapters one through three of this study focus mainly on westward expansion and the colonial legacy as these are found in Anne Bradstreet, Elizabeth Bishop, and Amy Clampitt.[1] Expansion, exploration, pilgrimage, conquest, desire, and linearity are powerfully emphasized in the works of these three writers as they grapple with and seek to revise in some instances the aggressive cultural constructs and metaphors found in the context of America, its creation, and its history. In order to try to obviate the typically linear Western mode of textual and historical analysis, chapter four cycles back again to Anne Bradstreet, followed by chapters on Bishop and Clampitt and their respective readings of nature in America. What is attempted here — which is to link and recycle the past to the present as well as to integrate as much as possible the thematic strands of culture and nature — is neither new nor flawless.

The first three chapters of this study focus on travel, geography, and cartography as underlying metaphors for the processes by which European culture has transplanted itself to the Americas. Obviously Anne Bradstreet thought about travel and geography as she set out for the New World in 1630 at the age of eighteen. The Puritan culture encoded in Bradstreet's poems often reveals how she imagines her relationship to that culture as well as to England far to the east. Bradstreet's eastward gaze is therefore worth noting. In these opening chapters, both Elizabeth Bishop and Amy Clampitt are read as poets who also gaze eastward to envision the largely

European past coming at them in their own times. Indeed, in certain instances we can see all three of these poets as facing the Atlantic to gaze eastward and into Western history, although Clampitt, as we shall see, complicates this orientation by traveling east to the island of Iona in order to look west at her own immigrant forebears in the heartland of America. Elizabeth Bishop focuses extensively on the themes of travel, desire, and geography; her preoccupations stem in part from a disrupted childhood that made it continually necessary to redefine *home* throughout adult life. Clampitt is also constantly on the move in ways that make the metaphor of travel — within the context of Western culture — significant and intriguing. More than either Bradstreet or Bishop, Clampitt perceives the landscape as a living organism subject to the actions of humankind, and like both she looks back on a ruptured early personal history. "The firstborn of Roy and Pauline Clampitt's five children," writes Mary Jo Salter in her Foreword to *The Collected Poems of Amy Clampitt* (1997), "never lost the sense of her early childhood as a paradise from which she was expelled" (xiii).

Much of what is presented in this study regarding Anne Bradstreet is given in the historical context, a context crucial to understanding not only the work of Bradstreet herself but also that of Bishop and of Clampitt, both of whom take up Bradstreet's themes and concerns. Certainly what Bishop and Clampitt do in their work vis-à-vis the origins and history of America is twofold, and intricately related to the way in which this book is organized. First, each takes up what Bishop calls the "Questions of Travel" that are rigorously — yet seemingly offhandedly — investigated throughout her poetry. In the context of Bradstreet's perilous voyage to the shores of North America, and also in the wider context of other European voyages of exploration and contact, Bishop examines, probes, and parodies the heroic traditions of travel that are elevated in the history of Western culture. Amy Clampitt carries on this work, albeit in her own singular way. For Clampitt, what she calls "transhumance" constitutes her "epic theme," her project being no less than a grand recapitulation of the westward migration of various peoples over the course of several thousand years (*CPAC* 22 and 358). This theme finds its crescendo in America's heartland, as well as California, where Clampitt's family settled and resettled in the nineteenth and early twentieth centuries.

Alongside the central theme of travel shared by Bradstreet, Bishop, and Clampitt is another that is just as important, and that indeed under-

3

lies and grows out of the whole discussion of Western culture: and that is how nature is understood and treated by such a culture. The "discovery" of the Americas by European explorers resulted in massive, irrevocable changes to the biosphere, changes that have reached crisis proportions in the twenty-first century. These changes grew directly out of the Western world view, largely globalized today, in which nature is treated as a resource to be exploited, arranged, and consumed. Such is the major focus of the last three chapters of this book.

Birds: A Concluding Remark

Birds haunt the poems of Anne Bradstreet, Elizabeth Bishop, and Amy Clampitt. Bradstreet's Philomel can be read as a poetic hybrid of the Old and New Worlds, a new kind of Old World bird emerging from the visionary forests of the eastern seaboard of North America. As such this "merry" bird beckons to Bradstreet as well as to Bradstreet's dedicated readers, giving both poet and readers a view of the risky oracular outside a culture that, in the twenty-first century, is still committed in many ways to the original Puritan project of the early seventeenth century. Although at certain points in this study it is argued that Bradstreet is a willing participant in the massive project of the Winthrop Fleet of 1630, she is far more complex than that. Indeed, the contradictions and turbulent cross-currents of Bradstreet's community in the New World are brilliantly articulated by Bradstreet herself. She is seldom single in her utterances, for which reason her poetry and her culture will be studied and debated as long as a readership continues to exist.

Elizabeth Bishop knew about the drawing power of the oracular in human experience. She also knew about birds. Her birds demonstrate her own search for transformation, as in "Over 2,000 Illustrations and a Complete Concordance" in which her speaker strains to espy signs and signals of the holy even in the tiny figures of birds that speckle the sky in the illustrations found in the big family Bible. The bird cage of "Questions of Travel" also reverberates with a wider Western cultural wish — often unfulfilled — to catch and keep the treasures, material, spiritual, and biological, that are exemplified by birds, especially the more exotic South American ones. Indeed, the symbolic birds of "Brazil, January 1, 1502" bolster this point: that birds can often represent Western dreams and projections of dreams about New World wilderness, from the jungles of Brazil to the temperate forests of what has come to be called New England, an appellation that has stuck for now.

If any one of these three American poets can be said to be poetically possessed by birds, however, it is Amy Clampitt. She reaches out to her birds as she reaches out to childhood, where the reality of the oracular lives under other names: play, wonder, curiosity, freedom, creativity, memory, the numinous. Reaching back into her personal as well as the wider cultural past, Clampitt often re-experiences the visionary and auditory power of childhood through birds.

Introduction:
A Community of Peril

The title for this introduction is taken from John Winthrop's "A Model of Christian Charity," written in 1630 on board the *Arbella* during its transatlantic crossing. While Winthrop used this phrase to underscore the risk that he and his Puritan cohorts were taking by transplanting themselves *en masse* to the new and alien land to the west, "A Community of perill" (Winthrop 287) has global implications for the twenty-first century. The global human community is one of peril: through its own actions it is itself imperiled, and it has imperiled nonhuman life along with it.

The planetary crisis occurring primarily in the form of climate change is the direct consequence of dualistic thinking about *nature* and *culture*.[2] These terms, which carry and contain a nexus of various historical ideas and which we see in play in the work of the three American writers examined in this study, continually need to be sifted, discussed, and clarified. The fact that these writers, Anne Bradstreet (1612–1672), Elizabeth Bishop (1911–1979), and Amy Clampitt (1920–1994), are women has no bearing on their distinction as poets, although it does heighten, for us as it did for them, the crucial issue of gender relative to landscape, ecology, and the biosphere. The fact that three centuries separate Bradstreet from the other two writers provides a compelling ecocritical opportunity: not only to read Bishop and Clampitt in terms of one another, which is the obvious and still unattempted task, but to do so in the larger frame of the immigrant and legacy poet, Anne Bradstreet.[3]

The human community is, whether we like to acknowledge it or not, involved and invested in the nature/culture complex, the relationship between human beings and their environment or the *biosphere*, which James Lovelock defines as "the three-dimensional geographic region where living organisms exist" (*Gaia* xi–xii). How humans see themselves as relating, or not relating, to the biosphere often dictates, at an unconscious level, the kinds of action that occur within a given geographical area. Such actions are deeply connected with what John A. Livingston describes as the "historic rejection of our own biology, which is commonly expressed as the human/Nature distinction" (Livingston 11). In America, this has been demonstrated quite dramatically since 1630, the year that Anne Bradstreet and the Winthrop Fleet arrived off the coast of what would become New England, at which time the entire human population was about 300 million persons (Gore 217). Almost 400 years later, America by itself has roughly that population out of a total global population of approximately 6.5 billion (217). Yet, disproportionately, America contributes 30 percent of the world's total carbon emissions into an atmosphere that is rapidly warming (Singer 14–20; Gore 250–52; Wilson *TFOL* 66–67).

If *biosphere* describes the three-dimensional living space every organism shares, then *ecology* is the study of the connections between living things as well as between living things and their environment. *Human ecology*, then, would analyze relationships between humans, between humans and nonhumans, and between humans and the environment. Human ecology, in other words, is the study of the relationship between human culture and nonhuman nature. Further to this, the *ecocritic* reads literary texts within the frame of ecology and human ecology; as such, he or she attempts to delineate how a specific text itself deals with nature and the human community, and how that relationship in a particular place and time actually works. Read and analyzed from this perspective, the play, poem, novel, essay, or film, given the global ecological crisis and seen in that context, does matter and does have an impact. The job of the ecocritic is to draw out that impact for everyone to see, discuss, and debate. Such is the framework in which, in this study, Bradstreet, Bishop, and Clampitt can be read and understood. The pages that follow will, in part, mount a repeated contextual inquiry into how these three poets receive, handle, and comprehend their own culture along with what Bill McKibben calls the "rupture with nature" (58).

Natura

Although the first half of this study presents chapters on Bradstreet, Bishop, and Clampitt that seek to uncover how these poets saw the west-

ward expansion of European culture primarily through travel and exploration, the word *nature* needs to be unpacked here and now. It is indeed
a term with baggage, one that Kenneth Clark cites as having "fifty-two
different meanings" (188) and that Raymond Williams argues is used wildly
and "contains ... human history" (70). In classical Latin, according to the
Chambers-Murray Latin-English Dictionary, the feminine noun *natura* literally means "blood-relationship [or] natural affinity," as in the affinity
found between members of a family or clan. The word here is primarily
relational, inclusive, open-ended and qualitative; it implies a material reality that is female, which is problematic in a patriarchal culture. Carolyn
Merchant has, in fact, addressed this issue head-on in the Introduction to
her masterful book, *The Death of Nature: Women, Ecology and the Scientific
Revolution* (1989).[4] Indeed, *natura* in the classical understanding, ends up
referring to *what is*: to the totality of existence, the universe, the cosmos.
Samuel Johnson, in his *Dictionary* of 1755, defined nature in this sense of
the word as "The state or operation of the material world." Raymond Williams states further that *natura* represents the world's "essential constitu-
tion" (68).

Few would explicitly understand the word *nature* in this way anymore; and given the ecological sensibility that has been growing at least
since the publication of Rachel Carson's *Silent Spring* in 1962, it is debatable whether we would want to embrace the concept again, or if we even
can or should. Advocates of what some call *holism,* which sees nature as
an indivisible whole that includes humans, will, if they are frank, admit
that there are grave problems attached to their idea, not the least of which
is the potential for fascism. Morris Berman has, for example, described in
detail how holism (also called *homeostasis*) could lead to totalitarianism
(286–298). It would, of course, begin quite innocently and perhaps even
in a time of crisis, such as the environmental one we are experiencing now.
Yet holism also does us the favor of evoking what Williams calls the "most
critical question ... whether nature included man":

> It is now well enough known that as a species we grew ... in our capacity
> to intervene. But we cannot understand this process, indeed cannot even
> describe it, until we are clear as to what the idea of nature includes, and in
> part whether it includes man [75].

As shall be argued here, much of the current attitude to and action against
nature operates from the premise that humans are excluded — set apart —

9

because they are unique, intelligent, conscious, technologically-gifted: in short, superior to other creatures. How this occurred and how it can be seen through the eyes of the three poets studied here constitute important themes of this book. In the background, holism beckons with the idea that humans are in fact included and that nature expresses itself through them, that, in the words of Rudolf Steiner, "The human being is a microcosm, a little world or universe" (150). This idea must be approached cautiously.

Holism appeals powerfully to the naive desire to reunite with nature, and it has powerful Romantic names attached to it, one of these being William Wordsworth, whose poetry — even a single line — draws the average reader out of his or her insulated, largely urbanized life and, imaginatively speaking, into the pastoral vales of eighteenth- and nineteenth-century northern England. All of this is wonderful and good. Undergraduate students in particular are drawn to *Lines Composed a Few Miles Above Tintern Abbey,* especially when Wordsworth hits his contemplative stride: "And I have felt / A presence that disturbs me with the joy / Of elevated thoughts" (110). This makes for rich classroom discussion, and indeed not a few students as well as teachers have felt the presence of which Wordsworth speaks, which in the same passage is described as a force that "impels / All thinking things, all objects of all thought, / And rolls through all things." Similar passages can be found in Wordsworth's long poem and spiritual autobiography, *The Prelude.* This constitutes Romantic Idealism both at its best and its most vulnerable: at its best because Wordsworth, as a worshipper of nature, reminds us of the sacrosanct quality of childhood, is a defender of children, animals, and the poor, and speaks to the profound postmodern yearning for nature, a yearning that can be traced to the late eighteenth century; at its weakest because Wordsworth describes his reunion with not wild but rather improved, already humanized nature. In the poem quoted above, his gaze extends toward and takes in the ruins of Tintern Abbey as well as "these pastoral farms, / Green to the very door" (108). Wordsworth notices the hedge-rows and the smoke rising from the small houses he looks down on. In short, Wordsworth's nature, as Raymond Williams has pointed out, is already processed (80) and has "an arranged design ... the real invention of the landlords" (154).[5]

But more than this, and to return to the danger that lurks in holism as it does in Romanticism — if nature "rolls through all things," including me and you, then inevitably as René Dubos argues, "whatever is, is right"

(Berman 287). It does not work to counter the destructive separation of humans and nature with the notion that humans can be one with nature and even constitute the highest conscious expression of nature, although such notions are often beautifully articulated; eventually someone with a propensity for pathological egomania will seize on that idea, declaring that through him (or her) all things really roll best, and the rest of us ought to listen and obey. Such a person would have no problem twisting the words and ideas of Wordsworth to his own ends. Alan Watts, his incisive critique of the view of nature historically espoused by Christianity notwithstanding, also proposes a holistic solution when he states, quite wonderfully: "I feel this whole world to be moved from the inside, and from an inside so deep that it is my inside as well" (46). Coming from Watts this is well and good; coming from, or ingested by, one who craves absolute power over others, it is dangerous.

But there is yet another reason why we cannot expect to regain a oneness with nature: it may be too late. As we shall see throughout this study but especially in the second half, both Elizabeth Bishop and Amy Clampitt at least imply that the human impact on nature may have passed the point of no return. Despite the noble optimism of Al Gore, who expresses the conviction in his public statements that we can still pull ourselves out of an irreversible warming trend by way of something like an eco Marshall Plan, other writers and thinkers share the view that we may have gone too far in the changes we have made to the biosphere. Bill McKibben, E. O. Wilson, James Lovelock, and John A. Livingston, for example, while not totally despairing, have all published dire and powerful tracts that outline the state in which we already find ourselves.[6] These writers see nature in terms that are more recognizable to a twenty-first century readership — as a separate, nonhuman, independent entity often relegated to wilderness parks and whose existence is threatened by human activity. McKibben argues in *The End of Nature* (1989), "Nature's independence *is* its meaning; without it there is nothing but us" (58), and in doing so demonstrates vividly how holism is a non-starter. In *The Creation* (2006), the deistic entomologist Wilson tries to reach an American Christian audience that would very much understand nature as a separate entity, although for different reasons, reasons that indeed make up a substantial portion of this study. For Wilson, nature is "that part of the original environment and its life forms that remains after the human impact" (*Creation* 15).

There is nothing new here, either in the definition of nature as separate from human culture or in the grave concern for the ongoing existence of what we understand nature, in this sense, to be. France's Jean Dorst, for instance, covered this terrain in his 1970 publication *Before Nature Dies*. And prior to Dorst, others such as Henry David Thoreau, John Muir, Aldo Leopold, Joseph Wood Krutch, and Rachel Carson (to name only a few) gave voice to a rising awareness of the vulnerability of nature. In the larger historical context, however, what is different is not that nature is separate — from the Neolithic period forward there is an extensive, documented record covering our diverging relationship[7] — but rather that fragile nature should be seen as separate during the current period. To McKibben, Wilson, and Roderick Nash, nature's independence is crucial to the health of the planet and it therefore needs protection and preservation, although — again — it may be too late. McKibben argues that "we [already] live in a postnatural world" (60). In *The Rights of Nature* (1989), Nash makes the case that humans have behaved with "prejudice against nature" (6) in much the same way as they have enslaved and discriminated against their own kind. He sees a revision of the relationship between humans and nature, calling it "arguably the most dramatic expansion of morality in the course of human thought" (7). Others are not so sure. Vine Deloria contends that "Developing a sense of ourselves that would properly balance history and nature and space and time is a more difficult task than we would suspect and involves a radical reevaluation of the way we look at the world around us" (59). For John A. Livingston, we are so rapidly moving towards a home planet that is essentially a park that conferring "rights" on nature not only becomes rather meaningless but also amounts to yet another means to extend Western human power over it, therefore making our dilemma even more daunting and problematic (175). Livingston is, at any rate, convinced that most creatures living in what is left of the wild "would just as soon go their own way and take their chances" (175).[8]

Livingston's position on this matter indicates just how critical this kind of discourse actually is, and it can be seen further when it is placed in a wider historical examination of the meaning of nature, especially as the term gets transported to the Americas from Europe during the period of exploration and colonization between the late fifteenth and early eighteenth centuries. When McKibben *et al.* passionately, poignantly defend independent, wild nature, the nature they mean is, as has already been hinted at above, what Raymond Williams calls "leftover nature" that is found "where industry [is] not" and that becomes the object of avid consumer desire and appetite: "to consume it as scenery, landscape, image, fresh air" (80–81). Nature has become so humanized and acted upon that it is arguably no longer nature but culture, and even the separated, "protected," "wild" part that has been granted rights, laudable and necessary as this may be, "ceases to be nature" (81). Well, says Williams, nature is really an aggregate of many things; it is "varied and variable" (85). It is different things in different epochs, and understanding what these different things are, and have been, could enable us to create "different relationships" (85). Indeed, we need to apprehend these "varied and variable" understandings of nature, not only as a gateway to Bradstreet, Bishop, and Clampitt but, more importantly, in order to proceed with the urgent ecological discourse that is already well underway, and to which this study makes its own modest contribution. Nature as morally depraved, as the heart of darkness and home of the spidermother (Watts 48), as the place where Timothy Treadwell is sensationally eaten alive by a Kodiak Grizzly (Herzog), constitutes one of these understandings, indeed a central one in Western culture that needs to be taken into account.

Nature as Depraved

Aboriginal peoples of North America do not conceive of nature as depraved. Culturally and linguistically, their understanding of nature is quite different from the post-colonial perspective held, consciously or unconsciously, by North Americans of European descent.[9] In his powerful study of the Arctic, *Arctic Dreams* (1986), Barry Lopez recounts how the far North was for centuries regarded by Europeans as a place of "incipient evil" and "the abode of the Antichrist" (17). The Inuit, writes Lopez, "who sometimes see themselves as still not quite separate from the animal world, regard us as a kind of people whose separation may have become too complete. They call us, with a mixture of incredulity and apprehension, 'the people who change nature'" (39).

It should be said here, as it could at many places in this discussion, that we have also been talking about culture all along. In point of fact, the word *nature* by itself at least implies a *culture* that can conceive of and name it: the two terms hinge on one another, are not actually separable, and although they come into conflict are not polar opposites of one another. But this is not holism. One of the central points of this study will be not that culture is a purposive expression of nature so that whatever it does is *natural* (and by extension permitted) but that culture generally has its biological, evolutionary origins in nature, and as humans reassess that fact the relationship with and understanding of nature changes. As Wilson puts it: "This is the cardinal tenet of scientific understanding: Our species and its ways of thinking are a product of evolution, not the purpose of evolution" (*Consilience* 34). It is, to be clear, Western, democratized, industrial, commercial culture that needs to get this right. Humans come from nature, as Darwin has shown, and the fact that this is still intensely and bitterly debated in America demonstrates the extent to which the Western brand of culture operates, at a basic level, on the premise that humans emphatically do *not* originate in nature.[10] Paul Shepard speaks directly to this issue when he states that "Nothing so clearly identifies the West as the distrust of the powers of the earth, focused at last upon the undomesticatable wildness within" (*Nature and Madness* 87). For many living in North America in the early twenty-first century, humans incontestably come from the perfect Father God who stands outside the imperfect Mother Nature who in turn, as St. Paul reminds us, "groans" with her inadequacies (Rom. 8:22). Only a culture identified with such premises could practise clear-cut logging or open pit mining. The term *nature* resonates with the largely Western, increasingly globalized cultural viewpoint, so much so that when we think of or say the word *nature* we are unaware of the fact that it takes artifice — culture — to do it. This implies the possibility of other, much-needed points of view regarding human beings and nature that grow out of other languages and cultures. Vine Deloria addresses this issue when he quotes Luther Standing Bear on the irony of the term *wild* in its application to nature in North America by European settlers: to aboriginals, nature was not wild but tame (90). Nature could only be wild to humans who had become domesticated, indoors creatures, who when they ventured outdoors brought their indoors conditioning and perspective along with them. Hence, as Standing Bear truculently observes, myths like the "Wild West" are created, promoted, and treated like fact (90), even by a twenty-first-century American president. Alan Watts touches on a related aspect of this when he argues that Christianity is a mostly indoors religion (26), separated from the natural world by stained glass.

So how does this connect to the notion of nature as evil? Western culture has been in conflict with nature for various reasons — most of them religious, political, and commercial — for a very long time. War produces extreme perceptions of the enemy based on fear and the innate desire to survive. It is well-known and documented that when humans come into conflict with one another each side devalues the other. Specific terms are employed literally to take the humanity — the positive value — out of the enemy, making him or her easier to destroy; after the conflict subsides, these terms are reevaluated and largely rejected as toxic so that it becomes incorrect to use them. Wartime appellations do not apply in the same compelling way once peace has been established for a period of time. Could it be that we have done something analogous in the relationship to nature, that indeed this war has been going on for so long that we have only fossilized responses to and conceptions of nature, which we mistake for truth? Do we, in other words, negatively stereotype and devalue nature? Can this be revised? Take a look, for instance, at the use of animal names in current conversational North American English. The majority of these appellations are pejorative. When you want to correct, insult, mock, or otherwise devalue another person, an animal word will often do the job. Although botanical names, such as *pansy* and *fruit*, are occasionally used pejoratively, the list taken from the animal world is extensive; it demonstrates a relationship to nature based on dominance, guilt, hatred, and fear. The word *animal* by itself has negative applications. We would often call a young male an *animal*, which means that he is uncontrolled, untrustworthy, stupid, and/or unsanitary. A male or female of any age who is known as an *animal* might be feared in the community (he or she could also be mentally and/or physically different). Numerous instances from literature in English exist. Louise Erdrich's aboriginal character Fleur Pillager provides just one potent example (in *Tracks* [1988]) as Fleur is perceived in animal terms by the white men who employ her in a slaughterhouse in the town of Argus, North Dakota. In English-speaking culture, specific animal pejoratives include (in no particular order) *pig, snake, sheep, cow, whale, swine, ox, goat, vulture, weasel, rat, slug, shark, monkey, ape, gorilla, wolf, dog, insect, beast, reptile, toad, lizard, ass, donkey, mule, lemming, leech,* and

15

bitch. Undoubtedly, this list is not exhaustive. The word *cougar*—a distinctly negative, sexist term — is employed in Canada and the U.S. to refer to mature single women looking for male partners. Similarly, a woman considered by men to be unattractive is called *coyote ugly.* A few terms such as *tiger* pay a putative compliment to one who is, or should be, aggressive. Others — such as *fox* and *stud*—also pay a compliment but in a way that is sexualized and implies not only admiration but repression in the one who uses the word, as though *in nature* promiscuity reigns supreme as opposed to *in culture, where we are,* where sex is highly codified. Some of the sexualized terms taken from nature are, of course, used *totum pro parte,* such as *beaver, pussy,* and *cock.*

Applied to a person, the word *wild* evokes any or all of the weaknesses and immoralities associated with nature and condemned in human society. Anne Bradstreet, as we shall see, came up against these issues. A wild woman is wanton, ungovernable, possibly even referred to as a slut, a term synonymous, according to the *Oxford English Dictionary,* with bitch or female dog. A wild man, on the other hand, is less pejorative, often denoting a solitary "outlaw" male who has either returned to or been discovered in the wilderness.[11] Such a man is viewed with a mixture of awe and pity, as though he were fallen from a respectable cultural height. He makes up for his lost status, however, if while in the wilderness he can reconstitute a kind of civilized life and thereby conquer nature, or if he can make his way by strength, courage, and cunning, such as can be seen in Robert Redford's Pilgrim character in the film *Jeremiah Johnson* (Pollack). Alexander Selkirk, Daniel Defoe's real-life inspiration for *Robinson Crusoe,* comes to mind as well, although Selkirk — despite his celebrity in England after surviving over four years alone on an island off the coast of Chile — was not anything like his Puritanized fictional counterpart. Feral children have been studied with a similar sense of curiosity and pity. What we call homelessness could also be seen as related to wildness despite being associated with cities, which are occasionally referred to as *concrete jungles.* This indeed points to a state of wildness or savagery that is located within the city and is not, as Andrew Light has shown, attached to a particular place; it possesses instead what Light calls "a cognitive dimension" (138) ascribed to animals and certain kinds of people, even if they are encountered within the city limits. Finally, the word *wilderness* itself, as Roderick Nash has carefully noted, has a Teutonic rather than a Romance language base, "[linking] it to the north of Europe, where uncultivated land was heavily forested" and a human could easily become disoriented (*WATAM* 2). First employed as a concept to describe errant human behavior (1), the noun *Wild(d)éornes* found in the *OED* refers to an environment that is desolate, savage, and uncultivated. E.O. Wilson, who has also unpacked this word, states that wilderness "was the realm of beasts, savages, evil spirits, magic, and the menacing amorphous unknown. The European conquest of the New World established the concept of wilderness as a frontier region waiting to be rolled back" (*TFOL* 144). Like Luther Standing Bear, Nash sees the term as representing a way of perceiving the world that is thoroughly engrained in colonial and post-colonial thinking (5–8). Erich Neumann has argued that such world views — in his case, "matriarchal or patriarchal dominance" — are largely unconscious and carry over into specific activities of daily life such as sexual positioning during coitus (97–98). The Puritan world view brought to bear on wild nature in the early seventeenth century can be analyzed in this way, as the first and fourth chapters dealing with Anne Bradstreet will show. This world view had a daily impact on family and community relations, specifically on attitudes toward non–Puritans (called *strangers*), women, children, and the dead.[12]

Christianity

Christianity in general has influenced the perception of and human impact on nature through three related doctrines, all of which can be seen in the brand of Puritanism transported to the eastern seaboard of North America in the early seventeenth century. The first stems from the *Genesis* mandate conferring power and authority over nature on to humans:

> And God said, Let us make man in our image, after our likeness: and let them have dominion over the fish of the sea, and over the fowl of the air, and over the cattle, and over all the earth, and over every creeping thing that creepeth upon the earth. So God created man in his *own* image, in the image of God created he him; male and female created he them. And God blessed them, and God said unto them, Be fruitful, and multiply, and replenish the earth, and subdue it: and have dominion over the fish of the sea, and over the fowl of the air, and over every living thing that moveth upon the earth [Gen. 1: 26–28].

This passage from the King James translation of 1611 conveys the mandate — given twice, both before and after the creation of humankind — that is responsible for much of the "undeniable potency of anthropocentrism and dualism in Western thought" (Nash *RON* 19). Indeed, the King James Bible itself, as Robert Graves has pointed out, drove seventeenth-century England into an intensely masculinized world view (peaking by the time of the civil war) that dominated the era as Protestant dissenters sought to eradicate counterviews, especially those of Mary-venerating Catholics: "The temporary reinstatement of the Thunder-god in effective religious sovereignty during the Commonwealth is the most remarkable event in modern British history: the cause was a mental ferment induced by the King James Bible" (Graves 406). The *Genesis* mandate quoted above elevates humans above and outside nature and charges them — repeatedly in the passage — with its thorough subjugation. It results in what Robert Pogue Harrison has called "Christian imperialism" (62), which has continued over many centuries and in its various denominations, willful or not, to nurture a massive rift between people and nature. Writers as diverse as the Christian scholar Lynn White, Jr., and the ethicist and defender of animal rights Peter Singer have outlined in detail the scope and magnitude of Christianity's dominative attitude to nature.[13] Indeed, this fact is so well-documented and addressed that it might be called common knowledge; people are certainly increasingly aware of it. Christians themselves are waking up to this issue — as can be seen in, for example, the rhetorical strategy employed by E.O. Wilson in *The Creation* (2006), in which he delineates the environmental crisis by way of letters to a fictional pastor of an American evangelical church. Not himself a Christian, Wilson by the very act of writing this book implies the power that the church in America has to alter thinking and change behavior patterns.

Still, there is much denial among Christians. Bill McKibben himself, coming out as a church-going Methodist in *The End of Nature*, ironically defends Christianity against the charge of anti-environmentalism. McKibben brings up Francis of Assisi, the *Book of Job*, and even John Muir as examples of Christian nature worship (76) — but these are clearly behavioral exceptions to the ideological rule of subjugation found in the Old and New Testaments. Many Christians throughout the centuries have loved nature (Amy Clampitt, for example) but nature-loving Christians do not in any way obviate the doctrinal facts foundational to the religious movement itself. It is indeed quite astonishing that McKibben, a Christian, so passionately promotes the separation of humans from nature, the very doctrine that has largely by itself brought much ecological disaster upon us, not in order to dominate nature but to save it, if possible. Is this an instance, ideologically-speaking, of calling in the fox to guard the henhouse? Certainly not. Yet if wild nature is to be preserved, and it must, some would contend that it ought to come from a different kind of thinking than the stewardship model traditionally offered by Christianity. In *The Revenge of Gaia* (2006), James Lovelock, for instance, has rejected "the Christian concept of stewardship [as] flawed by unconscious hubris": "Christians need a new Sermon on the Mount that sets out the human constraints needed for living decently with the Earth" (*TROG* 176). Others would add that it is only pragmatic to create a broad cultural dialogue with Christians, especially as they reevaluate two millennia of dogma about nature. If various arms of the Church can publicly apologize for the abuse of children, women, and aboriginals, perhaps the treatment of nature can also be reformed. Clearly, Christianity throughout the world has the opportunity before it to correct itself and repair the damage it has done globally. (The article, "Vatican Penance: Forgive Us Our Carbon Output," appeared in the *New York Times* on September 17, 2007; it reported that the Vatican has declared itself "the world's first carbon-neutral state" and a Vatican spokesman added, with no apparent irony, "The Book of Genesis tells us of a beginning in which God placed man as guardian over the earth to make it fruitful.")

Just how much of a challenge Christians face as they reevaluate their impact on the environment can be seen in the second, related doctrine or tenet that is central to Christianity in its relation to nature: history. This aspect of Christianity can certainly be seen in Anne Bradstreet's work as well as in Amy Clampitt's critical emphasis on the longstanding westward movement of European and Eurasian peoples, which she calls in the long poem *The Prairie* her "epic theme" (*CPAC* 358). History in Christianity is linear and progressive, moving from the act of creation towards the end times, from the fall of humankind and subsequent redemption through the sacrifice of Jesus Christ and on to the period of tribulation and final conflict called Armageddon, after which the Messiah will return in complete triumph to set up a new heaven and a new earth. Indeed, evangelical American Christians who especially like to emphasize the end of history vigilantly look for the signs and symptoms — earthquakes, wars and rumors of wars, plagues, trouble in Israel — that Christ in the four gospels claims will immediately precede the end of the world. St. Paul as well abjures his various congregations to be vigilant, expecting Christ to return suddenly and without warning. In *Reinventing Eden: The Fate of Nature in Western Culture* (2003), Carolyn Merchant describes Christianity's strong emphasis on linear time as a "grand historical narrative" (11), one in which women play a pivotal role in humankind's loss of a paradisal garden state of being: "With the Fall from Eden, humanity abandons an original 'untouched' nature and enters into history. Nature is now a fallen world and humans fallen beings" (17–18). Out of this loss and corruption, with Eve the original causal agent, Christianity has pursued and pursues Recovery, says Merchant, as a signal component of the overarching narrative, one that denigrates natural cycles of time, decay, and renewal, as it asserts the reality of transcendent, progressive time. Robert Pogue Harrison describes linear time as having an "unearthly openness" that "underlies, at the deepest level, the enduring hostility between the institutional order and the forests that lie at its boundaries" (8). This hostility, says Harrison, is "religious in origin" (13). Against the fact of entropy found in nature and within the human body itself, Christianity posits a progressive storyline that promises the ultimate triumph over nature, non-entropic resurrected bodies, and the return to the static or eternal paradisal order. Linear time, civilization, history, progress, development, economic expansion, resource management, patriarchy, and manifest destiny are some of the concepts that constitute a powerful and often unconscious world view that arguably finds a basis in Christianity. Vine Deloria gets at this when he outlines the significant differences between aboriginal and European understandings of time, place, history, and nature in *God Is Red* (1973). His telling claim that "reconciling history and nature is the question of this generation" is prescient and remains true decades later (59).

The third doctrine propounded by Christianity against nature is that nature is fallen, corrupt, depraved, immoral, and subject to death. The Second Law of Thermodynamics, which in Lovelock's formulation "states unequivocally that the entropy of an open system must increase" (*Gaia* 117), provides the scientific framework for Christianity's enmity with nature. As Lovelock puts it succinctly, "Since we are all open systems, this means that all of us are doomed to die" (117). To most humans, death is unwelcome and feared; to Christians, however, death without the hope of salvation is utterly unacceptable. As it is found in the material world, death is the enemy whose sting is neutralized by the physical resurrection of Jesus Christ; and because nature incorporates and promises death, often in a manner that seems horribly unfair, nature is unacceptable and seen as the enemy as well.[14] If a scientist such as Lovelock can describe entropy as inescapable, as "rul[ing] the whole of our universe," and "read[ing] like the notice at the gate of Dante's Hell" (116–17), Christians can derive tremendous comfort and drive from St. Paul's renowned New Testament words:

> Behold, I shew you a mystery; We shall not all sleep, but we shall all be changed. In a moment, in the twinkling of an eye, at the last trump: for the trumpet shall sound, and the dead shall be raised incorruptible, and we shall be changed. For this corruptible must put on incorruption, and this mortal *must* put on immortality. So when this corruptible shall have put on incorruption, and this mortal shall have put on immortality, then shall be brought to pass the saying that is written, Death is swallowed up in victory. O death, where *is* thy sting? O grave, where *is* thy victory? [I Cor. 15:51–55, *KJV*].

The destructive impact of these words on the human relationship to nature over the course of nearly two millennia is undeniable, though just how great the impact has been could well be immeasurable. The passage is nothing if not triumphal. It posits the imminent onset of a new, non-entropic reality in which the cycles of death and birth will no longer obtain. In the meantime, since nature is mortal and moldering, and even at times bites back, "she" can be possessed, plundered, exploited, appropriated, developed, managed, surveyed, contained, and improved. Even in non–Christians living and working in the postmodern world, actions and attitudes stemming from these concepts can frequently be found, implying a relationship to nature based on the Christian model of stewardship, which is innately proprietal. The steward looks after a thing until the rightful owner comes along to reclaim it, just as Christ outlines in his Parable of the Talents (Matt. 25:14–30). The good steward turns his charge or talents into something more; the bad steward buries his. The good steward is rewarded by the master; the bad one is punished. As the New World colonists were well aware, and as we shall see further on in this study, nature untended was theirs for the taking while nature that showed evidence of human grooming was, ostensibly, not.

The Grizzly Man Moment[15]

Ironically, in describing nature as subject to decay and death Christianity appears to have trumped Western science, which did not formulate the Second Law of Thermodynamics until the nineteenth century. The Christian Church, however, cannot lay sole claim to having anticipated the latecomer science. In Western culture as a whole, angst caused by the passage of time has been the focus of poetry, drama, song, and dance, not to mention prayers, rituals, and burial rites, since the beginning of recorded history. According to this view, at some point in the dim past, the upright hominid, *Homo sapiens sapiens,* acutely aware of death, disease, suffering, and loss, arrived at the notion that another reality outside the purview of his or her sensory detection equipment must exist. Altered states of consciousness and shamanic lore became, over great expanses of time, integral parts of the community that were passed from generation to generation, initially by oral transmission. In Classical Greece, Sophocles gives us the figure of Oedipus who, at the outset of *Oedipus Rex,* promises the plague-stricken citizens of Thebes (at the behest of the oracle at Delphi) that he will discover the agent responsible for their suffering, no matter what the cost. Oedipus himself is the agent, of course, and inescapably, tragically, he comes to know himself, stepping out into the light of pathetic self-knowledge that he must, painfully, share with the audience. Time, decay, pain, and loss, and the awful insecurity that attends these in Western consciousness, are central to *Oedipus Rex*, as they are to tragedy itself, the legacy of Sophocles and his competitor and colleague, Aeschylus. Life is grossly unfair. Nature can be brutal and harsh. The myth of Orpheus, as found in Virgil and Ovid, also bears this out. In fact, the ancient Western poets are in rough agreement about this. In Homer, Sophocles, Aeschylus, and the anonymous author of *Job* as well as in Horace, Virgil, and the *Beowulf* poet, audiences and readers have discovered accurate reflections of their own feelings about that hackneyed thing called the human condition. These poets tell us who we are in the world, and the news is ultimately bad: we die knowing that we die in a seemingly arbitrary world of ceaseless flux. Christianity enters this discourse as a late player, and its news is suddenly good. It offers salvation — the ultimate escape from the heretofore inescapable tragedy — by telling the story of the transcendent, utterly good and faithful Son of the Father God, who overcomes entropy by offering Himself as a sacrifice for all humankind. Death, the great and vicious enemy, and nature, the handmaid of death, are defeated. All Christians have to do is believe and wait for the end. Or as William Dunbar would cheerfully put it, "Man, praise thy Maker and be merry / And give not for the world a cherry."

It would be shocking if what we now call the biosphere could benefit from such a world view, and the Puritans, with their Calvinist heritage and accompanying doctrines of predestination and the absolute sovereignty of God, were nothing if not intense about their views on wild nature in the New World. The Puritans, indeed, took the three tenets discussed above to their logical extremes and practised these in their everyday lives, with a vengeance. America still lives with this legacy. We can give these sturdy Puritan questors conditional credit, however, on two levels: they understandably realized that the wilderness before them could not give them their morality[16]; and their brand of Christianity was not the first ideology to conceive of nature as threatening and in need of domination. Robert Pogue Harrison has, for example, written about the *Gilgamesh* epic in which the eponymous hero pursues and destroys the forest demon Huwawa who represents the real antagonist, the forest itself (14). Harrison uncovers a longstanding pre–Christian conflict between the forces of civilization and the environment. In other words, the rupture with nature goes back a long way, and in myth, legend, and folklore the relationship between humans and nature is repeatedly addressed.

Harrison writes about several of these ancient texts in *Forests: The Shadow of Civilization* (1992), including the tale of Diana and Acteon as told in Ovid's *Metamorphoses*.[17] With this myth, we can put a finger on what exactly John Winthrop and company feared, as the hunter Acteon, deep in the forest with his faithful dogs, comes suddenly upon the goddess of nature, whom Harrison describes as "invisible, intangible, enigmatic, cruel, reigning over the nonhuman reaches of the wilderness" (24). He is describing one of the oldest embodiments of the Great Goddess, who swiftly punishes Acteon for seeing her naked at her bath by transforming him into a stag that retains human consciousness: "What should he do? / Return home to the palace, / or find a hiding place deep in the woods? / Shame kept him from one course, and fear, the other" (Ovid 98). Acteon's questions at this place in the narrative point to the Western dilemma regarding nature at its core. We feel and fear that we can never return to what we must have once been, creatures inhabiting wild nature; at the same time, we feel and fear that we might well be returned to nature against our wills by some catastrophic transformation event. (Cormac McCarthy's *The Road* [2006] deals precisely with life in America after such an event.) Thus Acteon can neither return to the palace nor plunge into the wilderness, but can still engage in interior speech acts, even though his attempts to command his dogs come out as nonhuman noise. In his loss of mastery brought upon him by Diana, Acteon's beloved dogs — domesticated extensions of his power over nature — kill him. The Acteon story invites its audience to deliberate over its own alienation from its origins in nature; to consider the perils involved in getting too close to, seeing too much of, nature's mysteries before we are ready; to realize that humans cannot even partially meld with their animal past while retaining their apparently unique form of awareness: that, in other words, reintegration with nature — *holism* — is not possible, even though the idea is incredibly alluring.

From this perspective, we cannot really blame the domesticated Puritans of the Winthrop fleet, with their truly strange belief system, for feeling out of place on the shores of a seemingly wild, alien continent in the year 1630 or for throwing up fences and fortresses as fast as they could. But we can and must understand both them and ourselves. Boston and New York City have grown directly out of those colonial encampments, and much as we might cherish them in the aftermath of 9/11 we also need to reevaluate the idea of the city and what a city might be in the near future. The psychoanalyst James Hillman has had much to say about how we might reimagine the city as we also revise our relationship with nature, suggesting that we "imitate the process of nature rather than what the process has made, the way of nature rather than the things of nature.... We would remember nature in the way we construct so that nature echoes in the constructed object" (102–03). In *Biomimicry: Innovation Inspired by Nature* (1997), Janine M. Benyus outlines nine important ways in which Western culture must follow the lead of nature: "It is time for us as a culture to walk in the forest again. Once we see nature as a mentor, our relationship with the living world changes" (9).[18] For the first time in the history of humankind, more than half the global population lives in cities, a daunting fact (Lovelock, *TROG* 182). Four centuries after the first European landings on the shores of this continent, most North Americans have

24

yet to come to terms with themselves, their history, and their—for the most part—urbanized environment.

In some ways, it is a terrifying task. To acknowledge the nature of nature and the human place in it is to concede our limits and our biology. Timothy Treadwell, the subject of Werner Herzog's *Grizzly Man,* is arguably our Acteon. Filming himself standing mere feet away from giant Kodiak grizzlies, Treadwell demonstrates the enduring critical reality of the Acteon myth, a myth whose core dynamic is enacted at crucial points in the works of the three poets examined in this study. (These points are identified as Acteon moments in the last three chapters of this book. Bradstreet has her Acteon moment in her encounter with the nightingale, Philomela; the moment of transformation, though, is aborted. Bishop and Clampitt have several of these moments. Bishop encounters or portrays nonhuman life in "At the Fishhouses," "Crusoe in England," "The Moose," "The Fish," and "The Riverman": in the latter poem, she succeeds in getting below the boat, so to speak, of Western culture. Clampitt's Acteon moments are found throughout her poetry, as she is a poet arguably in search of transformation, as shall be seen especially in the final chapter of this book, where poems such as "The Cove," "Good Friday," and "The Sun Underfoot Among the Sundews" are examined.) Timothy Treadwell inevitably crosses the line that Western culture in particular has firmly established between human and nonhuman life. He gets up too close, and is finally eaten alive, although the audio recording of his demise is tellingly withheld by Herzog. Curious, enraptured, and outraged though the audience might be regarding a man who films himself living with giant bears in the wilderness of Alaska, the moment of Treadwell's consumption must remain arcane and indescribable, even though many creatures, including humans, devour and absorb other creatures as a matter of course. There is a controversial moral contradiction here that demonstrates vividly the belief that humans are distinct from and *other* than nature. It's okay to watch hyenas kill and consume a zebra foal in a *National Geographic* video. Treadwell is truly and even willingly transformed by Diana, but the rest of us cannot go there with him—that is beyond the pale. Thus it is understandable that, as Robert Graves has pointed out in *The White Goddess* (1948), Artemis—the Greek counterpart in some ways to Diana—is cast in a new role by Christianity as St. Artemidos (143), because she must be contained and controlled. Christianity has been very adept at co-opting

25

entities otherwise inimical to the Church and, in this case, the Church's stance on nature. Through Christianity in general, and through Werner Herzog's specific ethical decision made in the filmic text of *Grizzly Man* to withhold from the audience the audio recording of Timothy Treadwell's death, what biologist Lyall Watson calls dark nature is excised as much as possible from cultured human experience — although we do enjoy it as spectacle in a zoo or a documentary film, and we do ground many of our actions against nature in the notion that we mean to improve it.

We are an abyss away, it seems, from the so-called Romantic view of nature found in the poetry of William Wordsworth. And you do not have to be a Christian to see in nature something daunting and cruel that pushes you into the warmth of your kitchen and the easy familiarity of a humanized world view. The term commonly in use here is *anthropocentrism*. This word, however, at least in its usage, does not extend quite far enough. What we are discussing here is what could be called Acteon's Gift — the culture/nature divorce — although it is also Yahweh's Gift and the Gift of the Son of God: and what binds all three of these personages together is their maleness. Only a profoundly human *and* male-centered understanding of nature could be advanced in narratives like those found in *Genesis*, the letters of St. Paul, the Acteon myth, or *Grizzly Man*. In all of these, the female is either marginalized or demonized. Treadwell's girlfriend, killed and eaten immediately before Treadwell, is treated in the Herzog documentary as a puzzling helpmate to Treadwell. Her story remains peripheral to his, and while Herzog asks questions about her, he knows that the sensational, almost pornographic steps have been taken by none other than Timothy Treadwell, and this is what the audience wants to know more about: that "crazy" man-boy from California who cheerfully walks into the maw of a half-ton bear in the middle of nowhere. Indeed, there is something almost Christ-like about Treadwell's person and actions, not the least of which is his apparently solitary journey into wilderness to locate the truth about us and him and vulnerable wild nature. At any rate, his sojourn seems, and is meant to seem, his alone; the focus is almost all on him while his girlfriend gives silent witness. Christ-like, Treadwell seems to do it for all of us as we peer and peep into Herzog's handling of his story with its awful sacrificial denouement.

Northrop Frye's Telling Questions

In *Words with Power* (1990), Frye asks a series of questions concerning the nature of nature:

> But what does Wordsworth's gentle goddess who never betrayed the heart that loved her have to do with Tennyson's nature red in tooth and claw, with its ferocious and predatory struggle for survival? Even more, what does she have to do with the narrators in the Marquis de Sade, who, after some particularly nauseating orgy of cruelty and violence, appeal with equal confidence to nature to justify their pleasure in such things? Are there two natures, and if so are they separable? [246].

These are potent questions. They get at the central issue delineated by Raymond Williams and mentioned earlier in this chapter: that we cannot understand our own interventions "until we are clear as to what the idea of nature includes, and in part whether it includes man" (75). James Lovelock puts it similarly: "Is technological man still a part of Gaia or are we in some or in many ways alienated from her?" (*Gaia* 170). Until this issue is resolved, we will continue to front representations of nature that are mere projections and therefore partial; we will also continue to be in crisis. If we are not part of nature and nature does not include us, if we come about rather by way of what Daniel Dennett calls "sky-hooks," his metaphor for the religious institutional claim that the origins of humans and human culture are transcendent, then intervention in nature is our Promethean right and we may, by way of religion, a component of culture, make moral judgments on nature and proceed accordingly, either directly or indirectly, in our treatment of nature. If, though, we are part of nature and nature includes us, if we come about by way of another Dennett metaphor, "crane-making crane[s]" (339), if indeed "culture must have a Darwinian origin" (341), then the project for us humans relative to nature is entirely different: it means, in short, that the answer to Frye's last question is that there is *one* nature. One biosphere exists, but we habitually perceive in it two sides, two faces, William Blake's tiger as well as his lamb. But until now, we have acted in accordance with whichever perception — nature as tiger or nature as lamb — we have held to be true in relation to our convictions about ourselves as a species and about our values and where they originate. Misanthropic environmentalists will tend to see nature as the innocent victim and humans as tantamount to vermin. Fundamentalist Christians, on the other hand, will be inclined to see humans as immortal souls worth redeeming whose definitive mission includes the stewardship of nature — thus ensuring the destructive tradition of what E.O. Wilson terms "exemptionalism," which says that humans have a special status in the world (*Creation* 83). To separate the two sides and act as though one claim were true and not the other is to falsify the environment, and when we falsify the environment we inevitably do something disrespectful or foolish or both. One of the most important things eco-critics and readers can do, therefore, is to ask questions like those both Blake and Frye ask. Their questions imply and inspire other questions. Here is one that this study will pursue at certain points: How do writers falsify nature by showing one face only, and why do they do this?

In this context it is significant that a scientist such as James Lovelock has repeatedly called for a rapprochement with nature in its *totality* or what he calls Gaia — which is really the Great Goddess of the ancient world, Artemis, the Wolf-goddess (Graves 222) — although Lovelock is not the first or only one to put it in these terms. Using many of the animal appellations that we have already identified as pejorative, Robert Graves describes the Great Goddess as one who

> will suddenly transform herself into sow, mare, bitch, vixen, she-ass, weasel, serpent, owl, she-wolf, tigress, mermaid or loathsome hag. Her names and titles are innumerable.... [She is] the Mother of All Living, the ancient power of fright and lust — the female spider or the queen-bee whose embrace is death [24].

"Shakespeare," wrote Graves, "knew and feared her," and the bard attempts to dominate her through the character of Prospero in *The Tempest,* although Shakespeare is also "poetically just to Caliban, putting the truest poetry of the play in his mouth" (426). Erich Neumann calls her "the Great Mother Goddess" who is "the mother of all living things, of animals as well as men" (94 & 96). She is benign and life-giving as well as "the deadly devouring maw of the underworld": "For this woman who generates life and all living things on earth is the same who takes them back into herself" (149). Archeologist Marija Gimbutas, in *The Language of the Goddess* (1991), rejects Neumann's use of the term *mother,* opting instead for "the term 'Great Goddess' as best describing her absolute rule, her creative, destructive, and regenerative powers" (316). Gimbutas also refers to the "obvious analogy ... to Nature itself; through the multiplicity of phenomena and continuing cycles of which it is made, one recognizes the fundamental and underlying unity of Nature" (316). Graves, Neumann, and Gimbutas all agree that the Father God religions arrived quite recently, superseding and transforming the earlier cultures that understood the world in female terms. Writes Gimbutas, "There is no trace of a father figure in any of the Paleolithic periods" (316). Neumann argues that the throne on which the male deity is seated is originally the goddess herself— literally Isis, whose name means *throne,* so that the "king comes to power by 'mounting the throne,' and so takes his place on the lap of the Great Goddess, the earth — he becomes her son" (98–99). Father and Son, then, as we see them in Christianity, are cultural extensions of the goddess: they evolve out of her like the infant son on his mother's lap but then also betray her as they seek and finally claim transcendent power over her. These late male deities act to deny, reduce, contain, explain, and defeat her, finally making her available for technological manipulation, just as the beekeeper manipulates the Queen and her colony. Not only Graves, Neumann, and Gimbutas but others such as Robert Pogue Harrison and Carolyn Merchant have written extensively about the culture wars between the Great Goddess and the more recent patriarchal religions that drove her into the deep, dark recesses of what we call *wilderness,* that place of apparent confusion and disorder.

Marija Gimbutas sees "the Goddess reemerging from the forests and mountains ... returning us to our most ancient human roots" (321). Writing fifty years earlier, Graves demonstrates various attempts by goddess devotees to revive her at certain points in patriarchal history. Catholics have done this most obviously and recently with their adoration of Mary, which acknowledges and reveres the ancient sacred bond between the goddess and her male offspring. The British, as well, "have an unconscious hankering ... after goddesses" (Graves 406), but "The Puritan Revolution was a reaction against Virgin-worship" that became a warning to Catholics during the sixteenth and seventeenth centuries "to strengthen rather than weaken the festal side of their cult" (424). That this conflict of basic world views also has ecological consequences was certainly not lost on Graves during the late 1940s when he added a Foreword to *The White Goddess,* linking her fundamental power and place to poetry and ecology:

> [Poetry] was once a warning to man that he must keep in harmony with the family of living creatures among which he was born, by obedience to

the wishes of the lady of the house; it is now a reminder that he has disregarded the warning, turned the house upside down by capricious experiments in philosophy, science and industry, and brought ruin on himself and his family [14].

The Puritan rejection of the goddess can, in this framing of the discussion, certainly be seen as a part of a much larger culture war that extends, with threatening consequences, into the twenty-first century. Graves's use of the word *family* to identify the totality of living creatures on this planet, our *house* and home, recognizes the integrity of nature. Life is, as scientists such as Lovelock and Wilson remind us, balanced and unified, possibly even beyond our understanding. Indeed, it is we humans who, if it is not already too late, need a comprehension of ourselves in the world that meshes with nature unconditionally. Doing so requires a relentless reevaluation of Western culture and the moral and ethical assumptions it takes for granted relative to nature. As Wilson states in *The Future of Life* (2002): "The lady is our mother all right, and a mighty dispensational force as well.... Ancient and vulnerable, she will not tolerate the undisciplined appetite of her gargantuan infant much longer" (106–07).

ONE

Anne Bradstreet: Questions of "Travail" to New England

Anne Bradstreet and the Winthrop Fleet of 1630

When the *Arbella* finally got underway from the Isle of Wight on 8 April 1630, John Winthrop was that much closer to achieving his first significant objective as Governor of the Massachusetts Bay Company: "to passe the Seas (vnder Gods protection) to inhabite and continue in new England" (Winthrop 152).[19] After a frustrating delay of several weeks due to contrary winds, Winthrop could at last put into action his various maps and models for living in a largely unknown land. As his letters and journals reveal, this leader of a threatened minority in England was under considerable pressure to orient both himself and his passengers to their precarious new existence in the so-called New World.

The Winthrop Fleet consisted of eleven ships carrying approximately four-hundred seamen and seven-hundred emigrants, "the largest number of Englishmen sailing as passengers in one body across the Atlantic up to that event" (Banks 24). Not only did the *Arbella* have to steer the fleet over many miles of strange, often turbulent waters by hugging latitude 43° 15' north (Banks 41), but Winthrop was responsible for rallying his people as they struggled with seasickness, boredom, limited rations, cramped quarters, and scurvy, not to mention doubts and fears about the expedition's chances for success. Up to this point, only a few hardy explorers had tried to build colonies in New England and, other than the pilgrims who had settled in and around Plymouth during the previous decade, most had failed.[20]

Winthrop's knowledge of the New England coast was scant: he possessed a chart that, with a meager but accurate line, traced the coast for less than twenty miles from Gloucester to Marblehead (Winthrop 280).[21] But just as important as navigating the coastline was the task of accurately piloting the company of emigrants towards a promising settlement, and Winthrop partially accomplished this with his well-known "A Modell of Christian Charity," composed and delivered aboard the *Arbella*. In "[seeking] out a place of Cohabitation and Consorteshipp vnder a due forme of Government both ciuill and ecclesiasticall," the colony would be viewed by the outside world "as a Citty vpon a Hill" (Winthrop 293 & 295). As such, the new settlement would be a refuge as well as a beacon, providing both sanctuary from England's political and religious problems and a model for true Christian civility.

Even as eighteen-year-old Anne Bradstreet, on board the *Arbella* with her siblings, parents, and husband, disembarked at Salem Harbor, Winthrop's Massachusetts Bay Company was conscious of itself as set apart from, and yet culturally attuned to, England and English ways. Leaving behind "her comfortable life in the mansion of the earl of Lincolnshire, where her father, Thomas Dudley, had been steward of the earl's estate and her husband, Simon Bradstreet, had been her father's assistant" (Martin 20), Bradstreet later wrote — using words that been quoted many times since — how she "fovnd a new World and new manners at wch my heart rose, But after I was convinced it was ye way of God, I submitted to it & joined to ye chh., at Boston" (*CW* 216). From the day she left England forever until her death in 1672, Anne Bradstreet would lead a contradictory existence. Committed to — and, indeed, writing on behalf of— a community where "the care of the publique must oversway all private respects, by which not onely conscience, but meare Ciuill pollicy doth binde vs" (Winthrop 293), Bradstreet would, as Wendy Martin states, "[question] the validity of the Puritan voyage and [doubt] the existence of God.... The grievances that brought the Puritan expedition to New England were not Anne Bradstreet's but belonged to the two men she loved" (Martin 4 & 20).[22] Like so many other New England settlers, Bradstreet would find herself caught between personal and communal claims and values, and her reservations about the Puritan experiment would be compounded by feelings of ambivalence about the New World itself.[23]

The members of the Great Migration of 1630 were unique in so far as they constituted "a close facsimile of English society" (Anderson 26; see also Conforti 45). Once settled in the New World, their sense of identity became intensified as they found in the ocean what Edward Johnson called a great "ditch between England and their now place of abode" (Cressy 194–95). Joseph A. Conforti states:

> It would be hard to exaggerate the deep impression the sea made on early New Englanders.... Colonization originated with ocean voyages. For Puritans the physical-spiritual pilgrimage across the Atlantic remained a historic touchstone.... In [commercial port towns], the sea occupied a pivotal place in the Puritan imagination. The world, after all, was a "sea of sin." Early New England sermons and writings regularly invoked the sea in ways that resonated with both the moral bearings and the maritime activities of Puritan laity [74].

As the distance between themselves and England threatened to "uncode" them, the Puritans found it necessary "to erase the distance" by continually redefining their Englishness even though they had also in many ways rejected England as a viable place to live (Samuels 233–34). Ironically, as Michael Kammen has written, "At the outset, early American society may have been more 'traditional' in character than English society itself":

> Many who left England [during the 1620s and 1630s] did so in the certainty that God would destroy their homeland — a corrupt nation where few men honored their obligations to Him. Nevertheless, despite these forebodings of doom, despite their hostility, most colonists brought with them a great pride in being Englishmen [Kammen 183 & 144; see also Conforti 3].

Several historians and critics of Puritanism in the New World strenuously emphasize this point. David E. Stannard writes, "It has often been said that no one is more English than the Englishman away from home" (96).

Many of the people of the Massachusetts Bay Colony therefore saw themselves as a remnant salvaged from a homeland in danger of imminent destruction. Unlike the Puritans remaining in England, who broke up into different, often conflicting groups, the brethren in New England stressed the need for homogeneity within the community. In order simply to survive, they needed to safeguard their identities not only as Englishmen but also as Puritans, and they attempted to accomplish this by creating a monolithic "Community of perill" (Winthrop 287) in which the place of the individual would be subordinated.[24]

At the same time, however, the Puritan movement of the early seventeenth century required that its members be subversive, that the individual be able to assert himself[25] to the point of undermining political and religious orthodoxies. Central to the Calvinist belief system was, in addition, the transcendent reality of each believer's relationship with God unmediated by hierarchical institutions (Conforti 35). The Puritan emigrant's sense of self would be made even more acute by mere dint of boarding a ship to live elsewhere. As Wayne Franklin states, the traveler is "almost by definition an iconoclast; his departure, even if he goes in the service of 'home' purposes, hints not merely at the general authority of experience, but also (and more subversively) at the prospective power of individual life beyond the horizon" (Zuckerman 129). This force of the individual within the Puritan community clarifies the fact that its members saw themselves as pilgrims *en route* to an earthly as well as a heavenly destination, and that, indeed, pilgrimage was "the most powerful metaphor pervading Puritan devotion" (Anderson 86).

Yet, having boarded a ship in the Winthrop Fleet, the emigrant also agreed to submit "to the strictures of those he embraced as brothers. His very attachment to them placed his outward behavior under their ceaseless surveillance and made his most inward experience, the vicissitudes of his regeneration, subject to their scrutiny" (Zuckerman 130). If, at any time, the individual went beyond the bounds of belief or behavior as defined by the Puritan community — as did Roger Williams, Anne Hutchinson, and Anne Bradstreet's sister, Sarah Keayne — he or she would be excommunicated, which would entail either returning to England or joining another colony elsewhere in the New World.[26]

The Puritan traveler setting forth into the wild was therefore constantly negotiating with the paradoxical claims of self and community. Sacvan Bercovitch comments on the push and pull of these two forces when he explains "the relationship between the believer, *exemplum fidei*, and the community of the elect, the universal society of *exempla* fidei," as part of a

> a giant effort at cohesion and control, expressly opposed to the outburst of individualism that marks most of the other intellectual movements of the Renaissance. For as the Reformers condemned the institutional Catholic *imitatio*, so also, and just as virulently, they condemned the humanist doctrine of *imitatio hominis*, with its flaunted freedom of the intellect, its pagan

tributes to the splendor of the human body, and its extravagant claims for self-determination. Those tributes and claims rested on the vision of man as microcosm; the Reformers required a higher authority, an external absolute. "Every man, individually, is an epitome," they agreed; but they proceeded to distinguish between the natural and divine meanings of the term: "every natural man (who in a natural consideration is called *microcosmus*, an epitome of the world), in whose conscience God hath his throne ... may be called *microchristus*, the epitome of Christ mystical" [*Puritan Origins* 10–11].[27]

The Puritans' rejection of and separation from England defined the terms of travel towards, and eventual settlement in, a place whose very name — New England — suggested such idealism and tension. These contradictions, simultaneously involving subversion and submission, are readily apparent in a letter dated 21 August 1629 from John Winthrop to his father, who would remain in England:

> For the businesse of N[ew] E[ngland] I can say noe other thing but that I beleeve confidently that the whole disposition thereof is of the Lord who disposeth all alterations by his blessed will to his owne glory and the good of his, ... and for my selfe I have seene so much of the vanity of the world that I esteem noe more of the diversities of Countries then as so many Innes, wherof the travailer, that hath lodged in the best, or in the worst findeth noe difference when he commeth to his Journies end, and I shall call that my Countrie where I may most glorifie God and enioy the presence of my dearest freindes, therfore heerin I submit my selfe (laying by all desire of other imploymentes whatsoever) to the service of God, and the Company herin, with the whole endeavours both of body and mind [Winthrop 150–51].

Anne Bradstreet was just such a "travailer" during her forty-two years of experimental living in various communities in New England. The poems examined in this chapter disclose not so much the patterned musings of a woman fomenting rebellion as the kinds of contradiction and paradox typical of many members of the Puritan community that had migrated to the New World. Bradstreet is often represented as a dissident and early feminist; this reader's analysis of her poems, however, reveals that she also wrote as a committed member of the Puritan community in New England. As such, she articulated the difficult position in which many of her contemporaries found themselves. That she frequently delineated such a complex position in her poems precludes seeing her simply as a feminist rebel, no matter how much readers may be taken aback by this Puritan woman's refreshing, albeit occasional, forthrightness. Close textual analyses within the historical frame support the view that Anne Bradstreet continually balances a precarious position between the often conflicting needs of self and community. Although periodically she directly expresses doubt, and while she arguably defies her God in late poems such as her elegy for her granddaughter Elizabeth, more often than not she loyally speaks on behalf of the collective enterprise. There are substantial grounds for believing that she employs her poetic voice in the service of the powerful male forces of orthodoxy represented by her father. To refuse to set forth the Puritan ideology would be seen not only as an abdication of responsibility but as a threat to the community and a family embarrassment, and Bradstreet would thus be risking the fate of an Anne Hutchinson or a Sarah Keayne. For the colonial Puritan, "Poetry," as Perry Miller states, "existed primarily for its utility" (White 125), and it is no surprise that Miller quotes Bradstreet herself: "I have not studied in this yov read to show my skill, but to declare ye Truth — not to sett forth myself, but ye Glory of God" (*CW* 215). To declare the "truth" in seventeenth-century Puritan New England was, as we shall see, no simple exercise.

Traveling over three thousand miles to begin life anew in a strange land and under arduous circumstances, Bradstreet, like many of her fellow colonists, developed a more or less permanent feeling of being far-flung, of existing on the edge of the civilized world. The resulting "wistfulness, nostalgia, and disorientation," which David Cressy states "may have underlain the early history of New England, and may have been a common syndrome on the frontier" (Cressy 206), would naturally have tended to influence many aspects of life in the New World. In various ways throughout her poetry, Bradstreet voices her acute sense of separation, or distance, from a number of places and persons, many of them notably cast in terms of the parent-child paradigm: from Mother England, which she would never see again; from her father, Thomas Dudley, a stern, orthodox colonial governor whose death in 1653 elicits an intriguing elegy; from her grandchildren, whose untimely deaths make for dark nights of the soul that compel Bradstreet to question her beliefs; and, penultimately, from her God, who could inflict suffering with no apparent reason other than to teach her the vanity of all things, as well as to remind her of the possibility of the eternal separation after death that haunted the lives of so many Puritans.

Finally, and perhaps most significantly, Puritanism constantly threatened to separate Bradstreet from herself, and it was against this danger that she mainly struggled. For Anne Bradstreet, poetry helped to ease the pain of these various kinds of separation. By means of poetry, she could, covertly at times, imaginatively traverse the distances she would feel between, for example, New England and Old, or herself and a dead grandchild.

The Distance from England in 1642

"A Dialogue Between Old England and New" (1642) constitutes Bradstreet's attempt to come to terms with the distance between the mother country, where civil war had broken out, and the young colony, which, while rejecting England, continued still to depend on it for supplies, trade, settlers and, perhaps most importantly, a cultural and political identity.[28] During a period when news from abroad was dear, Bradstreet's "Dialogue" would reflect, and perhaps ease, the acute anxiety felt by Puritan colonists because of the conflict between Royalists and Parliamentarians.[29] "Dialogue" would, in effect, speak to a particular *audience,* bringing the wilderness community together through the elements of ritual and repetition central to the poetic act. Originally composed in 1642, but not published until 1650, "Dialogue," like all the poems in *The Tenth Muse,* was written first and foremost for Bradstreet's father, Thomas Dudley, and her husband, Simon Bradstreet. Closely connected to the poem's audience is the issue of *projection:* "Dialogue" demonstrates Bradstreet's ability to "imagine distance" in terms of England's stance towards its colony during a period of upheaval that threatened the colony's very existence (Samuels 248). For an explorer such as Captain John Smith, it was common to "[imagine] distance not from the point of view of his own distance from England but from the point of view of England's distance from himself" (Samuels 248–49), and this is precisely the strategy that Bradstreet adopts here. "Dialogue," finally, participates in the Puritans' creation of an orthodox reading of New England's colonial history that excludes a variety of others. The poem represents the perspective and interests not so much of Old and New England as of a specific group within the larger, heterogeneous colony led by John Winthrop and Thomas Dudley.

Although it stridently emphasized communal values, New England

Puritanism remained in many ways a culture of separation and solitude, and the pain and anxieties that attend separation insinuate themselves at many points within Bradstreet's poetry. While over the course of her poetic career she voiced her acute sense of separation from a number of places and persons, her articulation of distance from England itself is of fundamental importance — not simply because it naturally made her perception of loss keener while living in the New World but, more substantially, because the geographic distance from her homeland inevitably became entwined with the Puritan belief-system in her community. Much has been written and said already about Bradstreet's marriage poems and elegies, all of which deal in one form or another with her sense of separation from a loved one, be it her husband, Simon, who traveled frequently, or her father, who died in 1653, or the three grandchildren who died either in infancy or in early childhood. Rosamond Rosenmeier has made a thorough analysis of the theme of separation in the marriage poems, calling it their "most distinctive feature" (Rosenmeier 119). Less attention, however, has been paid to analyzing Bradstreet's attempt to surmount the distance between England and the strange, new world in which she and her fellow Puritans eked out their existence after 1630. Specifically, in "A Dialogue between Old England and New," Bradstreet wrote as a dedicated member of her community during a time when civil war was breaking out in England over the very issues that, in part, compelled emigration. By composing a "Dialogue" that would see Old England delineate a Puritan colonial point of view, Bradstreet not only reflected the acute sense of isolation felt by her fellow Puritans but also reminded her community of its original purpose "as a Citty vpon a Hill" and thus shored up its flagging self-esteem in a time of increasing political and economic uncertainty.

Contrary to what Elizabeth Wade White states in her biography of Anne Bradstreet, the "New Jerusalem of Winthrop's company" was *not*, by 1642, "sure of its continuing existence," even if it "had settled into a substantial human community" (White 157). Instead, more recent historical research indicates that as far back as 1632 rumors "about the impending collapse of the Massachusetts Bay Colony" were common in England (Cressy 23). A worried Thomas Dudley would write to the Countess of Lincoln that "they who went discontentedly from us the last year, out of their evil affections towards us, have raised many false and scandalous reports against us, affirming us to be Brownists in religion, and ill affected to our state at home, and that these vile reports have won credit with some who formerly wished us well" (Dudley 331). During the 1630s there was, in point of fact, a plethora of English viewpoints regarding the state of New England, but

> By 1637 the news was mostly bad, tainted by reports of 'error and faction' and the long-distance echoes of the Antinomian controversy. The leaders of the Bay Colony still attempted to limit the export of unfavourable news, to soften the impact of criticism, and to ensure that their spokesmen in London could control the damage, but contradictory and unflattering stories continued to leak out.... Rumour circulated in England again in 1640 to the effect that the Massachusetts Colony was about to fold. Migration faltered, even before the rapidly-evolving religious and political crisis in England transformed the situation. Sudden economic ruin and crisis of spiritual confidence beset the holy commonwealth, leading to a further evolution of its image in England. Some New England settlers, cold, depressed and disappointed, toyed with the idea of further migration to a more favoured place. Hundreds went back to England [Cressy 23, 24,& 26; see also Conforti 65].

Rather than a growing, prosperous colony with ship-filled harbors exchanging people and supplies, New England in 1642 found itself increasingly isolated by rumors and bad press as well as by the onset of civil war in England. If nothing else, there was an exodus of people returning to England that exceeded the number of new settlers (Cressy 201). So many important New England Puritans found themselves sailing eastward, both to escape tensions and to join the Parliamentarian forces in England, that the flux constituted what we would call "a brain drain," about which "John Winthrop was furious" (Cressy 200). On the other side of the Atlantic, "The end of migration to New England ... coincided with the resurgence of Puritan political power in England. Why travel 3,000 miles to create a new society when one could now remake the world at home?" (Anderson 18).

For those who remained in New England, "A Dialogue between Old England and New" would reflect the ways in which they would repeat and revise their reasons for emigration as well as interpret the crisis abroad in terms acceptable to the Puritan community. Thus Bradstreet's audience *circa* 1642 was primarily a New World one, even though the poem would eventually circulate in England.[30] What "Dialogue" was emphatically not was a poem that was "essentially feminine, for although the ladies employ the language of preacher, politician, and soldier in their conversation, one is constantly reminded that this is an outspoken discussion of a family crisis, between a mother and daughter who are as closely bound in affection as they are in blood" (White 160). On the contrary, because the female speakers converse in mainly masculine terms, they demonstrate the strength of a specific patriarchal audience located within the larger and diverse society of this time. The poem arguably discloses the subordination of the female — in this case in particular, a woman poet testing her craft — to concerns that are primarily male and Puritan. It is simplistic to argue that "Dialogue" reveals a bond of affection between the two representatives of Old England and New; rather, what is more in evidence throughout the poem is Bradstreet's desire, on behalf of her group, to put words in the mouth of England that express what she believes Puritan colonists would wish to hear and, indeed, what she herself believes.[31] Although what the poem delivers is, in part, the expression of a vital desire to remain connected — politically, culturally, and economically — to England, Bradstreet also makes the Puritans' reasons for dissension and exile abundantly clear.

When Old England, in response to her daughter's query, asks at the outset of the poem,

> Art ignorant indeed, of these my woes?
> Or must my forced tongue these griefes disclose?
> And must my selfe dissect my tatter'd state,
> Which 'mazed Christendome stands wondring at? [*CW* 141],

she begins to manifest a distinctly colonial perspective. In the interrogative, the mother-figure alludes to problems arising from the distance between herself and New England, making it plain that the colonial Puritans are apprehensive regarding their own lack of information and knowledge about events abroad. Such anxiety would, of course, stem from the trickle of news available to settlers in New England. The lines that follow raise questions about the connection between England and the colony, and reveal the Puritans' ambivalence about themselves and their relationship to England:

> And thou a childe, a Limbe, and dost not feele
> My weakned fainting body now to reele?
> This Phisick-purging-potion I have taken,
> Will bring Consumption, or an Ague quaking,

Unlesse some Cordial thou fetch from high,
Which present help may ease this malady.
If I decease, dost think thou shalt survive?
Or by my wasting state, dost think to thrive?
Then weigh our case, if't be not justly sad,
Let me lament alone, while thou art glad.

Through the mouth of Old England, Bradstreet asserts and clarifies Puritan distress about how events across the sea will reflect their identity and affect their future. The series of questions are essentially those of Bradstreet's audience about its own strengths and weaknesses vis-à-vis Old England. While they reflect the Puritan colonists' view that their cause is godly since they have access to a "Cordial" they can "fetch from high," that indeed they might well be comforted to some extent by their distance from civil strife, there is also the distinct suggestion that the settlers see a disquieting causal link between England's condition and their own increasing isolation.

The poem's questions, moreover, all focus on the issue of determinism, and are, in effect, Puritan questions regarding power, consolidation, and expansion in the New England theatre, i.e., Will the community in New England be subject to the consequences of English strife, or will it remain unaffected due to its godliness? The metaphors of "childe" and "Limbe" both imply contingency; New England is a part related to a larger whole without which it cannot survive. Each of the three queries above probes this issue in one way or another, and we can be sure that the subject of New England's affiliation with Old England was foremost in the minds of Bradstreet's audience. Colonial Puritans would be anxious about their isolation at the same time as they might feel "glad" about England's "wasting state."

In other words, the Puritans in New England felt that they stood to be both vindicated and isolated by the events unfolding across the Atlantic. And the litany of English history that ensues in New England's reply discloses the colonists' desire to prove that, more than a decade after the transatlantic crossing, they remain very much in touch with their English roots. Certainly New England goes to great lengths in her delineation of an English historical point of view, consoling homesick pilgrims by shrinking the distance between England and its colony. In twenty-two lines, Bradstreet has her speaker recite a tortuous short history of English wars from Saxon times to the present, the upshot being that New Englanders are still primarily *English* in their world view. Referring to herself as "Your humble Childe," New England evokes submission and demonstrates that she is more than able to "guesse" at the possible historical causes of Old England's current misery. But by thus displaying her ready knowledge of things English, New England also displays how her own identity still hinges on that of the mother country:

> Your humble Childe intreats you, shew your grief,
> Though Armes, nor Purse she hath, for your releif:
> Such is her poverty, yet shall be found
> A supplyant for your help, as she is bound.

The Puritan colonists' precarious position in relation to England is constantly implied. They are "bound" to England at the same time as they want to maintain their repudiation of her. Farther on in "Dialogue," New England goes so far as to take partial responsibility for her mother's "fearfull sinnes" even though, strangely, it is just these acts that the daughter claims have driven her into exile: "My guilty hands (in part) hold up with you, / A sharer in your punishment's my due" (145).

The extent of the ambivalence evident in "Dialogue"—of the Puritan colonists' conflicting feelings of yearning and self-righteousness—is also apparent in Old England's willingness to malign herself, especially for her past mistreatment of Puritans. Because Bradstreet imagines England's point of view, the dissection referred to in Old England's opening address is actually performed by proxy, not only to reveal New England's awareness of the homeland's "tatter'd state" but also to compel some kind of contrition, however fictitious. Curiously, such a strategy is not unlike what a child will do to address a perceived injury at the hands of a parent. Here England's tongue is indeed "forced" as Bradstreet enacts her community's official narrative, or story, of events abroad. Having responded to and confirmed her daughter's history of her wars, Old England makes a diagnosis of her current problems in terms that would not only exonerate but aggrandize the Puritan community in New England. Old England's putative "selfe-dissection" is truly a colonial Puritan analysis with a colonial Puritan agenda.

Neglected and almost forgotten in the maelstrom of events in England, the Puritan colonists were moved to anger and indignation, and thus the figure of Old England goes on to state:

> Famine, and Plague, two sisters of the Sword,
> Destruction to a Land doth soone afford;
> They're for my punishments ordain'd on high,
> Unless thy teares prevent it speedily [143].

As forces congenial to Puritanism waged a successful war on Charles I, a war which would ironically bring England "into its period of greatest permissiveness" (Ziff 80) and thus threaten the stability of Puritan New England even more, Bradstreet attributes to England a perspective that amounts to sheer wishful thinking. Fitting the current crisis into a Calvinist framework, she imagines New England as possessing the spiritual power to curb God's wrath and "prevent it speedily" from being visited on the motherland. Yet the reality of the situation, as Cressy observes, was that "Instead of a model 'city upon a hill,' New England was, by 1642, in danger of becoming a forlorn and distant side-show":

> the principal attraction of New England in those troubled times was its remoteness from the distress of public affairs in old England. New England had become a refuge rather than a beacon. John Winthrop, Jr., described the colonies as "an hiding place ... when their precious brethren have been so long under the hurries, hazards and sufferings of civil wars." New England could at least offer "settled peace and prosperity" in contrast to the confusions in "our dear native country," although Quakers, Baptists, Antinomians and Indians knew better [Cressy 28–29].

Cressy's final point — that even the notion of New England as a refuge for dissenters was a spurious one since the government was essentially a theocracy intolerant of heterogeneity — applies especially to "Dialogue."

The extent of the confession "forced" from the tongue of Old England must have made sweet reading for many New England Puritans:

> Before I tell the effect, ile shew the cause,
> Which are my Sins, the breach of sacred Lawes;
> Idolatry, supplanter of a Nation,
> With foolish superstitious adoration;
> And lik'd, and countenanc'd by men of might,
> The Gospel is trod down, and hath no right;
> Church Offices are sold, and bought, for gaine,
> That Pope, had hope, to find *Rome* here againe;
> For Oathes, and Blasphemies did ever eare
> From *Beelzebub* himself, such language heare?

> What scorning of the Saints of the most high,
> What injuries did daily on them lye;
> What false reports, which nick-names did they take,
> Nor for their owne, but for their Masters sake;
> And thou, poore soule, wast jeer'd among the rest,
> Thy flying for the Truth I made a jeast [143–44].

Even if one argued that the Puritan voice is justified here because Round-heads led by Cromwell would eventually win the war in England, this distinctly Puritanized English "history" reveals the extent to which Bradstreet projects a specific perspective across the Atlantic and back again. Such a point of view is also rife with fictions held by Puritan colonists about themselves, not least of which is the belief they had left England "for the Truth." Many historians today would agree with Charles Edward Banks "that a considerable part of the passengers of the Winthrop Fleet were loyal to the English Church and had no intent or desire to be a part of any scheme that pretended otherwise.... Many of them never joined the Puritan churches, nor became Freemen after their arrival" (Banks 22).[32]

If such a statement seems to contradict the more common assumption that settlers in general — or passengers of the Winthrop Fleet in particular — were of one mind in their reasons for migrating, or that they constituted a cohesive, revolutionary movement, "Dialogue" establishes itself as typical of the ruling party's resolve to inscribe and maintain a particular history of New England. "'Puritans,'" writes Cressy, "stride through the pages of popular New England history as if no one else was present" (Cressy 79). As Joseph A. Conforti puts it, "colonial New England was not an insular American city upon a hill, either at the time of its founding or in the course of its colonial development" (Conforti 3). Indeed, Lee Oser's statement that "We have learned to view Puritan religious orthodoxy not as an adamantine column, but as a crowded hall" (190) is indicative of the growing view that even within orthodoxy, schism and dissent were almost continuous from 1630 on. Additionally, Timothy Sweet points out that "the seeds of expansion were sown even in Winthrop's sermon on social cohesion":

> On the one hand, the colonists valued the organic society defined most famously by Winthrop's "Modell," with its images of the colony as a city on a hill and its inhabitants as a single body united in Christ. On the other hand, the Biblical rationale for colonization — God's command to Adam,

"againe renewed to Noah," to "increase & multiply, replenish the earth & subdue it," which the colonists interpreted as a mandate to settle what they considered to be unimproved lands — led to geographical dispersal [Sweet 58].

What emerges from this is the fact that Anne Bradstreet composed "Dialogue" not on behalf of a struggling, yet essentially unified New World community but, rather, on behalf of one Puritan group within a heterogeneous one at a particular time. With a vested interest in the civil war in England, this subversive, yet authoritarian group had to find ways to protect its image — and thus its power — as "a Citty vpon a Hill," and, as in any conflict, one of the most effective tools at its disposal would be propaganda.[33] Wendy Martin's assertion that "'A Dialogue between Old England and New' laments the devastating effects of male territoriality, ... [revealing] Bradstreet's distress about the waste and loss caused by the battles to demonstrate moral superiority" disregards Bradstreet's own complicity (Martin 38).[34] Martin too easily perceives Bradstreet as writing against the patriarchal grain, when in fact she is serving its purposes. Nothing more readily evinces Bradstreet's submission to the tenets of Puritan ideology at this point in her life than the disseminating tone of her poetic voice. This tone is most apparent as Old England castigates herself hyperbolically:

> For Bribery, Adultery, for Thefts, and Lyes,
> Where is the Nation, I cann't paralize;
> With Usury, Extortion, and Oppression,
> These be the *Hydra's* of my stout transgression;
> These be the bitter fountains, heads, and roots,
> Whence flow'd the source, the sprigs, the boughs, and fruits;
> Of more than thou canst heare, or I relate,
> That with high hand I still did perpetrate;
> For these, were threatned the wofull day,
> I mock'd the Preachers, put it farre away;
> The Sermons yet upon record doe stand,
> That cry'd, destruction to my wicked Land:
> These Prophets mouthes (alas the while) was stopt,
> Unworthily, some backs whipt, and eares cropt;
> Their reverent cheeks, did beare the glorious markes
> Of stinking, stigmatizing, Romish Clerkes;
> Some lost their livings, some in prison pent,

Some grossely fin'd, from friends to exile went:
Their silent tongues to heaven did vengeance cry,
Who heard their cause, and wrongs judg'd righteously.

Not only a jeremiad, "Dialogue" is also a call to arms, which again suggests Puritan New England's ambivalence about its own distance from English strife. Indeed, Sacvan Bercovitch significantly points out that here Bradstreet calls "for a holy war" (*Puritan Origins* 62). Even though a Puritan victory abroad would jeopardize New England's exemplary status, the crucial issue remains that "Religion, Gospell, here lies at stake" (146). The poem's frequently violent language is deployed at a time when "England was experiencing all the tensions created by the development within a single society of [the] two distinct cultures [of "Court" and "Country"] ... there were no secure monoliths in Jacobean and Caroline England" (Kammen 131). Thus Bradstreet has New England hope "That Right may have its right, though't be with blood," and zealously proclaim that

These are the dayes, the Churches foes to crush,
To root out Prelates, head, tail, branch, and rush.
Let's bring *Baals* vestments out, to make a fire,
Their Myters, Surplices, and all their tire,
Copes, Rochets, Crossiers, and such trash,
And let their names consume, but let the flash
Light Christendome, and all the world to see,
We hate *Romes* Whore, with all her trumperie [146–47].

Elsewhere in "Dialogue," Old England puns on the imprisonment and execution of her daughter's High Church enemies: "They took high *Strafford* lower by the head, / And to their *Laud* be't spoke, they held i'th' Tower, / All *Englands* Metropolitane that houre" (144–45). As White informs us, the four lines ending in "Romish Clerkes"

were deleted from the second printing of the poem. They refer to the punishments inflicted, at the behest of Archbishop Laud, on such writers as William Prynne, Henry Burton, and John Bastwick. Although the Court of Star Chamber, in which these men were tried, imposed many cruel sentences on nonconformists before its abolition in 1640, it never admittedly contained "Romish Clerkes," and Anne Bradstreet was well advised to cancel these lines while preparing the poem for its second appearance [White 163].

To English readers, such lines could have been seen as dangerous during the Restoration period that followed, when "The Puritan movement in

England disintegrated" (Conforti 99) and "extreme penalties were inflicted on the Regicides and other Puritan leaders, a number of whom were arrested and executed" (White 166).[35]

"A Dialogue between New England and Old" is less a dialogue than a representation of a narrow, fractious ideology striving to hold on to its sense of its own hegemony. As such, the poem excludes and abjures the *other*, i.e., Catholics, Laudians, Royalists, Muslims (Turks), and any other "Canaanites" (148), just as New England Puritans — no matter what dissensions they had to contend with among themselves — would often ostracize Quakers, Antinomians, Aboriginals, and anyone else "who found that in crossing the Atlantic they had not journeyed far enough to find liberty of conscience" (Anderson 118). The Canadian environmentalist John A. Livingston calls this kind of orthodoxy a form of "exotic ideology," a set of values introduced into a new environment with "an effect similar to that of a measles bug, or a goat, or a mongoose, or a sailor on first glimpsing one of Madagascar's extraordinary terrestrial lemurs" (Livingston 56):

> Such is the nature of world conquest by a system of ideas and beliefs indigenous originally to Europe, exotic everywhere else. It rests fundamentally on Western philosophy, science, and technology, together constituting a metaphysics peculiar to its area of origin. It is anointed and sanctified through the manifest truth of its extraordinary success in competition with ideologies indigenous to other parts of the world. Its advancement is understood to be necessary and inevitable [71].

One significant result of the introduction of "exotic ideology" is what Livingston calls *pseudospeciation*: "The invaders see themselves as qualitatively different from the invaded indigenous peoples, and behave accordingly" (56).

The Puritans' exclusive perspective is readily apparent in "Dialogue's" last words, spoken by New England. Having exhorted her mother "To sack proud *Rome*, and all her vassals rout," as well as to wage war on "*Turky*" and "*Gog*," New England concludes her depiction of England's glorious future as a champion of the Puritan cause throughout the world:

> No Canaanite shall then be found ith' land,
> And holinesse, on horses bells shall stand,
> If this make way thereto, then sigh no more,
> Farewell dear mother, Parliament prevail,
> And in a while you'l tell another tale [148].

The last two lines suggest the triumph of the official colonial Puritan perspective as it becomes institutionalized in England and from there proliferates via official codes and narrative structures. The end of "Dialogue" therefore envisages the repression and destruction of alternative perspectives at the same time as it elevates its idealized own. If another tale is to follow, then it will constitute a sequel to this one, the implication being that "Dialogue" possesses primary status as a kind of *Logos* or "first word" from the New World. "Tale," however, connotes the power of the imagination to create fictions and fantasies. As such, "Dialogue" also reveals itself as one expression of the colonial Puritan desire to be heard and noticed abroad. In the final analysis, the poem is not a dialogue but a powerful projection of the dreams, wishes, and fears of New England Puritans.

Writing about the Puritan colonists, Michael Zuckerman points out: "Saved and damned, Christian and heathen, civilized and savage, white and black were counterpositions that came congenially and, indeed, compellingly to the colonists, as though they could redeem their own enigmatic identities by disparaging the identities of others.... Thus these settlers came to know themselves by their negations" (Zuckerman 143). Part of a community that, defining itself by what it was not, still desperately needed to retain its ties to England, the author of "Dialogue" tries to traverse the distance between homeland and colony by imagining the English point of view. But in doing so, Bradstreet cannot help but make that perspective both English and Puritan, as a consequence of which all other points of view, both abroad and at home, are necessarily denied existence. Rosamond Rosenmeier's statement that "The relationship of mother to daughter is initially presented as extremely close — *symbiotic* might describe it" (Rosenmeier 47) is accurate only in terms of such a rhetorical strategy. In other words, when the mother says (to quote the same passage that Rosenmeier does), "And thou a childe, a Limbe, and dost not feele / My weakened fainting body now to reele?" (141), the implied symbiosis is a poetically conjured one. It allows the Puritan New England government, led by men like John Winthrop and Thomas Dudley, to continue to validate its own existence and to believe in itself as vitally connected to English concerns.

While it is true that "Dialogue" repeatedly signals how deeply the Puritan colonists yearned for, and worried about, England, the sense of partisanship, of difference and distance from home, remains so ingrained that the longing and distress are always qualified, if not at times magnified. Old England's speech indicates colonial concern but like the rest of the poem the perspective also reveals the need for vindication. The mother-figure speaks of "My plundered Townes, my houses devastation, / My ravisht virgins, and my young men slain," but with that she also appeals to the strength of her daughter's "child-like love": "For my relief now use thy utmost skill, / And recompence me good, for all my ill" (146). New England's qualified response again manifests the tripartite agenda that underlies the entire poem: "Your griefs I pity much, but should do wrong, / To weep for that we *both* have pray'd for long" (146, emphasis mine). These words imply, as well as speak to, the audience of Puritans in New England; attribute to Old England a distinctly Puritan point of view; and in so doing exclude the other perspectives whose existence is nevertheless suggested all along.

Bradstreet's Problematic Relationship with Thomas Dudley

In many ways, New England colonists not only replicated the divisions and tensions they had left behind in England but encountered new ones as well. Despite the goal of establishing a unified, coherent community based on Calvinistic precepts, Puritans found themselves facing problems of faction and turmoil, problems that stemmed in part from the very issue of having to negotiate relationships with "strangers." Joseph A. Conforti points out that, "Most commonly, *stranger* referred to all non–Puritan inhabitants, whether white, black, or Native American" (4). As Anne Bradstreet wrote to her children, "god will haue vs beholden one to another" (209). Such thinking was deeply embedded in the Puritan psyche, with its instinct for preservation; and, indeed, Bradstreet herself was quite adept at warding off the possibility of her own exclusion from the community. She would have witnessed the debacle surrounding Anne Hutchinson and felt acutely the anger of Thomas Dudley towards her sister, Sarah Keayne: both these women had "been excommunicated from the church and ostracized by the community for speaking their minds in public" (Martin 17; see also Conforti 93).

If Bradstreet wanted to speak her own mind, she had to be careful not to offend her father, who, while encouraging her to read and write poetry, also took it upon himself to keep the community purged of subversive elements (Dudley 315; Cressy 45 & 85; Oser 189–90). In her dedication of *The Tenth Muse* to Dudley, Bradstreet "assumes the persona of the obedient daughter" (Martin 16) but, more than that, the epigram also evokes the bonds of obligation and submission that compelled her to move to the New World in the first place: "From her, that to your selfe more duty owes / Then waters, in the boundlesse Ocean flowes" (*CW* 6). The subtle tension contained by these lines is understandable in view of the sense of debt felt by Bradstreet. Rosamond Rosenmeier calls these lines

> A typically cryptic and typically complex Bradstreet statement: the "duty" owed by daughter to father appears to be greater than the ocean. In her phrasing of this "debt," however, the daughter suggests that the debt is lost in the "boundless" body of water to which it belongs. After all, how does one separate waters from an ocean? This debt is more like a great source that the father and daughter share than it is like a specific sum to be paid or duty to be performed [Rosenmeier 41].

Bradstreet expands on the subject of her debt and obligation to her father in "To her Father with some verses" (CW 183–84), a poem whose main features Lee Oser astutely observes are "more characteristic of the 'Tribe of Ben,' the very un–Puritan Cavalier school" even while "Puritanism speaks through every line" (189–90). How much the death in 1653 of Thomas Dudley, Anne's first reader, would see that debt discharged is up for further analysis and debate, as the influence of Dudley surely continued to impact his daughter's poetic positioning even in a mature meditation like "Contemplations." This issue may be partly understood as hinging on Bradstreet's need to balance and recognize public and private claims upon her throughout her writing life. In his essay entitled "Anne Bradstreet's Poetic Voices," Kenneth Requa persuasively separates Bradstreet's poems into public and private works (150–166). Joseph A. Conforti adds to this the fact that "love and passion pervaded the marriage covenant" (61) and that these emotions are obvious in Bradstreet's love poems to her husband, Simon. Published in 1650, *The Tenth Muse* is made up of poems composed for a circle of readers within and outside her immediate family unit; as such, these would not easily jeopardize Bradstreet's position as a poet who was both a Puritan and a woman since, as has already been demonstrated relative to "Dialogue," Bradstreet wrote with such an audience in mind.

On the other hand, *Several Poems*, which contains all the private pieces, appeared in 1678, six years after Bradstreet's death. Of these latter poems, certainly the majority were written after 1653. As the editors of *The Complete Works of Anne Bradstreet* (1981) state in the Introduction: "The most significant development in her new writings after 1650 was a turn toward a more personal mode of expression, away from the formality of her already published work" (McElrath, Jr. & Robb xx).[36]

Thomas Dudley's death constituted a profound loss to the Puritan establishment, but how much it freed Bradstreet to articulate herself more freely, knowing that her first reader was no longer around to peruse her work directly, is unclear. Certainly in the years that followed her father's death, she would elegize more intensely, expressing more doubt and anger and less caution and restraint while grieving the death of a loved one. Just as certain is the fact that Anne Bradstreet seldom wrote without also resorting to the cryptic mode of utterance identified by Rosenmeier and which Bradstreet likely learned to employ early on as a strategy both for and against her first reader, Thomas Dudley. Whether she would do so in a way that also reflected incremental changes in New England Puritanism, such that — for instance — the practice of austerity increasingly gave way to ritual and ornamentation, invites inquiry and is part of the project here. David E. Stannard comments, for instance, on changes in Puritan burial practices, linking these to a wider cultural shake-up, and providing an intriguing context in which to read Bradstreet's elegy for Dudley:

> Prior to mid-century, there is no extant evidence of New England's Puritans taking much care at all to even mark the graves of their deceased. While it is possible that some sort of wooden markers may have been employed in the early years, it is a striking phenomenon that only in the mid-1650s did New England's cemeteries begin to become populated not only with bodies, but also with carefully carved stones to indicate the sites of burial. By the 1660s the popularity of this practice was widespread, and the stones themselves had grown increasingly large and the carvings on them more elaborate [Stannard 116–117].

Thomas Dudley's last testament provided his family with an unequivocal reminder of the kind of life he had led and, by implication, enjoined them to continue to do likewise: "I have hated & doe hate every falce way in religion, not onely the Old Idolitry and superstition of Popery, which is weareing away, but much more, (as being much worse), the newe heresies, blasphamies, & errors of late sprange upp in our native Country of England, and secretly received & fostered here more then I wishe they were." Likewise, a poem found in his pocket concluded: "If Men be left, and otherwise Combine, / My Epitaph's, I DY'D NO LIBERTINE" (White 296–97). Simple and stark, this epitaph evokes the kind of tension that Anne Bradstreet would not resolve satisfactorily but that nevertheless informs her best poetry. For Dudley, such tension — between the claims of the individual and those of the community, as signified by "Combine" and "LIBERTINE" — seems to have been less problematic. Throughout the years of his role as a colonial leader, Dudley remained true to his vision of what it meant to be a Puritan: "We are not like those which have dispensations to lie; but as we were free enough in Old England to turn our insides outwards, sometimes to our disadvantage, very unlike is it that now, ... we should be so unlike ourselves" (Dudley 332).

Turning the "insides outwards" was to the Puritans a proclamation in itself of freedom from pretension, and in the first part of the seventeenth century it entailed the renunciation of any kind of embellishment. Hence when Anne Bradstreet begins her elegy, entitled "To the Memory of my dear and ever honoured Father, Thomas Dudley Esq" (*CW* 165–66), she tries to make it immediately clear that she is not straying from the path of decorum: she is "By duty bound, and not by custome led / To celebrate the praises of the dead." In the face of death, early Puritans looked on elaborate memorials and funeral ceremonies as not only improper but possibly blasphemous, since no one but God could actually know the condition of the departed soul (Stannard 99; Geddes 110). "To celebrate the praises of the dead," then, was to take a risk, for it assumed that the soul had all along been saved for paradise even though Calvinists rigidly believed that most people were predestined to be damned for eternity. Of course, Puritans on both sides of the Atlantic wrote elegies, and the New England custom established by the mid–1640s of attaching verses to the coffin or hearse (or throwing them into the grave) of the departed circumvented the dearth of graveside prayers, eulogies, and sermons. But as Stannard says of Bradstreet's elegy for Dudley, "By comparison with others, Bradstreet was being positively emotional": "the overwhelming tendency was to resist such sentiments" (154–55). To this Cheryl Walker adds, "Elegies, too, were pared and pruned to exemplify the pattern of Christian piety. The poet grows in stature as he comes to speak for the public and political rather than the lyrical self" ("In the Margin" 111). Indeed, Walker here evokes the complexity of Bradstreet's ideological positioning, what Oser calls "her crippling self-consciousness" (193–94), within her community both before and after Dudley's death.

Stating that her elegy stems from being "duty bound," Bradstreet still manages to retain a hold — albeit a precarious one — on Puritan propriety. Patriarchal New Englanders would understand that Dudley was her "Father, Guide, Instructor too, / To whom I ought whatever I could doe." Just as no one "knew him better," so too there was no "greater debtor" than this daughter of Thomas Dudley, and the poem, in fact, is viewed by Bradstreet as a kind of final payment: "But now or never I must pay my Sum; / While others tell his worth, I'le not be dumb." Bradstreet is also careful to point out that, besides being zealous, humble, and "Truths friend," Dudley had renounced all worldly pursuits:

> High thoughts he gave no harbour in his heart,
> Nor honours pufft him up, when he had part:
> Those titles loath'd, which some too much do love
> For truly his ambition lay above.
> His humble mind so lov'd humility,
> He left it to his race for Legacy:
> And oft and oft, with speeches mild and wise,
> Gave his in charge, that Jewel rich to prize.
> No ostentation seen in all his wayes,
> As in the mean ones, of our foolish dayes.

Finally, what Bradstreet says about Dudley's life of austerity and strict adherence to basic Puritan precepts creates ironic tension in the poem, a tension that may have been present at many Puritan gravesides. "No ostentation" is dealt with by the public broadside sheet that is nonetheless "only ... rarely used by the author as a 'Vent hole' for grief. Elegies expressed public sentiments" (Geddes 159). Writes William J. Scheick, "they were not designed to survive this occasion, and that they did not is evident from their scarcity today.... The elegy was funerated" (298). The New England funeral elegy, unlike its English counterpart, "plumbed the depths of the collective self" and was customarily left in the grave (290).

Bradstreet's elegy may also be seen as ironic insofar as it tests the Puritan concept of "due distance" between parents and children. As Stannard has shown, "The prescribed and common personal relationship between parents and children was one of restraint and even aloofness" (57). "Due distance" enabled Puritans to cushion themselves against the possible death of a loved one, either parent or child, but it also prevented too much emotional attachment to one who might well be destined for eternal damnation (Stannard 57–8).[37] Thus Bradstreet presses the limits of traditional Puritan practice if she fails to keep her emotional distance from her father. Here she assumes her father's salvation — "For he a Mansion had, prepar'd above, / For which he sigh'd and pray'd & long'd full sore" — and expresses her grief with a "mournfull mind, sore prest."

Wendy Martin's observation that "Bradstreet struggled to write poetry in a society that was hostile to the imagination; nevertheless, she was able to express the range of her feelings" more than ever points to the paradoxical circumstances in which Bradstreet wrote (Martin 9). These circumstances provide the context for understanding the Puritan parent-child paradigm that governs so much in Bradstreet's life and work: not just her relationship with her father but, as we have already witnessed, the New World Puritans' sense of relatedness to Mother England. This core paradigm also dictates, as we shall see presently, the careful fury Bradstreet evinces in her poetic lamentations over the deaths of her grandchildren. Indeed, Anne Bradstreet can be seen as straining to stake out a cautious, politic position from which she can speak with an integrated voice informed by both her private and public selves, as though anticipating what Alan Watts, writing from the coast of California three centuries later, would argue concerning the civilized response to the spontaneity of children:

> We ... make the mistake of socializing children, not by developing their spontaneity, but by developing a system of resistances and fears which ... splits the organism into a spontaneous center and an inhibiting center. Thus it is rare indeed to find an integrated person capable of self-controlling spontaneity, which sounds like a contradiction in terms.... Spontaneity is, after all, total sincerity — the whole being involved in the act without the slightest reservation — and as a rule the civilized adult is goaded into it only by abject despair, intolerable suffering, or imminent death [Watts 112].

Certainly Watts's analysis of the split organism, divided into "spontaneous" and "inhibiting center[s]" that alternately relinquish and take control, depending on the context, can be applied to Anne Bradstreet. From this perspective, Bradstreet's elegy for her father invites a reading in the context of a transitional New England society, especially in the latter half of the seventeenth century. We can add it to the earlier elegies and "David's Lamentation for Saul and Jonathan," which Rosamond Rosenmeier identifies "as the first poetic fruits of New England's declension" (86), although we should be cautious about the notion that Puritanism in seventeenth-century New England underwent straightforward "declension." As Conforti makes clear, it was never that simple, even after 1660 when the prospect for "Puritan reform in the homeland perished," although Conforti does attribute to second-generation Puritans "more of an *Americanized* collective consciousness" (98). Isolated by English strife and mired at times in economic decline, Puritan New England struggled in its relationship to Old England and, as Stannard points out, "in unsettled and unstable societies ... the loss of an individual [in this case, Dudley] is simply much more disruptive to the social order" (128).

> As long as the New Englanders maintained their identities as Englishmen, as long as English Puritanism provided a model and England promised an eventual home for them, as long as they felt themselves part of the forces of history at work in their homeland, the Puritans of New England were culturally and psychologically at one with their relatives and friends on the opposite side of the Atlantic. But once these ties were severed, if not formally at least conceptually, New England's Puritans were on their own. The existence of such a break became apparent within two decades of settlement, by the turn of the 1650s [122–23].

Thus Bradstreet's elegy for Thomas Dudley may be seen as part of a social and cultural transition that is both private and public.[38] As Stephen Fender adds, describing Dudley's final parting with Anne's sister, Mrs. John Woodbridge, in 1648, five years before Dudley's death, "There is something in his depression that is almost fatalistic, as though New England is decaying along with him, its lifespan to be measured on the scale of the human fourscore and ten" (Fender 275). Not only would Bradstreet find herself separated by death from the direct influence and authority of her father (he will no longer be around to "*try*" her verses [Rosenmeier 54]), but the Puritan community in New England would lose one of the leaders of the original Winthrop Fleet — "His Generation serv'd his labours cease; / And to his Fathers gathered is in peace" — and thus find itself ever more separated from England and English Puritanism. A new generation of New England Puritans would come of age that "did not simply shed [its] Puritan skin to reveal Yankee souls" but that was nevertheless "more ... *Amer-*

ican" (Conforti 98). As such, this generation "ritualized death as only the most non–Puritan of pre–Restoration Englishmen would have dared to do. In meeting death, it seems clear, [New England Puritans] encountered something their English ancestors never had. What they encountered was themselves and their profound sense of tribal vulnerability" (Stannard 119–22).

Such vulnerability is seen in the epitaph for Dudley with which Bradstreet's elegy closes:

> Within this Tomb a Patriot lyes
> That was both pious, just and wise,
> To Truth a shield, to right a Wall,
> To Sectaryes a whip and Maul,
> A Magazine of History,
> A Prizer of good Company
> In manners pleasant and severe
> The Good him lov'd, the bad did fear,
> And when his time with years was spent
> If some rejoyc'd, more did lament.

The several martial images here — describing Dudley as "a shield," "a Wall," "a whip and Maul" — suggest not only how keenly New England Puritans felt threatened by difference and diversity but also the kinds of cultural paradigms they would apply to the massive "wilderness" theatre in which they now played out their individual and communal lives. As a "Patriot" now ensconced within his "Tomb," Dudley would become part of his own "Magazine of History," another figure or "weapon" in the store of personages and events that would be represented later by Puritan writers such as Cotton Mather. In view of this, the irony of Anne Bradstreet's epitaph for her father seems to mount. It is written with the characteristic doubleness that Rosenmeier identifies as a major a feature of Bradstreet's voice, and it also resonates with the complex relationship Bradstreet had with her father and with the "difficult task" of composing his eulogy (Rosenmeier 13, 87, & 91).

Losing Grandchildren in the New World

One of the most anthologized of Anne Bradstreet's poems, "In memory of my dear grand-child Elizabeth Bradstreet" (*CW* 186–87), dispenses with communal requirements to question privately the elusive ways of the

Puritan God in the New World. Written over a dozen years after the death of Thomas Dudley, this elegy displays a more complete disregard for public questions of predestination and "due distance" than "To the Memory of my dear and ever honoured Father." While, according to Stannard, many Puritan parents and guardians still saw "the large number of acknowledged 'reprobate infants'" as irrevocably damned, and while many others were "'putting children out,' both to early apprenticeship and simply extended stays with other families ... [in order to maintain] the necessary distance between parent and child" (Stannard 52 & 58), Anne Bradstreet earnestly lamented the death of her year-and-a-half-old grandchild. Indeed, like Ben Jonson's "On My First Son" (written over fifty years earlier), Bradstreet's elegy for Elizabeth diverges from Christian tradition to display a subtle yet intense fury over the arbitrariness of "fate," which for Jonson is "Exacted ... on the just day" and for Bradstreet is guided "by [God's] hand alone" (Jonson 762).

In Bradstreet's poem, the concept of predestination is implicated as a source of irony and personal anguish instead of being viewed as an intellectual and theological concept to be upheld publicly and applied to the majority of the population. Although separated from Elizabeth by death, Bradstreet uses language that intimates a deeply-felt connection to the child at the same time as it camouflages a heretical rejection of divine will:

> Farewel dear babe, my hearts too much content,
> Farewel sweet babe, the pleasure of mine eye,
> Farewel fair flower that for a space was lent,
> Then ta'en away unto Eternity.
> Blest babe why should I once bewail thy fate,
> Or sigh thy dayes so soon were terminate;
> Sith thou art setled in an Everlasting state.
>
> 2.
> By nature Trees do rot when they are grown.
> And Plumbs and Apples throughly ripe do fall,
> And Corn and grass are in their season mown,
> And time brings down what is both strong and tall.
> But plants new set to be eradicate,
> And buds new blown, to have so short a date,
> Is by his hand alone that guides nature and fate.

Bradstreet's stance in this poem has been the subject of considerable debate. Critical opinion has ranged from Wendy Martin's, that "Although Bradstreet's sorrow threatens to overwhelm her, the second stanza expresses resigned acceptance of Providence" (Martin 69), to Randall W. Mawer's, that "The conclusion resulting from these meditations ... is not resignation ... but high, righteous anger, all the more fearful in its ability to disguise itself" (Mawer 210).[39] Taking Robert Daly and others to task for seeing it as a "mere tract," Mawer gets to the crux of the poem when he states, "If blame is to be placed, the blame is God's, and that surely is cause for grief" (Mawer 213 & 211).

Bradstreet begins her elegy by stressing the painful contrast between reality and desire. The heavily-accented first two feet of lines 1 through 3, with the thrice-repeated "Farewel," underscore the pain of separation felt by Bradstreet, who, at first glance, seems to berate herself for having invested too much emotionally in the relationship. But "my hearts too much content" also contains nuances of anger directed at a culture that values the practice of "weaned affections" (Miller 172). Instead of interpreting the death as a divinely-ordained purgative experience, Bradstreet makes the clause subtly sardonic by juxtaposing it with the repeated "Farewels" and by frankly admitting having done away with "due distance" to commit the sin of vanity by making the "sweet babe, the pleasure of mine eye." The question posed in the first stanza remains unanswered in the second only if the reader is looking for some kind of resolution typical of Puritanism. Ann Stanford observes that the poem does not "lead into a conventional Christian apotheosis.... The reply is closer to Herrick and the Cavaliers than to most Puritan poetry" ("Dogmatist and Rebel" 85). That Bradstreet's elegy contradicts Puritan convention is precisely the point. With its anguished question directed at the Puritan God in a triplet that ends with an Alexandrine —

> why should I once bewail thy fate,
> Or sigh the dayes so soon were terminate
> Sith thou art setled in an Everlasting state

— her elegy for Elizabeth has more in common with Jonson's for his son, which poses a similar question:

> Oh, could I lose all father now! for why
> Will man lament the state he should envy —
> To have so soon 'scaped world's and flesh's rage,
> And if no other misery, yet age?[40]

Bradstreet, in fact, goes well beyond Jonson in her criticism of divine justice (Jonson 762). While Jonson concludes by vowing that "what he loves may never like too much," Bradstreet portrays the natural order as one in which all living things are born, grow to maturity, and die, when "time brings down what is both strong and tall." The point, of course, is that the dead grandchild, like "plants new set" and "buds new blown," does not fit into this pattern. Ultimate responsibility rests, as Bradstreet sees it, not with the human subject to love judiciously, but with God, for it is "his hand alone that guides nature and fate."[41] With such a rebellious conclusion, Bradstreet places herself in direct opposition to the orthodoxy represented by her father. By aligning herself with a stance on the problem of suffering and entropy that is more Cavalier than Roundhead, she separates herself from a theological position in which she herself, as a fallen creature, would shoulder the blame for feeling the loss of her equally-depraved grandchild.

Bradstreet once again seems just able to contain her anger in yet another elegy for a deceased grandchild, "On my dear Grand-child Simon Bradstreet":

> No sooner come, but gone, and fal'n asleep,
> Acquaintance short, yet parting caus'd us weep,
> Three flours, two scarcely blown, the last i'th' bud,
> Cropt by th' Almighties hand; yet is he good,
> With dreadful awe before him let's be mute,
> Such was his will, but why, let's not dispute,
> With humble hearts and mouths put in the dust,
> Let's say he's merciful, as well as just,
> He will return, and make up all our losses,
> And smile again, after our bitter crosses [*CW* 188].

As in her elegy for Elizabeth, albeit with less effect, Bradstreet subverts Calvinist dogma even as she pays it lip service. The semi-colon in the fourth line punctuates the contradiction found in an omnipotent deity who "crops" infants like "flours," but is nonetheless "good." Bradstreet thus reveals her awareness of the ancient dilemma felt by those who have believed that God is both sovereign and just. There is, of course, irony in the fact that she then immediately proposes to her audience that "let's be mute" when she obviously intends to speak her mind. Such a strategy results in sarcasm, a departure from the politic code more carefully employed in other, earlier poems. In dissident fashion, with her "[mouth] put in the dust," Bradstreet conspires with the like-minded element in her readership but without overtly saying anything heretical: "Let's say he's merciful, as well as just." Unlike Bradstreet's father, who had died "fully ripe," these infants are likened by their grandmother to "plants new set," "buds new blown," and "Three flours, two scarcely blown." Not even the possibility of heaven is really consoling, so that Bradstreet merely gestures wearily in the appropriate direction: "Such was his will, but why, let's not dispute."

With the often turbulent attitudinal changes that her poetry exhibits towards her culture, Anne Bradstreet's writing strategy frequently involves an attempt to come to terms with an acutely uncomfortable sense of separation from the Old World. She not only desired to heal the wounds of travel but also prevent such injuries from recurring in various other ways. Accompanying her endeavors to overcome distance is, moreover, her ambivalence about the whole Puritan colonial project. Then again, this ambivalence had been imported as well as inherited by many early colonists like Bradstreet. As Michael Kammen observes, "Colonization seemed one way to resolve ... tensions bred from pluralism; but it would sometimes aggravate them instead, and ofttimes create new ones from the old matrix" (Kammen 138). From this perspective, then, the *Arbella* can be seen as a metaphor for failed escape from contradiction.

Two

Elizabeth Bishop:
To Dream Our Dreams —
Questions of Distance
and Desire

Travel as Travail; the Impact of Darwin

Like Anne Bradstreet, Elizabeth Bishop concerned herself with the meaning of distance and place in order to fulfill certain longings. If John Winthrop possessed a scant cartographic outline of the coast near Boston by which to guide his fleet of colonists, Bishop employed a variety of colorful maps as metaphors for desire, the kind of desire — for the unknown, the sacred, for new patterns of human ecology, and for home — that has often propelled travel and questing. As Barry Lopez writes, maps are "expressions of a wish for something better, for an easing of human travail" (283). In an era of environmental crisis, maps are, moreover, being rapidly revised to acknowledge and protect living spaces for nonhuman life (Wilson "Problems Without Borders" 164–66). For Bishop, though, the need to overcome distance and find a place to call her own was less overtly ideological than — albeit just as personal as — it was for Bradstreet and company. Bishop was the solitary wanderer observing and questioning the passing details of the moment, and searching for a sacred place in which to feel at home in spite of the fact that she did not always believe it could be found. Her celebrated questions of travel are also questions about what it means for humans, a rogue species, to be at home at all — to have found that object or place of desire located at a specific point in space and time, only to abandon it for yet another far-off goal.[42]

In her poems about travel, distance and desire are entwined, mainly because for Bishop travel was a matter of fulfilling personal desire, of moving towards some far-off goal. At the same time, Bishop's poems reveal how desire is thwarted, denied, or deferred during travel. The seemingly casual language she employs helps to take the edge off disappointment, but also signifies the modernists' dilemma concerning the formal expression of the desire for meaning. Bishop attempted to solve this problem by articulating it, returning again and again to expressing a wish for what could no longer be had, using a language whose apparent nonchalance became a device both for expressing desire and for surviving disappointment and pain.

Along with cartography and geography, travel constitutes a primary theme of Bishop's work, from her early poem "The Map" to "Santarém," published in 1979, a year after her death. The titles of three of the four volumes that appeared during her lifetime — *North & South* (1946), *Questions of Travel* (1965), and *Geography* (1976) — reflect this theme and reveal how consistently and consciously Bishop worked it into her art. Not surprisingly, such an obviously crucial aspect of Bishop's poetry has been the subject of much critical attention, most notably by Lorrie Goldensohn, Bonnie Costello, Anne Colwell, and Susan McCabe.[43] Bishop's critics, fellow poets, and biographers have thoroughly examined her difficult childhood,[44] finding in it the determining factors behind her celebrated lifelong search for home. These details are, of course, crucial to understanding Bishop's work, illuminating such poems as "First Death in Nova Scotia," which appears in the "Elsewhere" section of *Questions of Travel*, and the late "Pink Dog," in which Bishop's friend Lloyd Schwartz says we can catch a glimpse of the poet's tortured psyche as she describes the sight of a hairless dog on the streets of Rio de Janeiro: "You are not mad; you have a case of scabies / but look intelligent.... poor bitch" (*CP* 190).

While the rigors of questing constitute a major feature of Bishop's writing, providing one significant intertextual link to Bradstreet's "travail," Bishop's poetry can be read not just as a record of such "travail," but as a reckoning of the yearnings that cause one to undergo the kind of suffering implicit in this older word for travel. Eric J. Leed describes "travail" as "the paradigmatic 'experience,' the model of a direct and genuine experience, which transforms the person having it":

We may see something of the nature of these transformations in the roots of Indo-European languages, where *travel* and *experience* are intimately wedded terms. The Indo-European root of experience is *per (the asterisk indicates a retroconstruction from languages living and dead). *Per has been construed as "to try," "to test," "to risk" — connotations that persist in the English word *peril*. The earliest connotations of *per appear in Latin words for "experience": *experior* and *experimentum*, whence the English *experiment*. This conception of "experience" as an ordeal, as a passage through a frame of action that gauges the true dimensions and nature of the person or object passing through it, also describes the most general and ancient conception of the effects of travel upon the traveler. Many of the secondary meanings of *per refer explicitly to motion: "to cross space," "to reach a goal," "to go out." The connotations of risk and danger implicit in peril are also obvious in the Gothic cognates for *per (in which *p* becomes an *f*): *fern* (far), *fare, fear, ferry*. One of the German words for experience, *Erfahrung*, is from the Old High German *irfaran*: "to travel," "to go out," "to traverse," or "to wander...." These crossings of words and meanings reflect one of the first conceptualizations of travel as suffering, a test, an ordeal — meanings explicit in the original English word for travel: *travail* [Leed 5–6].

Given this kind of etymology, the word *travail* certainly applies, as we have seen, to Anne Bradstreet's risky voyage from England to the New World. Bradstreet, however, was obviously willing to make this journey because she shared, albeit reluctantly at times, in her community's need to search out a new land and create a new community. While Elizabeth Bishop might not completely identify with the communal aspects of this particular goal, she well knew what it was like to want to go somewhere. Like her sandpiper, she seemed always to be "looking for something, something, something" ("The Sandpiper" *CP* 131). Although by Bishop's time there were fewer geographical frontiers, and thus fewer opportunities and/or demands for heroic individual and communal action (in the Old World imperialistic senses of those words —*frontier, heroic, action*), she could ask in "Questions of Travel": "Oh, must we dream our dreams / and have them, too?" (*CP* 93).

To ask such a question is surely to risk disappointment, and Bishop's unpretentious terms hide neither her courage nor her ambition. In fact, in her poems dealing strictly with notions of travel, she repeatedly returns to the ways in which desire is contained, configured, and, most importantly, frustrated, in a world where seemingly everything has already been mapped and explored. In the novel *V* (1961), one of Thomas Pynchon's characters states: "'[Tourists] want only the skin of a place, the explorer

wants its heart. It is perhaps a little like being in love. I had never penetrated to the heart of any of those places, Raf. Until Vheissu. It was not
till the Southern Expedition last year that I saw what was beneath her
skin.' 'What did you see?' asked Signor Mantissa, leaning forward. 'Nothing,' Godolphin whispered. 'It was Nothing I saw'" (204). Like Pynchon's
Godolphin, whose very name suggests mythopoeic longing, Bishop's
speakers reveal how the ancient voyager's desire to reach the Happy Isles
or find the Holy Grail remains vital but without the kind of fulfillment
enacted and promised in ancient texts. This apprehension regarding travel
in the modern era, so prominent in Bishop's poems, can also be found not
just in *V* but in a number of literary texts that appear from the nineteenth
century on, including but not limited to Herman Melville's *Moby-Dick*,
Robert Browning's "Childe Roland to the Dark Tower Came," T.S. Eliot's
"Journey of the Magi," Joseph Conrad's *Heart of Darkness*, and James
Joyce's *Ulysses*.

What sets Elizabeth Bishop apart from these other writers is her use
of casual language, language that acts as a distracting veneer to the compelling and stark underlying issues. The significance of Bishop's usage
becomes all too apparent when we compare it to that of Charles Darwin,
whose life and work, particularly *The Voyage of the Beagle* (1836), she
ardently admired. In a letter to Anne Stevenson, Bishop makes this celebrated comment:

> reading Darwin, one admires the beautiful solid case being built up out of
> his endless heroic *observations*, almost unconscious or automatic — and then
> comes a sudden relaxation, a forgetful phase, and one *feels* the strangeness
> of his undertaking, sees the lonely young man, his eyes fixed on facts and
> minute details, sinking or sliding off into the unknown. What one seems
> to want in art, in experiencing it, is the same thing that is necessary for its
> creation, a self-forgetful, perfectly useless concentration [Millier 246].

As others have already noticed, here Bishop gives us an unusual look into
what for her was a confirmation of her own genius for observation. Like
Darwin, she reveled in the ephemeral details of the world, recording what
Darwin called "the most trivial signs of change" (Darwin 154). Readers of
The Voyage of the Beagle will know what Bishop means by "endless heroic
observations," and will therefore also understand how Darwin impressed
and influenced a like-minded young poet over a century later.

Bishop's use of the word *heroic,* however, signals an important dis-

64

tinction between Darwin's sense of observation and her own. It would, in fact, be better to refer to Bishop's endless observations as unassuming precisely because, in contrast to Darwin, no monumental purpose is ever explicitly announced as being behind them. The glaring dearth of monumental purpose is indeed exactly Bishop's point. Darwin's use of language, on the other hand, constantly implies grand mission and motive. He and the crew of the *Beagle* are like "the navigators of old" (154), and at key points throughout *The Voyage* the young Darwin seems almost overwhelmed by his own observations. In the following passage, for instance, Darwin uses a cartographic simile that is strikingly like Bishop's penchant for employing map metaphors, but Darwin's perspective is noticeably elevated:

> We spent the day on the summit, and I never enjoyed one more thoroughly. Chile, bounded by the Andes and the Pacific, was seen as in a map. The pleasure from the scenery, in itself beautiful, was heightened by the many reflections which arose from the mere view of the Campana range with its lesser parallel ones, and of the broad valley of Quillota directly intersecting them. Who can avoid wondering at the force which had upheaved these mountains, and even more so at the countless ages which it must have required, to have broken through, removed, and levelled whole masses of them? ... all-powerful time can grind down mountains — even the gigantic Cordillera — into gravel and mud [221].

Here Darwin goes beyond "minute details" to ask a question apparently more sublime in scope than what we might expect of Bishop who, for example, asks in "Filling Station," "Why the taboret? / Why, oh why, the doily?" (*CP* 127). If she often appears not to take her travels seriously, it is because the desire she shares with a writer such as Darwin can no longer be articulated and implemented in his terms, not to mention those of other explorers Bishop admired, such as William Bartram, Richard Burton, and Alfred Russell Wallace. Her poems may evoke and incorporate older notions of the voyage but they do so mainly to clarify a single reality: that desire and experience are no longer (if they ever actually were) integrated during travel.

Bishop's use of apparently relaxed language thus indicates a transformation in the scope of travel, from heroic and auspicious to modest, unsure, and even skeptical, a change exemplified by her attempt in 1951 to take a cruise to Tierra del Fuego, to see there the cruel, entangled, rocky landscape where Darwin met with "savages" whose desolate way of life he found astonishing.[45] In contrast to Darwin's mission as ship's naturalist, Bishop's journey was much more of a strictly personal odyssey. Apart perhaps from Marianne Moore, Bishop had no John Stevens Henslow compelling her to travel in search of raw empirical data and to report back regularly by way of letter. Instead, as Lloyd Schwartz indicates, "Her compass kept pointing her south, to a warmer, more colorful, less puritanical climate" (89). In fact, Bishop's journey to Tierra del Fuego, far from ever being accomplished, was aborted during a stopover in Rio de Janeiro: "Wandering through the city, she ate some cashew fruit that she had bought from a street vender, and had a violent allergic reaction. She was hospitalized, and had to give up her 'dream-trip to the Straits of Magellan, et cetera.' The ship sailed on without her. She stayed in Brazil for nearly twenty years" (Schwartz 89).

Part of the difference between Bishop and Darwin as travelers also lies in the fact that Bishop was never sure she had a home to which to return. As we have seen in Anne Bradstreet, the idea of home, of course, plays an integral role in the mind and memory of the traveler, and Bishop frequently discusses home. Darwin writes at the close of *The Voyage* that he struggled with homesickness throughout the expedition. Home for Darwin was represented not only by the memory of familiar landscapes, friends, and family, but also by the notion of "a harvest, however distant that may be, when some fruit will be reaped, some good effected" (434). Such thoughts helped to keep him going for almost five years. Bishop, on the other hand, regardless of her admiration for Darwin or her love for the Nova Scotia of early childhood, was the "touring foreigner, in the place but not of it, wanting to 'stay forever' but finding it impossible" (Millier 47). As Bishop wrote in a letter to her friend and fellow poet, Robert Lowell: "I guess I have liked to travel as much as I have because I have always felt isolated & have known so few of my 'contemporaries' and nothing of 'intellectual' life in New York or anywhere. Actually it may be all to the good" (*Letters* 154).

Here, as in her poetry, Bishop's seemingly casual idiom carries serious implications, implications readily apparent in the poems discussed in the rest of this chapter. The discussion that follows concentrates on two main tasks: 1). to sort out and clarify what Bishop appears to say about the kind of yearning that precipitates travel, and about how such desire is constantly frustrated or put in question; and 2). to recognize the ways in which she alludes to an older and seemingly more stable but also destructive tradition of travel whose language and images speak of satisfying desire through conquest and acquisition. More specifically, this desire will be seen as a desire for place, for what Anita Desai calls "spirit of place or 'feng sui,'" a Chinese term defined by Robert Graves as "spiritual atmosphere" (Desai 101). Desai goes on to make a statement that, here, partly applies to Bishop also: "I tend to move into areas with a particularly strong *feng sui* and ... occupy my time spent in these areas by writing about them.... I lay claim to this nose for *feng sui* as part of my equipment as a novelist" (Desai 101). Although Bishop too certainly had a "nose for *feng sui*," her quest was never so easily successful as Desai's seems to have been.

Reaching for the Interior: Western Mythic Metaphor, Part 1

If Bishop incorporates older expressions of travel in her poems, she does so in order to express their collapse in terms that are either ironic or comic. Her poetry supports Vine Deloria's critical claim that "Western history is written as if the torch of enlightenment was fated to march from the Mediterranean to San Francisco Bay" (Deloria 68). Her work subtly but consistently alludes to and subverts what might be called a high tradition of travel that contrasts sharply with an actual array of seemingly trivial details. This ideal tradition, which embraces exploration and exploitation and is beckoning as well as elusive, provides the backdrop, the large canvas, to all the celebrated Bishopian minutiae.

"Over 2,000 Illustrations and a Complete Concordance" begins by referring directly to this tradition and the way in which it has been preserved and idealized: "Thus should have been our travels: / serious, engravable" (*CP* 57). What follows describes what the speaker has seen, read, and desired in a biblical text that is accompanied by elaborate pictures and a concordance, all meant to take readers through a kind of guided tour of traditional western thought and dogma — "our Christian Empire." The hyperbolical title of the poem suggests the scale of the ideal to which the speaker brings her mind and desires, having experienced travel herself. Yet she also positions herself apart from these patterns in which experience is idealized and sublimely arranged, even though she remains intrigued by the arrangement. Her speaker describes the Seven Wonders of the World as "tired / and a touch familiar" precisely because the destinations they represent have been so long framed by various traditions that glorify and inscribe the act of travel as a progressive venture in linear time. The quest is therefore assumed to be "serious" and "engravable" when, in fact, it may not be.

The glorification of travel implied in such visual representations as those found in the speaker's family Bible indicates an older, traditional belief in a transcendent ordering power. Standing over against the frail human scene, such a power — the power of the divine — acts as a stabilizing force that makes the various human situations coherent and unchanging. As a result, "the human figure" becomes crystallized, static, "in history or theology." Bishop's diction, her use of words such as "files," "diagram," "engravable," "cobbled," "brickwork conduits," evokes a model for human experience that is carefully ordered and purposive; and central to this model is "the Site" — "the Tomb, the Pit, the Sepulcher" — where death itself is conquered. "The creation of holy sites and a sacred literature," writes Eric Leed, "occurred from the fourth century on. The sacred sites demonstrated the truth of the text, while the text supplied meaning to the sacred site" (142).

David Kalstone sees in this poem a disjunction between childhood desire and adult reality, as the speaker goes on to juxtapose the biblical vision with the stark and sometimes frightening reality of her own travels. Citing one of Bishop's childhood memories of reading her "grandfather's Bible under a powerful reading-glass," Kalstone states: "in the formal arrangement of Bishop's poem, such memories are strictly cordoned off from adult life, unavailing, displaced as a childlike fantasy" (130). Leed's comment on the ties between holy site and sacred text, however, supplies us with a clue to an additional approach to "Over 2,000 Illustrations." Along with the child/adult rupture identified by Kalstone, the poem also enunciates the discovery of the gap between text and site, and as such goes beyond the biographical to describe, and thus engrave in its own way, what has become of travel as a mythic metaphor for Western experience. Although Anne Colwell sees the poem doing this in comic terms — "The tone and diction of the first stanza poke fun at the desire, present equally in both poet and reader, for a knowledge invulnerable to time, ... affirmed by the whole culture" (102) — there is a serious, almost elegiac sense of loss that is also evoked as the modernist text, almost in spite of itself, supplants the sacred site that it wistfully, childishly longs for. In this sense, "Over 2,000 Illustrations" is indeed about growing up, about the necessity for a culture, this culture, to grow out of and learn from its own past.

If Anne Bradstreet's experience of travel three centuries earlier included dislocation, it was also replete with spiritual hopes and consolations, the greatest of which was the creation of the community of pilgrims as a "city upon a hill." Bishop, on the other hand, records how such hopes and consolations elude one's grasp. In "Over 2,000 Illustrations," the speaker's express desire to locate a sacred site is, in this poem at least, not just unfulfilled but nullified, dashed. While Bishop's speaker conveys a sense of community in her use of the first-person plural, the actual travels she describes contain none of the tensions between self and community found in Bradstreet's "Dialogue Between Old England and New." Bishop's use of "we," rather than evoking any contradictory claims of group and self, supports the speaker's disillusionment with travel. If she does speak on behalf of another, the speaker does so in order to describe a shared sense of incongruity, of not having a communal and therefore shared sense of values rooted in the past. During real travel, she says, one finds holy sites "not looking particularly holy," and this discovery, which constitutes the nadir of Bishop's poem, frightens the speaker "most of all." It is terrifying; it invites denial. It also recalls Thomas Travisano's point that "[Bishop's] New England Baptist background, with its lingering imperative to work out an individual accommodation with God, and to read God's providential message in the landscape, underlies the poem and lends it urgency" (Travisano 121). Rather than confirm what the biblical text has always "Granted," "a page alone" or "a grim lunette," not to mention "God's spreading fingerprint," actual travel, with its visits to holy places, has brought the speaker to experience things such as "An open, gritty, marble trough, carved solid / with exhortation."

Like the biblical post-resurrection grave of Christ, this tomb is empty; but it is empty not because of the numinous but because of the passage of time, which Bishop's traveler notes in a manner that quietly parallels Darwin's eloquent description of what "all powerful time" can do. For Darwin, such observations led to radical theorizing about the mutability of nature and the nature of change. For Bishop's speaker, the revelation this experience brings regarding the brutal reality of death leads to irony. (Indeed, although Darwin himself does not wax ironic, irony may be seen as one inevitable consequence of his thought.) Next to the grave, readers are told, is a travel guide, a tour operator named Khadour dressed "In a smart burnoose" and looking on "amused." The speaker's other experiences leading up to her visit to this sacred site are almost equally ironic. They take note in the same wry and quiet way of the effects of time and of how unyielding belief systems (culture) can willfully ignore the fact of change (nature): "at Volubilis there were beautiful poppies / splitting the mosaics; the fat old guide made eyes." The speaker also sees "little pockmarked prostitutes" filling "the brothels of Marrakesh," and this vignette is juxtaposed with an Englishwoman "informing us / that the Duchess was going to have a baby" while "In Dingle harbor ... / the rotting hulks held up their dripping plush."

Such anecdotal accounts, strung together as they are, constitute the speaker's experience of a world where life vies with death rather than triumphs over it.[46] There is no Resurrection experience here but rather a catalogue of details that blatantly defy desire; hence, the speaker's record of her travels acts as the disconcerting foreground to a "vast and obvious" biblical tapestry. In the opening line of the third part of the poem, Bishop's speaker states, "Everything only connected by 'and' and 'and,'" acknowledging how the reality of travel is based on an arbitrariness for which she has had little preparation. While the various characters and constituents of the biblical illustrations are suspended by threads, filed, cobbled, or otherwise ordered, the speaker's actual experiences seem haphazardly serialized. Her poetic "engraving" of her journey, such as it is, is "*only* connected by 'and' and 'and'" [emphasis mine].[47]

But this realization also preludes a return to her contemplation of "the heavy book," makes her want to open it once more, as she did when she was a child (if we keep Kalstone's reading in mind), and as she has done at the very outset of the poem itself. The speaker repeatedly returns to the book because it has instilled in her a deep-seated desire for transcendence and order. She still yearns to see the evidence for these even though what she has witnessed during her travels stands in stark contradiction to what she has read. The repeated invocation, "Open the book," is therefore laden with child-like wonder and the longing for enchantment. Touching the pages of the old family Bible "pollinates the fingertips," causing the speaker to ask a wounded and wondering question, precisely as a child might, "Why couldn't we have seen / this old Nativity while we were at it?" These lines resonate with the kind of desire found at the end of the first passage, where the speaker sees "God's spreading fingerprint" in the embellished pages of the Bible, only here she explicitly recognizes how the book mesmerizes — indeed, how its power is analogous to the erotic in so far as it "rubs off" and "pollinates the fingertips." If there are signs of sexual intimacy and fertility here, it is because the Bible promises life and love, and records at great length who begat whom. As far as Christians are concerned, the "old Nativity," Christ's miraculous entry into the world, is the genealogical high point of the post–Adamic world, and the speaker's aching question — "Why couldn't we have seen / this old Nativity while we were at it?" — echoes Eliot's speaker's in "Journey of the Magi," "[W]ere we led all that way for / Birth or Death?," and presages the "questions of travel" that Bishop will pointedly ask further on in her career (Eliot 110).

The enchanted tableau the speaker wishes she could have seen with her own eyes represents her unmitigated desire for epiphany "while we were at it." It is an image of perfect domesticity that fulfills the biblical promise of immortality; it is, in point of fact, another holy site, one which would "demonstrate the truth of the text" and thus belie the numerous, frightening images of death encountered by the speaker during her travels. But this wish for epiphany and confirmation also brings up the issue of seeing, of the meaning of the traveler's eye. Observation, especially the observation of minutiae, has thus far brought disillusionment, irony, and anxiety. Dreadful entropic details meet the eyes of the traveler: "the dead man," "the dead volcanoes," "rotting hulks," and "little pockmarked prostitutes." Indeed, the speaker goes so far as to observe how others look at things in the real world: "the fat old guide made eyes"; "Khadour looked on amused." Against these is "a family with pets" illustrated in "the heavy book," while the poem's last line brings up a different kind of looking. Seeing "this old Nativity" would constitute another order of observation, which the speaker has never experienced (except in her reading). She calls such looking "infant sight" not because it already has incipient existence but because its birth is contingent on seeing the miraculous. Such looking cannot exist without its proper object, even though the speaker can imagine its happening and can ask a question for which there is no answer but the gap between text and site, nature and culture, dream and reality.[48]

Thus the illustrations are "sad and still," the speaker noting how there is "Always the silence." The word *infant* stems from the Latin *infans*, meaning "unable to speak." If travel is about seeing, then the speaker cannot, in the final analysis, describe what she has not seen, although she can intonate her desire to look on something for the first time. After all, such desire is what motivates the traveler to test limits, push boundaries, and report to others what he or she has witnessed. But again, Bishop's speaker is quite clear about what she has not witnessed, so that "Over 2,000 Illustrations" does not contribute further to the gap between text and site: instead, it describes that gap and, as a text itself, is unwaveringly honest in its attempt to be accurate and true to the experience of the traveler. At the same time, the poem also freely acknowledges the traveler's dreams, frustrated as they are.

In "Arrival at Santos," the first poem in the "Brazil" section of *Questions of Travel,* Bishop begins with a pointed, unflinching question that, like "Over 2,000 Illustrations," contrasts acutely with the mundane details that greet her eyes as her ship approaches port after what she calls "eighteen days of suspension" at sea:

> Oh, tourist,
> is this how this country is going to answer you
>
> and your immodest demands for a different world,
> and a better life, and complete comprehension
> of both at last, and immediately,
> after eighteen days of suspension? [*CP* 89].

Couched in terms that seem simple at first, Bishop's question is a bold, humorous one. "Oh, tourist," with its combination of mock-epic apostrophe and holiday light-heartedness, aptly sums up her attitude. "After eighteen days of suspension" at sea, Bishop finds a scene that fails to meet her expectations, expectations which would have arisen not just during "suspension" but possibly while reading Darwin's *Voyage* and which are now juxtaposed with the disappointing scene before her. Darwin, who we already know was reminded of "the navigators of old" as his ship approached the shores of South America, makes the following comments shortly after arriving in Brazil: "In England any person fond of natural history enjoys in his walks a great advantage, by always having something to attract his attention; but in these fertile climates, teeming with life, the attractions are so numerous, that he is scarcely able to walk at all"; and "every form, every shade, so completely surpasses in magnificence all that the European has ever beheld in his own country, that he knows not how to express his own feelings" (*Voyage* 22 & 27). This is infant sight indeed. By contrast, Bishop qualifies what she sees with adjectives such as "meager," "sad and harsh," "frivolous," "feeble," and "uncertain." Her presentation is matter-of-fact: "Here is a coast; here is a harbor; / here, after a meager diet of horizon, is some scenery." This, as Susan McCabe has also noticed, "strips topography of the romance of travel and arrival" (149). Bishop's use of the pathetic fallacy in describing the landscape she encounters indicates the level of her disappointment. The mountains are "impractically shaped and — who knows? — self-pitying"; they are also "sad and harsh beneath their frivolous greenery."

Such disappointment also recalls Anne Bradstreet's much-discussed uncertainty when she reached New England aboard the *Arbella* in 1630, finding "a new World and new manners at *wch* my heart rose." Elizabeth Bishop's heart rises too as she expresses dissatisfaction with ports in general. They "are necessities, like postage stamps, or soap, / but they seldom seem to care what impression they make." Like Bradstreet, Bishop recognizes and yields to the necessary and usual rites of passage; but while Bradstreet eventually submits to what is a practical necessity ("after I was convinced it was ye way of God"), Bishop creates a comic moment by depreciating her "immodest demands" with some pragmatic advice: "Finish your breakfast." For Bishop all the paraphernalia surrounding arrival might be "ye the way of God," but if it is she does not explicitly say so, saving more direct talk of God for the poem that follows, "Brazil, January 1, 1501." At this point, her main concerns are the practical ones that so defy and deflate her "immodest demands," and out of which she continues to create a comedy of manners that parodies conventional representations of arrival.

Exactly how Bishop creates a parody may be seen by comparing certain parts of "Arrival at Santos" with Anthony Smith's recounting of the official discovery of Brazil by Pedro Cabral "at the hour of Vespers" on 22 April 1500:

> A party went ashore in a single boat, and Nicolau Coelho became the first man from that fleet to walk upon the land that would become Brazil. He reported back to his commander that the people he encountered were ami-

able, naked and curious, never having seen such foreigners before.... On 26 April, Low Sunday, Cabral went ashore, together with a large number of priests and friars from among his complement of 1,200 men. He had no stone (*padrão*) to mark the place, as was customary on voyages of discovery, but made the carpenter construct a wooden cross to serve as a token of possession. This was erected on 1 May after a Mass had been celebrated. He then named the land, not knowing if it was a huge island or a continent. *Terra da Vera Cruz* was his choice: Land of the True Cross [Smith 5].

Because they are often strategic representations of seeing things for the first time, accounts of arrival are nearly always writ large, representing the triumphant fulfillment of desire or domination. Thus, in accounts of "discovery," places are marked, rituals observed, and there is an accompanying evocation of magnitude or destiny—what Bishop calls the "immodest demands for a different world, / and a better life, and complete comprehension / of both at last." Barry Lopez touches on something like this when he discusses the heroic voyager's prospect of arrival, which often makes the land into an adversary even before arrival has occurred (358). This takes place because landscapes are evaluated beforehand, at home, and are the products of imagination, desire, and the explorer's relationship to "the larger society" (390) of which he or she is a part.

Along with her "fellow passenger named Miss Breen," Bishop too is seeing the Brazilian landscape for the first time but her rhetoric pokes fun at desire, at the idea of arriving itself, and at the traditional colonial emblems signifying arrival and possession: "So that's the flag. I never saw it before. / I somehow never thought of there *being* a flag." Likewise, as we have seen, her first impressions are anything but grandiose: there was a flag "all along," and the currency will "remain to be seen" by other tourists. Her mode of arrival occurs in plain contrast to the prowess implied in Smith's account, just as her comic vision contrasts sharply with the "infant sight" yearned for in "Over 2,000 Illustrations":

> And gingerly now we climb down the ladder backward,
> myself and a fellow passenger named Miss Breen,
>
> descending into the midst of twenty-six freighters
> waiting to be loaded with green coffee beans.
> Please, boy, do be more careful with that boat hook!
> Watch out! Oh! It has caught Miss Breen's
> skirt!

All the traveler desires on a larger scale is here subordinated to the necessity for movement from one craft to another, but the competent seventy-year-old Miss Breen, a police officer and therefore in this context an almost slapstick representative of law and order, gets caught on a boat hook. She and the speaker worry about their whiskey. Like the irony that abounds in "Over 2,000 Illustrations," this poem's comedic tone stems from the incongruity between wish and reality — between the speaker's "immodest demands" and the practical need to "gingerly ... climb down the ladder backward" without getting snared or falling. Bishop's use of the present tense accentuates the awkward everyday reality of travel ("There. We are settled.") as does the unusual — for her — enjambment breaking a single letter from the place name for Miss Breen's home. Language at customs will slip across the page like the damp postage stamp.[49] For the time being, larger desires are laid aside — "The customs officials will speak English, we hope, / and leave us our bourbon and cigarettes" — but the poem ends with an unmistakable gesture towards grappling with these ever-present yearnings as soon as possible: "We leave Santos at once; / we are driving to the interior."

With this final line, "Arrival at Santos" reconfigures the dichotomy between reality and dream with an analogous one between surface and interior. With its flag, currency, and customs officials, Santos is merely the skin of Brazil, which is why Bishop likens it to "the unassertive colours of soap, or postage stamps" since both these products are made only for contact with surfaces and both call forth the kind of slippery thinking and perceptions that can arise when binaries are invoked. The poem that follows thus beckons to the reader, inviting her or him on a promising quest into both history and jungle. The journey back in time seems directly proportional to the trip into the natural world of the rainforest. Indeed, at the outset "Brazil, January 1, 1502" implies a loss of the sense of current, civilized time as the speaker takes an imaginative excursion over four centuries into the past to envision the first Portuguese conquistadors' encounter with the Amazon rainforest and its native inhabitants: "Januaries, Nature greets our eyes / exactly as she must have greeted theirs" (*CP* 91). The natural dynamic is active. But what the jungle, the interior, offers is not the fulfillment of "an old dream of wealth and luxury," but rather an endless series of surfaces the speaker compares to a "hanging fabric."

Susan McCabe, glossing the epigraph by Kenneth Clark with which this poem begins, locates the fascinating connection between landscape and art that forms the background to the poem. Both McCabe and Clark are quoted here:

> Early medieval art disregards nature as either irrelevant or shuns it as either irreverent or terrifying; it is only the domestication of nature into garden that allows landscape to emerge:
>
> > Natural objects, then, were first perceived individually, as pleasing in themselves and symbolical of divine qualities. The next step towards landscape painting was to see them as forming some whole which would be within the compass of the imagination and itself a symbol of perfection. This was achieved by the discovery of the garden — be it Eden, or the Hesperides, or Tir-nan-Og — it is one of humanity's most constant, widespread and consoling myths.

Here McCabe makes an interesting point, arguing that Bishop — acting from the desire for the ideal that informs her poems about travel — is guilty of the same sins as the colonizers: "The conquistadors cannot 'see' the landscape: it appears before them as a tapestry, and Bishop implicates herself along with the present-day colonizers, as caught up in the same composition of the landscape as paradise" (153–54). The speaker's "we," argues McCabe, states that nature greets them "exactly" as it must have to the Spanish; that is a given, although it must pointed out that the first-person plural also includes readers. And yet a value is brought to bear on nature too. Roderick Nash comments extensively on this in the context of the Puritans, for whom wilderness constituted "a dark and sinister symbol" (*WATAM* 24); which is to say that so-called wild nature is given a value and perceived according to that value, no matter what it is in reality. Bishop's speaker therefore inhabits the value as she enters the rainforest and the rainforest greets her: it is not the exact rainforest but, rather, the exact experience of being met by it. John A. Livingston, writing in the context of a discussion of Darwin, comments on the Western, colonial process of observation, which is actually projection and evaluation and which he calls "the traditional perceptual lenses" with which we "receive and apprehend the world":

> if Nature were *not* an economistic marketplace, then it would not be in our preferred image, and if it were not in our preferred image, then we would have no way of predicting and controlling it. We would have no way of domesticating it — of bringing Nature into the orbit of human power, of making it *just like us* [91].

Raymond Williams also speaks to this when he states that arrangements of nature are connected to "centres of power" (151).

To return to the poem, suffice it to say that Bishop's speaker — again, using the collective "we" — observes "big leaves, little leaves, and giant leaves," "every square inch filling in with foliage," which she compares to a painter's canvas, "fresh as if just finished / and taken off the frame." The speaker's perception of the scene before her is at least partly contained by the art metaphor of frame and canvas, so that even though she observes a multitude of vulnerable surfaces that can be torn or "ripped away," this observation, sympathetic though it may be, is powerfully shaped by its own aesthetic trope. This is not, however, a failure of perception but rather a part of the poem's point: that the figurative devices used both to apprehend and describe nature are so deeply engrained that they are almost inescapable, no matter how acutely aware of them we might be. Indeed, many of us do exactly that whenever we employ the term *nature*. Meanwhile, nature — whatever that amounts to — comes to us just as it always has done. Self-consciously participating in the conventional western idea of the goal-oriented journey, Bishop's speaker, along with her traveling companion, is not at any point able to extricate herself entirely from these ideas. How, indeed, could she be expected to? All that the poet can do is resort to comedy and, sometimes, to parody. Hence, if she implicates herself she does so as if to say that she cannot take herself out of this — we are all implicated every time we travel, every time we employ the term *wilderness* or *park*. And there is guilt involved. Here she imagines the conquistadors tearing through the jungle "Directly after Mass, humming perhaps / *L'Homme armé*, or some such tune." "[M]addening little women" become the focus of desire, aboriginal women who are elusive, "retreating, always retreating, behind [the hanging fabric]." As in "Over 2,000 Illustrations," the traveler's desire is seen in sexual terms, although here those terms do not describe a pollination of the fingertips but rather a rampage through layers of rainforest. Colwell, writing about both "Arrival at Santos" and "Brazil, January 1, 1502," also notes this element of sexuality: "In both poems, the movement from the entrance to the interior, from the orifice to the center, has an insistent element of sexuality" (131).

Thus, this poem too, like "Over 2,000 Illustrations" and "Arrival at Santos," indicates how the objects of desire remain potent, intangible, and elusive, no matter how much they seem to correspond to "an old dream."

The dream remains firmly embedded in our modes of perception, which can be very dangerous in the rainforest. "Brazil, January 1, 1502," to be sure, points out how one of the great hazards of travel and exploration has been madness; and what chronicles there are of the European exploits by, among others, the Pizarro brothers, Francisco de Orellana, and Lope de Aguirre during the sixteenth and seventeenth centuries certainly support the poem's contention. One thinks too of the aging and desperate Walter Raleigh released from the Tower of London by James I in order to find South American treasure — only to fail, to see his son killed, and to return to England (and to the Tower, awaiting execution) in disgrace.

Twentieth-century accounts of excursions into the Amazon Basin also confirm Bishop's observations regarding travel and desire. Simon Schama recalls a boyhood fascination with fluvial origins and El Dorado:

> Had I reached back further in the literature of river argosies, I would have discovered that Conrad's imperial stream, the road of commercial penetration that ends in disorientation, dementia, and death, was an ancient obsession. Before the Victorian steamboats pushed their way through the scummy waterweed of the Upper Nile and the Gambia, there had been Spanish, Elizabethan, and even German craft, adrift up the Orinco basin, pulled by the tantalizing mirage of El Dorado, the golden paradise, just around the next bend [5].

In *Amazon Beaming*, which documents Loren McIntyre's 1968 discovery of the true source of the Amazon River, Petru Popescu describes how the rainforest has lured travelers for centuries:

> [McIntyre] dreamed that he was airborne — not in a plane but hovering by himself, like a balloon, above a vision of jungle and mountains looking like an oversized map. It was a dream, and in his dream he knew it. A vast stretch of jungle spread out beneath him, emanating a rich phosphorescence, as if lit from underneath. That phosphorescence was the jungle's own richness. The intricacy of its life-forms. That was why Pizarro and Orellana and so many others had feverishly searched here. It was all here, that treasure. Generations of predecessors had simply misnamed it, but in his dream McIntyre recognized it instantly. It suffused the greenness of the jungle, while the distant mountains blew their godlike breath on it. An invisible force swelled up the mountains from within, making them pregnant with a captive message [61].

What Popescu alludes to here is, again, the rampant eroticism — seen in terms of "treasure" — found in the Amazon jungle, which in the fifteenth and sixteenth centuries started to become the object of desire for European explorers. Early Spanish and Portuguese explorers created images to represent the forest's vitality and also to make it concrete in their own most basic terms, which included legends of Amazon women and lost cities of gold and which were, in turn, rapidly decomposed by jungle realities. As Bishop explores such traditional terms of travel, she can indeed seem to capitulate to them; on the other hand, she is no more co-opted by them than, say, Popescu is as he uses a cartographic metaphor or refers to treasure in the above passage. McIntyre, he tells us, instantly acknowledges his dream as dream, even while he is still in it. Atop a mountain more than a century earlier, Charles Darwin likewise sees "Chile, bounded by the Andes and the Pacific, ... as in a map." Darwin too is well aware of his own mode of perception and of the imperial history of European travel and exploration of which he is a part. Barry Lopez speaks to this when he states that "mental geography becomes the geography to which society adjusts, and it can be more influential than the real geography" (294). Elizabeth Bishop, similarly, must include such heady experiences, fed by desire and the tropes that evoke it, in her poetic travelogue. She cannot finally stand completely outside the quest images preceding her.

In her late poem "Santarém," gold is mentioned four times as Bishop remembers her visit to the town of that name at the "conflux of two great rivers, Tapajos, Amazon" (*CP* 185). In the poet's memory, Santarém becomes the apotheosis of desire, the place where she wishes to pause and consider that this might constitute a kind of quest fulfillment: "That golden evening I really wanted to go no farther." Here again the narrative takes us backwards in time, except that now it is personal history that is also being explored, and the speaker finds herself recalling, and alluding to, various forms of treasure, all of which make her want to stay put. She remembers "a sky of gorgeous, under-lit clouds, / with everything gilded," and here too are streets of gold, of a kind: "The zebus' hooves, the people's feet / waded in golden sand."

Published posthumously in 1979, "Santarém" recounts the fulfillment of desire according to memory. In effect, what this poem describes is the kind of sacred site sought after in the earlier "Over 2,000 Illustrations" and alluded to with a wistful, half-humorous question in "Arrival at Santos." Here Bishop states: "I liked the place; I liked the *idea* of the place" (emphasis mine). She goes on to make a fleeting comparison to the Garden of Eden before realizing that Eden had "four [rivers] / and they'd diverged. Here only two / and coming together." As Bonnie Costello notes, "Bishop insists this is *not* Eden, even as she makes the comparison" (173). It is interesting to take in the fact that in "Santarém" a female voice obliquely identifies the place as Edenic, a landscape Carolyn Merchant describes as "spring-fed, river-based, and irrigated" (14), as though a descendant of Eve — "the mother of all living" (14) — were reclaiming her matrilineal legacy and knowledge. Of course, Bishop does not make such a claim in this poem; instead she twice replaces the word *church* with the more majestic and pontifical *Cathedral*, underscoring the presence of Christianity in the Amazon rainforest and by extension a longstanding schema that has clearly preceded the poet, in which women are identified with nature and both are dominated and exploited by a powerful male-centered culture. Indeed, the Cathedral is seen as the epicenter for miraculous events that according to folklore transcend the natural order. But Bishop also takes into account historical facts, facts which would seem to support her image of Santarém as a unique and also tainted place. Parenthetically, she inserts the fact that certain Confederate families had settled in the town after the American Civil War because "here they could still own slaves." Brilliant colours meanwhile accompany the remembered gold of the town. The American settlers "left occasional blue eyes"; the "stubby palms" have "flamboyants like pans of embers"; there are also "buildings one story high, stucco, blue or yellow, / and one house faced with *azulejos*, buttercup yellow"; the zebus are blue, as is "the blue pharmacy"; and on the river is a "schooner with raked masts / and violet-colored sails."

Bishop, however, knows that the town of Santarém cannot, despite its exotic beauty, be objectified as a sacred site. It is the poet's vulnerable perspective — her own most basic terms — as much as the place itself that is extraordinary and easily mis-applied, and Bishop makes this distinction clear by prefacing her description of the town with a disclaimer: "Of course I may be remembering it all wrong / after, after — how many years?" From the outset, the town is viewed as a site that is lost in time, a kind of El Dorado, imbued with enchantment; and like El Dorado and other legendary places reputed to exist in the Amazon River Basin, Santarém takes on mythical qualities as the traveler recalls her visit there. "Gilded" and "burnished" by the effect of time, Santarém remembered almost becomes like the holy places illustrated in the large Bible of Bishop's childhood.

Here, near the end of her life, she indicates how memory continues over the years to become charged with desire, so that Santarém attains the same status as the big pictures emblazoned across the pages of her grandfather's Holy Book. Yet Santarém's sacred quality cannot be assumed or taken for granted, even though the poem offers less of the cutting irony found in "Over 2,000 Illustrations."

If "Santarém" begins with a disclaimer, it also ends with an admission of subjectivity that furthers the tenuous condition of Bishop's memory and thus too of the poem itself. The poet recalls seeing an old wasps' nest in "the blue pharmacy." She describes it as "small, exquisite, clean matte white, / and hard as stucco"; readers can see in it an image of natural craft and transformation, just as the pharmacist who gives her the nest as a memento of her journey can be seen as a jungle sage and alchemist. This spell, though, is presently broken:

> Then — my ship's whistle blew. I couldn't stay.
> Back on board, a fellow-passenger, Mr. Swan,
> Dutch, the retiring head of Philips Electric,
> really a very nice old man,
> who wanted to see the Amazon before he died,
> asked, "What's that ugly thing?"

Like the other poems discussed so far, "Santarém" describes the traveler's desire for what the Canadian writer Maria Campbell calls "power places"[50] — places that invoke the past, in this case with its "old dream of wealth and luxury"; that give answer to "immodest demands for a different world"; or that beckon us to look "our infant sight away." But each of these possibilities proves, in Bishop's poems, consistently elusive or limited; and "Santarém" is no exception, even though it hints at more of a sense of fulfillment than the earlier poems do.

Certainly to a poet so preoccupied with detail, such an experience would be put to the test, and this is what Bishop does in "Santarém," or rather what Mr. Swan does for her. Besides the "question of travel" that prefaces the poem — that, indeed, clearly signals Bishop's doubt and uncertainty about her own experience — there is also one that provides an epilogue, so that "Santarém" as a whole is sandwiched between questions concerning subjective judgment and fallibility. Indeed, what "Arrival at Santos" does for the experience of arrival, "Santarém" does for departure — all with the mindful modernist poet as seemingly relaxed (but in truth quite cautious) travel guide. Bishop appears to be asking what we often must ask of travel narratives regarding accuracy and embellishment, and it thus follows that she also throws the poem — and poetry — itself into doubt, as the poem itself becomes a fragile object commemorating a journey, indeed much like the wasps' nest that the pharmacist in his blue pharmacy gives her. This nest, which evokes Bishop's desire for home, is to another traveler, Mr. Swan, a puzzling and "ugly thing." Swan travels because he too is propelled by desire, "want[ing] to see the Amazon before he died," yet he questions the validity of the poet's "golden evening" by interrogating the very thing she carries away from it as a souvenir. (The end of this late poem, like the man Bishop describes, also jokingly reverberates with the cliché *swan song*, for it is poignantly his song — his search — as well.) In contrast to the magic of the blue pharmacy, Swan — carefully described as "really a very nice old man" — is an energy magnate who represents Western power. After his subversive question, the wasps' nest will stand for doubt and tenuousness as well as verification and fact, and as uncertainty becomes part of the whole experience Bishop necessarily includes it. She has no choice. From another angle, we might say that Bishop's experience becomes less real but more emphatic once she boards her ship and that Mr. Swan, despite his romantic name (like something out of a poem by Yeats), is a trope for the mundane, the pragmatic, and the commercial, as opposed to "Two rivers full of crazy shipping." And this poet is nothing if not pragmatic.

Bishop's doubts about ever satisfying the desire that motivates travel are also expressed in another late poem, "The End of March," which appears in *Geography III* (1976). Here, rather than carry away a wasps' nest, she walks along a beach in order to see her "crypto-dream-house, that crooked box / set up on pilings, shingled green" (*CP* 179). Like the nest, however, the house possesses unique characteristics that simultaneously attract Bishop's attention and arouse her inherent skepticism. The speaker states parenthetically, as an aside to herself and the reader, that "Many things about this place are dubious." The house has what Bonnie Costello calls "The end-of-the-road quality" (170), partially indicated by the railroad ties that "[protect] it from spring tides." Although Bishop's speaker, walking along the beach with at least one other person (a kind of community), implies having been to the house before, boarded doors and windows prevent her from entering it again. Hence, as in "Santarém," she cannot verify her memory of the place, and her trip along the beach becomes analogous to the seemingly endless "wet white string," which finally does end as "a thick white snarl." Not surprisingly, then, Bishop's description of the house ("a sort of artichoke of a house, but greener"), and of what she would do were she able to live there, has a dreamy, colorful quality next to the chilly, vacant beach where "Everything was withdrawn as far as possible." The string that she calls a "snarl" (and that is also "a sodden ghost") is attached to nothing: the speaker asks whether it might be an old kite string but cannot see a kite anywhere. The house, by comparison, appears connected to something behind it. Certainly it is no accident that Bishop twice uses the word *dream* to describe this tantalizing, idiosyncratic place, or that she sees it in bright, primary colours, as she did the town of Santarém, in contrast to the white disconnected string, the dark water, and the darker sky — "the color of mutton-fat jade."

Moreover, what Bishop imagines doing in this house is sharply dissimilar to the laborious activity of travel evoked and described in so many of her other poems. Correlating to her odd dream house (and contrasting acutely with the kind of life signified by Mr. Swan), she imagines a state of mere being, of rest and contemplation, which seems always out of reach and yet always drawing her on, like the "lengths, endless, of wet white string" or, as at the close of the poem, "the lion sun," which momentarily appears and makes "the drab, damp, scattered stones/ ... multi-colored." Unlike the coils of string, the electrical wires would, in this "proto-dream-house," connect Bishop to a power source "off behind the dunes," giving her "A light to read by." Interestingly, the Western technological power Mr. Swan represents appears again in this poem as quite necessary to the poet's imagined state of well-being. Light and vision, in fact, inform her depiction of life in this house more than anything else. Here she would "look through binoculars" and "watch the droplets slipping, heavy with light." These images of light, together with that of the "lovely diaphanous blue flame," evoke a spiritual and creative refuge from the mundane and the workaday, a sacred site not unlike the others discussed thus far.

Finally, besides the string, Bishop also notes "a track of big dog-prints (so big / they were more like lion-prints)." By the end of the poem, these two images are conjoined with that of the sun — the ultimate source of light and life — to create a myth of fulfillment in keeping with Bishop's contemplative ideal. She imagines

a sun who'd walked the beach the last low tide,
making those big, majestic paw-prints,
who perhaps had batted a kite out of the sky to play with.

Like the house, however, such a vision is perfect but impossible, so that "The End of March" closes with an image of mythopoeic happiness that, typically for Bishop, can never be fulfilled.

To find such a place, where one can contemplate the minutiae of existence and "write down useless notes," is also the object of travel in "Questions of Travel," probably Bishop's most definitive poem on the subject. Appearing immediately after "Brazil, January 1, 1502" and chronologically preceding "The End of March" by a decade, "Questions of Travel" indirectly links the two with its allusion to the seventeenth-century philosopher and scientist, Blaise Pascal. "I have often said," wrote Pascal in his *Pensées*, "that all men's unhappiness is due to the single fact that they cannot stay quietly in a room. If a man who has enough upon which to live knew how to live pleasantly at home, he would never journey abroad, either on the sea or to besiege a fortress" (Pascal 70). Here and elsewhere in *Pensées*, Pascal argues that humans require distraction, which they find in travel, because they cannot tolerate being alone with their own thoughts since their thoughts inevitably turn towards questions about ultimate meaning that they know they cannot answer.

At first glance, Bishop appears to take issue with Pascal on the meaning of travel: what is for him a flight from an unbearable reality is for her a quest for an unattainable ideal. Yet if travel, according to Pascal, is motivated solely by the need to escape angst, it is, according to Bishop, fuelled by the desire to experience "a sudden golden silence," which amounts to the same thing. With its oblique reference to gold, "Questions of Travel" hints at what the conquistadors might really have sought after, however outrageously they may have behaved. At the same time, it also anticipates the "proto-dream-house" of "The End of March," in which the speaker longs to live alone in quietude even though she, like Pascal, knows this is difficult, if not impossible. Thus, in the final analysis, Bishop and Pascal do not diverge as abruptly as they initially seem to: both, in fact, point to travel as a metaphor for the act of searching for that "something, something, something" which proves consistently elusive.

Travel as an act of questing also helps to answer the poem's central question, "Why don't we stay at home?" "Questions of Travel" paraphrases this question in a variety of ways:

> Is it right to be watching strangers in a play
> in this strangest of theatres?
> What childishness is it that while there's a breath of life
> in our bodies, we are determined to rush
> to see the sun the other way around?

To be sure, the issues here are potently similar to those raised by Anne Bradstreet in "A Dialogue between Old England and New." Like Bradstreet, Bishop tries to imagine her situation from the point of view of home: "Should we have stayed at home and thought of here? / Where should we be today?" For both writers, such questions are in part caused by the stresses and discomforts of visiting alien terrain. As she does in "Arrival at Santos," Bishop expresses uncertainty, except that here her doubt is due to a glut of stimuli and movement rather than a "meagre" coastline and port. She is overwhelmed: "There are too many waterfalls here; the crowded streams / hurry too rapidly down to the sea." Just as the barren scene in "Santos" propels a drive into the interior, so the flux here invokes the more comforting thought of stasis signified by home, even as it perhaps makes doubtful the possibility of destination. To the beholder, only the mountains, which "look like the hulls of capsized ships," remain static; everything else, including Bishop herself, keeps "travelling, travelling" such that her habitual sense of time is affected.

From this unfamiliar scene of constant movement, Bishop, like Bradstreet, turns her thoughts homeward in order to sort out the connection between here and there. In contrast to Bradstreet, however, Bishop is not concerned with shrinking distance. The "long trip home" does not daunt her. Rather, she wishes to know what it is that prevents her from staying home and whether, in Pascalian fashion, she should not have stayed home in the first place. The desire that moves Bishop to travel seems insatiable, almost greedy, and of course here again Bishop links herself (quite knowingly) to the conquistadors and thus to an older conception of travel: "Oh, must we dream our dreams / and have them, too? / And have we room / for one more folded sunset, still quite warm?" Indeed, Bishop is well aware that what motivates travel is often the questionable desire to possess and to penetrate that which is "inexplicable and impenetrable," and that there is infantile pleasure involved in discovery — what is "instantly seen and always, always delightful." Not just the Spanish and Portuguese conquistadors but also the New England pilgrims and, later still, Charles Darwin felt the need to push the boundaries of the known in order to gather and possess land, gold, lumber, knowledge, and so on. Additionally, since at least the Victorian era, the desire of tourists "to consume [nature] as scenery, landscape, image, fresh air" (Williams 80–81) has underscored tremendously the reasons for travel.

Hence, Bishop feels the enormous weight of Pascal's admonition to stay at home, not because, as Thoreau would say (342), home contains the world in small and therefore makes travel unnecessary, but because travel stems from unhappiness and therefore inevitably involves intrusion and destruction. Yet Bishop travels nonetheless, partly because the notion of home is itself implicated in her questions, especially the last one: "Should we have stayed at home, / wherever that may be?" Home for Bishop is dislocated and ambiguous even more than it is for Bradstreet; there is no "sitting quietly in one's room" as far as Bishop is concerned because she has yet (in terms of this poem) to find one in which to sit. Perhaps "Questions of Travel" finds its power and eloquence in the fact that Bishop seems to see home in macrocosmic terms, which would place her at the other end of the continuum from Thoreau and, like him, Annie Dillard (Dillard 74–5).

If the dimensions of home are global for Bishop, then her connections backwards in time, as well as outward in the present, are all the more intensified. Human history is, in point of fact, a mere snapshot in "a quick age or so, as ages go here," and thus Bishop's reasons for travel, transformed from her questions of travel, are casually given in journalistic fashion. Almost like the longed-for, imaginary existence in the "crypto-dream-house" of "The End of March," travel itself contains unexpected, fragmentary moments which are later connected by the writer's dashes on the page. Although these remembered moments are all that travel can offer, they are sufficient. Although sacred sites and holy places remain elusive, such moments, unexpected and often beautiful like "the trees along this road," may make the journey itself a sacred one. As in "Sandpiper," Bishop finds herself making do with the various, seemingly insignificant details along the way, all of which she is happy to have noticed.

Like the imagined experience of living in her "crypto-dream-house," there are also moments of illumination that spark creativity, such as the "sudden golden silence / in which the traveller takes a notebook." What the poet on her journey "writes," however, is inconclusive, except that the choice of where to go *"is never wide and never free. / And here, or there ... No. Should we have stayed at home, / wherever that may be?"* Such a question could not have been asked in this way by an Anne Bradstreet or a Charles Darwin, both of whom could, and did, measure their experiences of travel against more stable textual, religious, and cultural constructs, even though they also both interrogated them in ways that have left controversial, much-discussed legacies. By Bishop's time, such constructs, religious and even scientific, had come apart and become open-ended. Hence, she is left to ponder "blurr'dly and inconclusively." The "connection" she makes in "Questions of Travel," "between the crudest wooden footwear / and, careful and finicky, / the whittled fantasies of wooden cages," is crucial to our understanding of her position because it is here that she points out the age-old way in which travel is connected to, and informed by, myth. Here, indeed, is history, since so much of it has been made by the men in "wooden clogs" who revamped and contained what they found in the New World according to the designs they brought with them: "a bamboo church of Jesuit baroque." Viewed thus, the connection between cages and clogs evokes the kind of question asked consistently by Bishop throughout her work as more than a mere personal diversion. Her central question — whether to stay home and "[whittle] fantasies" or to don clogs and venture forth — carries an historical weight that transcends the personal. Her poems account for how such "whittled fantasies" have taken shape and imbedded themselves historically through the actions of other travelers. Yet, as shall be seen in the other chapter in this study that focuses exclusively on the poetry of Elizabeth Bishop, they also take note of how culture intersects with, and ultimately tries to possess, the natural world. Bishop herself follows in these older footsteps with a sense of irony, the irony of one accompanying a Miss Breen or a Mr. Swan: not so much to conquer and possess, but rather to sift through the details of other journeys and, with that, to weigh and to know the desire that made them happen. Although the teleology of travel has changed radically by her time, Bishop nevertheless thoroughly understands the power of these old objectives.

THREE

Amy Clampitt: "Distance is dead"

Westward-Trekking Transhumance, History, and Globalization

In an interview, Amy Clampitt describes herself as "a poet of place," a remark that she rapidly qualifies:

> Elizabeth Bishop began life in Nova Scotia (if I'm not mistaken) and can hardly be said to have settled anywhere. I feel a certain kinship with her nomadism, if that is what it is: though I've been based in New York for many years, I feel less and less as though I really *lived* anywhere. Is that kind of uprooting possibly an American tradition?... The more I think about this question, the more intriguing it becomes. Whatever answer there may be, I suspect, will have some relation to being native to the Midwest — and having left it. And then looking back [*Predecessors* 163–64].

Aside from the issue of whether dislocation is *generally* an American tradition, Clampitt's question provides a starting point for this chapter, one in which her connections backward in time to Elizabeth Bishop and Anne Bradstreet may be realized and examined. Certainly a specific tradition of uprootedness can be traced through these writers, who are, to use Clampitt's word for the title of her only volume of essays, among her *predecessors*. But just as important is the fact that Clampitt's preoccupation with flux and the loss of cultural memory — or, more precisely, the loss of cultural awareness of memory, since memory for Clampitt always seems to reassert itself, however disguised — places her on the edge of the modernist camp with its ironies and backward gazing.

Even more than either Bradstreet or Bishop, Clampitt sees herself and her own personal migrations and meanderings in the context of vast his-

torical movements — or *processions*, another of her terms — whose
significance is threatened by the forgetful present age. As she writes in
"Nothing Stays Put": "All that we know, that we're / made of, is motion"
(*CPAC* 340). For Clampitt, as for both Bradstreet and Bishop, a strong
sense of personal rupture, loss, and exile accentuates the need to understand the past with all its predecessors, and to hold it consistently in the
current of her own time where it can be examined at will. This is what
she calls "the livingness of the past," without which "it's hard to see how
the world we live in can have any meaning" (*Predecessors* 3). Indeed,
Clampitt's penchant for remembering details and working them into a
much larger act of cultural recollection constitutes the central part of her
mythical thinking, a concept which Mircea Eliade describes as a

> progressive return to the "origin" by proceeding backward through Time
> from the present moment to the "absolute beginning...." [Mythical think-
> ing involves] a meticulous and exhaustive recollecting of personal and his-
> torical events.... Here *memory* plays the leading role. One frees oneself from
> the work of Time by recollection, by *anamnesis*. The essential thing is to
> remember all the events one has witnessed in Time [88–89].

The resemblance in Clampitt's work to Bradstreet's urge to collapse
time and space can be seen in the former's focus on what she calls
"westward-trekking/transhumance," poetically surveyed from a broad
range of vantage points (*CPAC* 22). More than three centuries after Bradstreet, Clampitt sees the ongoing, still-fluctuating aftermath of a huge
westward movement of humanity begun millennia before the voyage of
the *Arbella* in 1630. In the image of a lighthouse on the eastern seaboard
of North America, she observes "a point of view / as yet unsettled," and
still therefore backward-looking, as though "the coast of Maine had Europe
/ on the brain or in its bones" (*CPAC* 107). Like Bradstreet, Clampitt displays a certain homesickness, a longing for ancestral homelands, but she
is also keenly aware of how the extensive westward procession has impacted
non–Western cultures as well as the biosphere.

Although to look backward is clearly her inclination, Clampitt's
poetic and myth-making virtue lies in her ability to go well beyond nostalgia — for her own childhood, for instance — to examine the historical,
colonial processes that brought her family to the American midwest. Doing
this from a wide variety of perspectives (the road, the air, rail, boat, the
terminal) and locations (from Greece to Great Britain, Maine, and Cali-

fornia),[51] she also takes note of the altered nature of travel itself, going so far as to include the elevator car in "Homer, A.D. 1982" (*CPAC* 177). Although still arduous at times, even in the bus that follows a walking tour taken by Keats (298), overcoming distance is no longer an act mostly of the poetic imagination, a kind of wish-fulfillment. It is a concrete fact that now, urgently, must be accounted for culturally and ecologically.

In the poem containing the allusion to Keats, actually the title poem for the 1990 volume *Westward,* Clampitt contemplates "the collapse of distance" brought on by technological change (297), using diction that at times emphasizes her ties to Bishop ("the flyblown exotic place, / the heathen shrine exposed"). John A. Livingston describes this effect — this loss of the sense of distance — in terms that include the biological when he writes that "it is becoming one homogeneous world": "There is abroad in the biosphere a growing, creeping and crawling *sameness* that is the utter antithesis of ecological and evolutionary process" (39). In *One World* (2002), Peter Singer describes, in the economic terms of globalization, the westward process that Clampitt captures poetically:

> For most of the eons of human existence, people living only short distances apart might as well, for all the difference they made to each other's lives, have been living in separate worlds.... Now people living on opposite sides of the world are linked in ways previously unimaginable.... As technology has overcome distance, economic globalization has followed. In London supermarkets, fresh vegetables flown in from Kenya are offered for sale alongside those from nearby Kent. Planes bring illegal immigrants seeking to better their own lives in a country they have long admired. In the wrong hands the same planes become lethal weapons that bring down tall buildings [9–10].

In her late poem "Hispaniola," Clampitt describes the "westward-spreading" sugarcane industry as "a topography / of monoculture" that eventually encompasses Asia, Africa, the Carribean, and South America:

> huger and huger
> deforestations
> making way for
> raising cane   to be
> holed   planted   cut
> crushed   boiled
> fermented or
> reduced to crystalline

> appeasement of mammalian
> cravings   slave ships
> whip-wielding
> overseers [*CPAC* 366].

The indictment is massive. It reverberates with Carolyn Merchant's statement in *The Death of Nature* that "Between 1500 and 1700 an incredible transformation took place.... Nature, women, blacks, and wage laborers were set on a path toward a new status as 'natural' and human resources for the modern world system" (288). In *The Global Food Economy: The Battle for the Future of Farming* (2007), Tony Weis illuminates the sugared relationship between Europe and the Third World when he states: "[T]he combination of coffee or tea plus sugar connect[ed] the exploitation of working people across continents in an especially intimate way — the products of slave, indentured or bonded labour and exploited peasantries in the colonies 'quelling hunger and numbing outrage' in the European working class toiling in the ghastly mines and factories of the age" (Weis 89).

Here, of course, Clampitt also intersects with Bishop, whose "Over 2000 Illustrations and a Complete Concordance" juxtaposes the historical, Western ideals assumed in travel with the modern inescapable reality: "Thus should have been our travels: / serious, engravable." Clampitt sees in her own immigrant ancestors a similar yearning for sacred sites, "for the pristine, the named, the fabulous" (*CPAC* 299), and she approaches the gradual disintegration of this ideal of the far-off with a casual irony that pays tribute to Bishop without mimicry: "We know nothing / of the universe we move through!" (*CPAC* 132–33). In the age of the machine, transhumance — a term Clampitt borrows from Fernand Braudel's *The Mediterranean and the Mediterranean World in the Age of Philip II* — has become "anonymous of purpose," like the westward crawl of traffic on a mid-western American freeway (*CPAC* 21); or as evoked from the vantage point of any number of buses in what we might call the Greyhound poems, all of which take their cue from Bishop's "The Moose."[52] Clampitt, one might argue, continues the work of Bishop, taking up where she left off in her poetic anatomy of culture and its ecological impact.

But true as this could be, Clampitt cannot be said to be a mere student or imitator of Elizabeth Bishop, as she certainly parts company with Bishop in her use of language. Despite occasionally resorting to a casual idiom, Clampitt's voice is distinctly her own, her language much more

91

thick and formal than Bishop's. Although Clampitt's view is shaped by modernism, particularly in its penchant for the past, it is not constrained by the "conciliatory impulse" that Seamus Heaney sees as Elizabeth Bishop's signature:

> This conciliatory impulse was not based on subservience but on a respect for other people's shyness in the face of poetry's presumption: she usually limited herself to a note that would not have disturbed the discreet under-song of conversation between strangers breakfasting at a seaside hotel [Heaney 101].

For Clampitt, the reticence in twentieth-century poetry is the legacy of T.S. Eliot, or, rather, the legacy of two world wars and numerous other fragmenting traumas given memorable expression by Eliot and discussed by Heaney in his essay on Bishop: as a result of which, Clampitt argues, "an entire generation of poetic arbiters took it as their function to insist on our not insisting" (*Predecessors* 20). Yet she notes Eliot's own aspirations:

> From the diffidence of J. Alfred Prufrock he had come round unmistakably to wanting, like old Wordsworth, to fill a room. Could he do it? Could it be done? Or are we all condemned to go on twittering in the hedges, hoping somebody will be kind enough to pause and listen? [21].

Clampitt's answer to these questions, with which she concludes the essay "T.S. Eliot in 1988," is "I think we still don't know" (21).

With the death of Clampitt in 1994, and the publication of her *Collected Poems* in 1998, it is quite possible that concerning *her* work we do now know the answer to the last question. For what has been written about Clampitt to date points to the fact that her *oeuvre* constitutes no "twittering in the hedges." As David Perkins describes her in *A History of Modern Poetry*:

> She is not a poet of penetrating single insights but of lavish ongoingness; one thing leads her to another; or, more exactly, she has several things in mind at once and they all evolve simultaneously. She is a poet of wit, fecundity, and rich ornament, and her chief defect is the excess of her virtue, for she can overburden her syntax, losing momentum in amplification and decoration [632].

Hence the long modernist period, in Clampitt's view, must be encompassed by a much wider historical picture, one which allows her to choose from a broad, rich linguistic marketplace. Not that she views words as commodities made for consumption, though she knows that *ipso facto* they are: but in this, the age of information and globalization, language for Clampitt has become deregulated, accessible. Thus she uses the disparate tongues of entomology, botany, biology, zoology, history, philosophy, technology, ecology, psychoanalysis, and commerce, as well as the words of predecessors, even though at times this becomes "a grope" and at others signals decadence (*CPAC* 331). As she observes in "Nothing Stays Put" concerning her local supermarket, "The exotic is everywhere" (339).

"Clampitt, who grew up a Puritan and can still sound like one," writes one reviewer, "recoils from this unmerited glut ('we are not entitled')" (Morrison 30). True as this is, Clampitt's diction can be said to be as historically broad, dense, and embracing as the various vantage points taken in her poems, recalling Eliot's remark in his essay "The Metaphysical Poets" about the ability of the major poet to make associations between seemingly incongruous things (Eliot 1063). Consciously composing in the context of her predecessors, Clampitt sees travel in terms of mass migrations of peoples and their cultures, and she habitually does this from her seat on a bus, train, taxi, or plane, or while simply strolling down a street in Manhattan. Her tendency to juxtapose now and then, to put a contemporary hook in the history of questing, reverberates with the modernist sense of loss. At the same time, Clampitt acknowledges the legacy of the modernists via *transhumance*, a concept open to the charge of obscurity were it not for her own detailed awareness of specific historical trends such as the westward one from eastern Europe and the Mediterranean over the last two millennia. And certainly by placing herself and her family history in the foreground, she avoids the merely academic, including her own lineage in a brutally honest disclosure of what westward-questing humans have done.

Modernism, again, becomes in Clampitt's view merely a recent facet of the historical backdrop, a small segment in time of the total westward coursing of humanity, and therefore gives voice to merely one period of loss and alienation among others. "A Procession at Candlemas," one of the seminal poems in the breakthrough volume of 1983, *The Kingfisher*, which catapulted Clampitt late in life on to the American literary scene, ruminates over the North American landscape in terms of the freeway, renovating the trope *road* as Whitman would *grass* in the previous century. As such, "A Procession" opens with an expression of loss that is at once personal, intimate, yet poised for the historical as well as the mythical:

> Moving on or going back to where you came from,
> bad news is what you mainly travel with [*CPAC* 21].

The passage that follows immediately places the familiarity of the interstate in the context of transhumance, which Clampitt wastes no time in
making literally and historically concrete by describing the endless lines
of vehicles as

> the bison of the highway
> [that] funnel westward onto Route 80, mirroring
> an entity that cannot look into itself and know
>
> what makes it what it is.

Here already is the articulation of what for Clampitt is arguably *the*
American problem: that America is cut off from the past even as the past
is incessantly re-enacted; that America's inheritance is partly one of ignorance, because the forces that went into its creation are also the self-serv-
ing ones responsible for revising history, as Clampitt portrays vividly in
the late poem "Matoaka" where she exposes "the shadowy predatory
tentshow / we know as history" (*CPAC* 375) in her lament for the First
Nations woman many Americans call Pocahontas and know from Disney.
At the same time, however, the problem of history and what history means
is not only an American one anymore but rather one America represents
in the age of globalization. Other Western — not to mention non–Western — nations are certainly aware of globalization as threatening to their
own histories, written and oral. It is also important to acknowledge here
the distinction between the mythical and the fictive, that it is the latter
which glibly replaces and stands in for important originary myths that
express a particular culture's sense of itself as unique, meaningful, and
located in nature. In the midst of a technological explosion, the old pastoral dreams to which the poet's mind reverts in "A Procession at Candlemas" cannot be said to be lost because even the sense of loss itself is now
arguably gone in America. One cannot, in this new world "anonymous of
purpose," lose the thing one never knew one had. The past therefore
becomes an absurdity invoked by the corpse of a "mother curtained in
Intensive Care," "lying dead" in a sterile environment, even as the auto-
mobile/bison are a part of the past — and doomed — without their passengers knowing it. The rupture is simply that great, but the speaker, asking
at one point "Where are we?," seems to grasp it.

In fact, the speaker (and it is reasonable to assume she is Clampitt) is a passenger aboard one of these mythical/historical creatures of the highway, resting for the moment by "a Stonehenge / of fuel pumps ... drinking" a hydrocarbon, while

> The sleepers groan, stir, rewrap themselves
> about the self's imponderable substance,
> or clamber down, numb-footed, half in a drowse.

Like the dreamy collective portrayed in Elizabeth Bishop's "The Moose," the sleepers' hobbled consciousness here presents itself as bewilderingly incongruous next to the speaker's aching awareness of both them and herself, and of the context in which they all take their journey together. Clampitt is an alien here, her mind at first "blank" in her reluctance to look at what she sees, bound by fear as well as horror of the ignorance around her. Yet she displays no hint of arrogance either: she just knows what she knows.

And what she knows at this point, while waiting for her bus to refuel, is that it is Candlemas, February 2nd, which the other passengers on the bus will recognize as Groundhog Day. Understanding Candlemas is essential to understanding this poem and what it is that Amy Clampitt wants to evoke, what she calls "the fabric of the backward-ramifying / antecedents." Candlemas by itself is backward-looking by its very nature, although at the same time — as an institutional fiction — it also appropriates and buries older traditions and mythic realities. Cosmologically, it falls on a cross-quarter day midpoint between winter solstice and spring equinox (Graves 168). Prior to the spread of Christianity, the date was known as *Imbolog* or *Imbolc*, as it was called by the Celts (Gimbutas 110–111). To the latter, especially the Irish, *Imbolc*, meaning "in the belly," was "a feast of purification" associated with Brigit who "watches over childbirth" (110), while for the Greeks the date was associated with the myth of Persephone and Demeter (Baring 367–374). In any event, February 2nd was seen as a watershed day when the darkness of the passing winter was put behind one, and spring, with its promise of returning light, new crops, and wild botanical growth, could be anticipated again. Robert Graves adds that Candlemas is associated with the Rowan tree, the "tree of life," and that "In Ireland and the Highlands February 2nd is, very properly, the day of St. Brigit, formerly the White Goddess" (168; see also Gimbutas 110–111).

The advent of Christianity and the Christian calendar saw the replacement of the pagan *Imbolc* with Candlemas, commemorating the meeting of the Christ child with the old man Simeon in the temple, after Mary's requisite purification (Luke 2:26). With the presentation of Christ in the Temple of Jerusalem, a new age is announced, the meeting between the infant and the old man, called *Hypapanti* by the Greeks, marking "the encounter between the passing heathen world and the new beginning in Christ" (Ratzinger 25). Co-opting the meaning and even some of the rites of *Imbolc* (and other pagan rituals associated with February 2nd), Candlemas begins to evoke not just these older rites of passage, nor the New Testament ones involving Mary, Christ, and Simeon, but *change* itself. Hence becoming, evolving, succession, memory, and amnesia are all built into Candlemas. Writing on behalf of Catholics, Pope Benedict XVI states (without irony):

> Accordingly this day was made into a feast of candles. The warm candlelight is meant to be a tangible reminder of that greater light which, for and beyond all time, radiates from the figure of Jesus. In Rome this candlelit procession supplanted a rowdy, dissolute carnival, the so-called Amburbale, which had survived from paganism right into Christian times. The pagan procession had magical features: it was supposed to effect the purification of the city and the repelling of evil powers [Ratzinger 26].

Thus Candlemas casts off old ways by conquering them, even as the day itself, with its ancient cosmological significance, is about casting off, purification, rekindling, and is today unwittingly acknowledged when the status of the groundhog's shadow is sought every February 2nd:

> If Candlemas be fair and bright,
> Come, winter, have another flight.
> If Candlemas brings cloud and rain,
> Go, winter, and come not again.

What is viewed as lost in "A Procession at Candlemas" is the ability to remember itself, with Candlemas itself ironically invoked as the watershed of loss, even as the processions that have traditionally preserved memory are carried on unconsciously. Hence Clampitt sees "A Candlemas of moving lights along Route 80," but whether these lights carry with them the hope traditionally associated with spring is doubtful; they are, after all, the lights of fossil-fuel-burning vehicles. So there is only the refuel-

ing bus and the loss it presupposes, what the speaker tellingly calls, with
Firestone spin, "The lapped, wheelborne integument, layer / within layer,
at the core a dream of / something precious." The rituals of the past continue to be enacted but only to embody "the pristine seductiveness of
money," the old god Mammon, even though of course little of this is realized. Again, it is the notion of change itself, the knowledge of flux as an
ineluctable part of existence and with that the awareness of the old in the
new, that is lost.

Clampitt juxtaposes old and seemingly new in the contrasting images
of the terminal's name, Indian Meadows, and its cafeteria showcase with
its glittering jellies, "gumball globes, [and] Life Savers." The latter "plop
from their housings / perfect, like miracles." This "nowhere oasis" marked
by absence and "without inhabitants" still has a history in its name, albeit
one that is anglicized and that echoes with loss and irony. Here is a fossil
landscape that continues to bear witness to how North American aboriginals, according to Vine Deloria, perceived creation "as an ecosystem present in a definable place" (77). The same cultural forces that, deeply
imbedded with Christian thought, have created what Clampitt calls
"bison[s] of the highway," have also caused the flight of peoples native to
North America:

> The westward-trekking
> transhumance, once only, of a people who,
>
> in losing everything they had, lost even
> the names they went by, stumbling past
> like caribou, perhaps camped here. Who
>
> can assign a trade-in value to that sorrow?

To be sure, the latter question is the third of six posed by the speaker,
the poem's two sections of twenty-four tercets each dividing the set of
questions equally. In order to see and examine them clearly, they are set
out here as prose:

I

Where are we?
What is real except what's fabricated?
Who can assign a trade-in value to that sorrow?

II

Who can unpeel the layers of that seasonal returning to the dark where

97

memory fails, as birds re-enter the ancestral flyway? [emphasis mine]
  Where is it?
  Where, in the shucked-off bundle, the hampered obscurity that has been
for centuries the mumbling lot of women, *did the thread of fire*, too frail
ever to discover what it meant, to risk even the taking of a shape, *relinquish
the seed of possibility*, unguessed-at as a dream of something precious?
[emphasis mine].

The first question is posed in the context of the moving traffic, its
metaphorical and historical implications discussed here already. The second comes between the two images of "a Stonehenge / of fuel pumps" and
"the cafeteria showcase," adding a teleological dimension to the first question. And the third follows the naming of the terminal, Indian Meadows,
and the loss that that act of power — naming — implies for indigenous peoples of North America.

Against this, Clampitt posits another image at the end of section one:
"The monk in sheepskin over tucked-up saffron / intoning to a drum,"
which "becomes the metronome"

> of one more straggle up Pennsylvania Avenue
> in falling snow, a whirl of tenderly
> remorseless corpuscles, street gangs
>
> amok among magnolias' pregnant wands,
> a stillness at the heart of so much whirling:
> beyond the torn integument of childbirth,
>
> sometimes, wrapped like a papoose into a grief
> not merely of the ego, you rediscover almost
> the rest-in-peace of the placental coracle.

Here indeed is a bundle of images: the monk, the drum, the metronome;
the diaspora up Pennsylvania Avenue toward the American seat of power;
the oxymoronic snow seen as corpuscles; street gangs among magnolias;
childbirth, a papoose, and the placenta seen as a wicker boat. In part,
Clampitt's point is to call complexity and chaos into the reader's mind and
so recreate contemporary experience as she brings the poem's first movement to a close. The metronome of Christianity, of Candlemas, contrasts
with the "straggle" and "whirl" of the current age (replete with discordant
images of the past) when street gangs run "amok." Christianity, it seems,
continues to preside over and regulate history with all its fabrications, even
though it maybe one of them.

Over against this human activity is the natural world, offering a possible refuge from the dispersals of history. But this is also "backward-ramifying," or at least what Clampitt finds (as she moves "beyond the torn integument of childbirth" to "the rest-in-peace of the placental coracle") is a biological reversal that only "almost" takes her out of the "whirling." In the final analysis, she cannot quite get to that tranquil state, the *before* to this scattered *after*. She appears to assume its actual existence as a non-ego, non-historical objective reality, one that "sometimes ... you rediscover almost...." It is outside time; hence, it cannot quite be articulated, recalling what Eliot would write in *Burnt Norton* just before the onset of World War II, that "Words strain, / Crack and sometimes break, under the burden" (Eliot 194).

Clampitt's fourth question, "Who can unpeel the layers...?," follows her return to history, myth, and memory in a backward reaching to the Greek classical myths and rituals pre-dating Christianity and Candlemas. This too, she acknowledges, is difficult, if not impossible:

> Of what the dead were, living, one knows
> so little as barely to recognize
> the fabric of the backward-ramifying
>
> antecedents, half-noted presences
> in darkened rooms: the old, the feared,
> the hallowed. Never the same river
>
> drowns the unalterable doorsill.

The allusion to Heraclitus' doctrine of flux clarifies the extent of the problem, since all human activity, no matter how far back in time one tries to reach, includes the backward look to "the old, the feared, / the hallowed." On one level, the fourth question seems to ask, "Was it ever any different?" Even the ancient Greek cults faced this question, of origins, of stepping out of time, and whether it could be done by humans: "Athene, who had no mother, ... had her own wizened cult object." But around Athene, and attending to the "Athenian foundation myth" (Connelly 59) inherent in her character, was also the annual procession: "to whom, year after year, / the fair linen of the sacred peplos / was brought."[53] Gimbutas points out in her study of the goddess that even Athene — indeed, *especially* Athene — conceals earlier female figures: "Most strikingly visible is the conversion of Athena, the Old European Bird Goddess, into a militarized figure carrying a shield and wearing a helmet. The belief in her birth from the head of Zeus, the ruling god of the Indo-Europeans in Greece, shows how far the transformation went — from a parthenogenetic goddess to her birth from a male god!" (Gimbutas 318).

Posed in the context of the gender transformation of the gods, the fourth question, with its migratory simile, tenuously and ironically connects the time of the ancient Greeks to that of modern America. In contrast to the darkness into which memory instinctively returns, and as though to answer the question posed in the poet's mind during the long night of travel by bus, there is

> Daylight, snow falling, knotting of gears:
> Chicago. Soot, the rotting backsides
> of tenements, grimed trollshapes of ice
>
> underneath the bridges, the tunnel heaving
> like a birth canal.

The "fair linen of the sacred peplos," the robe offered annually to the wooden image of Athena, is set against "wall-eyed TV receivers" in another terminal where the bus comes to rest temporarily. Likewise, "wildflower-/ hung cattle" have now been reduced to "feedlot cattle," and the "nubile Athenian girls, [and] young men / praised for the beauty of their bodies" are, in this distant era, "unloved, the spawn of botched intentions."

The modern landscape, as Clampitt sees it from her place on the bus, lies dormant, if not outright dead: "gray," "cadaverous," "frozen," "dragnetted in ice." The sight of this terrain precipitates the final pair of questions: "Where is it?" and the convoluted final one quoted above. Syntactically, the subject of both these questions is "the thread of fire," which of course refers the reader back to the beginning of the poem, with its allusions to Candlemas evoked by the procession of vehicles moving along the interstate in the gathering dark: "to carry fire as though it were a flower." The appropriation of history and myth entrenched in Candlemas, and what that has meant for women especially —"such a loathing / of the common origin"— is also paramount in the final interrogative. Their "seed of possibility," set aside as a result of the dominant Judeo-Christian tradition, can only be wondered at and grieved over — like "the westward-trekking" native Americans whose cultures and languages are, in many cases, irrevocably lost.[54]

But for Clampitt, despair cannot be the final word, even though she sees in the "long-unentered nave of childhood" a microcosm of women's history in which women are categorized as a lower form of life along with animals (Merchant *DON* 143). In her own memory, which she calls "that exquisite blunderer, stumbling"

> like a migrant bird that finds the flyway
> it hardly knew it knew except by instinct,

she locates "the untouched / nucleus of fire." Regarding the oft-used term *instinct,* John A. Livingston quotes Gregory Bateson, who calls it an "'explanatory principle' which explains everything and nothing.... Wild, whole beings would appear to have full sensibility not only to local signs, but also to the greater orchestration which they themselves will now perform. It may not be preposterous to suggest a consciousness of biospheric self" (Livingston 116). This "biospheric self" for Clampitt constitutes "the lost connection," which she finds in the memory of "a small / stilled bird, its cap of clear yellow / slit by a thread of scarlet." It is only in this personal recollection that the poet — who finds similar evocations of meaning in the image of the bird in several other poems, most notably "The Kingfisher," "A Hermit Thrush," "A Whippoorwill in the Woods," "Syrinx," and "Sed de Correr" (*CPAC* 42, 272, 313, 363, 420) — can resolve and restore the loss indicated by both the "the wizened effigy" and "the mother / curtained in Intensive Care." Both are hallowed by Clampitt's striking memories of childhood, memories that frequently involve birds and that point to what we call *nature* as the place where the macro memory of both women and America can be recovered.[55]

Geologic Time and the Westward Quest for Living Space

In "The Quarry," found in the same volume as "A Procession at Candlemas," Clampitt continues to delineate her theme of westward expansion. Here she sees "the stagecoach laboring" in the context of prehistory found in the rock faces of an abandoned quarry (*CPAC* 55). Covering vast periods of geologic time in the opening of this poem, Clampitt makes the westward movement of humanity appear as what it is: a piece of minutiae, a ludicrous and humbling "pinpoint." And only from such an extreme point of view, beginning outside and prior to human history, can she demonstrate the absurdity of the objectives and aims held by the progenitors of westward trekking. Unlike "A Procession at Candlemas," there is no lamentation in this poem, but rather a dazzling, sardonic inspection of Western culture given in the context of geologic time. Even the image of the stagecoach, given at the outset of the poem, is seen as absurd in its arrogance and presumption: unwittingly, it labors "through mud / up to the hubs" where fishes once swam "through the Eocene." As in the Candlemas poem, stasis is seen as assumed when, in fact, the only constant is change. This Clampitt calls

> a flux
> that waterlogs the mind, draining southeastward
> by osmosis to the Mississippi.

The "flux" becomes a metaphor for the imagination's failed attempt to grasp, to cope with, the concept of prehistoric time: "[N]o landmarks to tell where you are, / or who, or whether you will ever find a place / to feel at home in."

Hernand De Soto, also discussed here in Chapter Five in the context of Elizabeth Bishop's "Florida," is one of two central historical figures in "The Quarry," the other being Lyman Dillon. Like Dillon, who "drove a plow southwestward / a hundred miles — the longest furrow / ever," De Soto represents the long thrust westward from Europe. Searching for gold and the lost city of El Dorado on behalf of seventeenth-century Spain, he typifies the greed behind the earliest European forays into the Americas. Clampitt calls it "the corrupt / obsession," passed on to others in the wake of De Soto's death by drowning in the Mississippi, his corpse fouling the waters in more ways than one before being "Flushed finally / out of the heartland drainpipe." Culturally and historically, the flushing is open to question:

> Will
> some shard of skull or jawbone, undecomposed,
> outlast his name, as the unquarried starfish
> outlast the seas that inundated them?

For now, ironically, Clampitt remembers and preserves the name De Soto as a landmark to help tell us, her readers, who and where we are.

The tripartite structure of "The Quarry" reflects Clampitt's repeated attempts to dig through layers of history and prehistory. As in "A Pro-

cession at Candlemas," it is only in the context of Western linear time
that flux becomes, if not completely comprehensible, at least somewhat
coherent and meaningful to its audience. Hence, each of the three stanzas in "The Quarry" begins with the Clampittian reach backward to
attempt to recover the past. At the outset of the poem, the speaker tells
us, "Fishes swam here through the Eocene." This is followed by the opening words of the second verse paragraph, which establishes the second-
person address: "No roads, / no landmarks to tell where you are." Finally,
the third begins,

> Think back
> a little, to what would have been,
> without this festering of lights at night,
> this grid of homesteads, this hardening
> lymph of haste foreshortened into highways:
> the lilt and ripple of the dark,
> birdsong at dusk augmented by frog choirs
> already old before the Eocene.

Each initial posing of the prehistorical gives way to the more recent and
historicized human narrative. The image of the stagecoaches moving
through the heartland like "prairie schooners" provides the foreground to
the distant Eocene. Eastward and earlier than the stagecoach era is De
Soto's decomposing corpse, leaving a legacy, his name a landmark in Western culture. Likewise, the third and final verse paragraph moves through
time once more, as though to scan it yet again as though it were a
palimpsest. Frog choirs give way to "wickiups / now here, now there," as
aboriginal peoples are "edged westward / year by year, hemmed in or
undermined, / done in finally by treaties." This, in turn, gives way to the
most recent figure of Lyman Dillon (complementing De Soto in the previous paragraph) who

> starting at Dubuque, drove a plow southwestward
> a hundred miles — the longest furrow
> ever.

Prehistoric past meets "belly of the future" in the marble dome of the capi-
tol at Des Moines, Iowa, quarried somewhere in the heartland, though
Clampitt is careful to point out in an endnote that the original capitol at
Iowa City was made of native limestone (*CPAC* 437). In the poem's final

three lines, the dome acts as a crux, one that "overtops / the frittered sprawl of who we are," while the legendary El Dorado, precipitating so much lust for travel, remains undiscovered.

In the "Heartland" section of *The Kingfisher,* where "The Quarry" is found, "Imago" extends the preoccupation with human movements and their consequences in time. Here Clampitt ponders her own evolution and ancestral background filled with "Nomads," from whom she inherits her penchant for moving on, "stowed aboard / the usual nomadic moving van" (*CPAC* 59). Even here, among personal memories, she alludes to her fascination with the prehistoric, in this case a "chipped flint" found in a furrow. Clampitt's strong sense of being an outsider is also given direct, autobiographical reference in "Black Buttercups," which appears in the second volume, *What the Light Was Like* (1987), where the month of March is "the farmer's month / for packing up and moving on" and "the verb *to move* / connoted nothing natural." Here the speaker remembers what it is like, at ten, to leave a loved farm:

> The look of exile
> foreseen, however massive or inconsequential,
> hurts the same; it's the remembered
> particulars that differ [*CPAC* 125].

Related personal memories appear in "Urn-Burial and the Butterfly Migration," where the speaker compares the intense growth and change of her childhood with the repose of a now-deceased brother:

> We scattered. Like the dandelion,
> that quintessential successful
> immigrant, its offspring gone
> to fluff, dug-in hard-scrabble
> nurtured a generation of
> the mobile, nomads enamored
> of cloverleafs, of hangars, of
> that unrest whose home —*our*
> home — is motion [*CPAC* 132].

In the final poem of *The Kingfisher,* "The Burning Child," addressed to a Jewish friend whose grandparents were killed in a Nazi concentration camp, Clampitt describes her paternal grandparents' nineteenth-century journey across America in the context of the horrific trans-European journey that her friend's relatives endured in the century following. The two disparate rides by rail (one a journey to gold-crazed California from Iowa, the other to certain death in the camps and gas chambers of World War II Europe) together make up a pair of seemingly disparate recent additions to the massive flux of humans that *The Kingfisher* envisions spreading westward over centuries:

> I think of how your mother's
> people made the journey, and of how
> > > unlike
>
> > my own forebears who made the journey,
> > when the rush was on, aboard a crowded
> > train from Iowa to California, where,
> > hedged by the Pacific's lunging barricades,
> > they brought into the world the infant
> > who would one day be my father, and
> > > > ... chose
>
> > to return, were free to stay or go
> > back home, go anywhere at all —
> > > > not one
> outlived the trip whose terminus was burning [*CPAC* 102].

That Clampitt posits these together at the end of *The Kingfisher* is disturbing, and no coincidence. As "unlike" as these two journeys are (one including birth and return, the other imprisonment and death), they still share the same narrative structure, implying a common historical root in the imperial desire for land, wealth, and power. The quest narrative outlining the nineteenth-century American Dream is folded within, sandwiched between, the structure of what would follow in the twentieth in Europe: that is, the Nazi's Final Solution. Despite the freedom Clampitt's grandparents had to "go anywhere at all," their story is qualified by the construct of other journeys, also by rail, which saw the Jewish people nearly destroyed by Nazi Germany. Both journeys find a common progenitor in sixteenth- and seventeenth-century Spain, Portugal, France, Holland, and England, and the broader European desire for gold and space: this latter what Hitler would come to call *lebensraum,* a "living space" for the German people in the vast areas of Eastern Europe, the Ukraine, and Russia.

Looking West from Iona

The dual themes of the westward and the backward, with both poet and reader looking east to understand them, are also prevalent in Clampitt's final two volumes, *Westward* (1990) and *A Silence Opens* (1994).[56] "Westward," a major poem in the 1990 volume, provides a significant addition to the exploration of distance undertaken by both Anne Bradstreet and Elizabeth Bishop. Bradstreet's need, as discussed in Chapter One, to collapse the vast distance between England and New England becomes for Clampitt a *fait accompli* as she travels across the English countryside on her way to the island of Iona, where the sixth-century monk, Columba, established a western outpost for Christianity. The opening sentence of the poem abruptly puts Bradstreet's earlier dilemma — the quandary of the American position relative to the rest of the world — in stark perspective: "Distance is dead" (*CPAC* 297). For Clampitt, indeed, there are new and growing problems now, brought on by the rapid technological advances in travel and the consequent acceleration of the cultural conquest underway during Bradstreet's era. That "A generation / saw it happen" requires close scrutiny.

In order to explore her theme of westward expansion and thus to recover as much of the past as she can, Clampitt's own journey takes her east to an English airport (she mentions both Gatwick and Heathrow), after which she is en route to Iona "doleful, unlulled / by British Rail," the trains at Euston station the "overleapers of the old slow silk route." The rapidity of technological change has changed everything else along with it. As in the earlier "A Procession at Candlemas," Clampitt is again brooding over the loss of origins — a similar problem to that faced by Bradstreet and the early colonists, but now on an endemic scale and brought on by "manglings, accelerated trade routes / in reverse." While for Bradstreet there was the distant presence of England to the east, with its powerful cultural codes, for Clampitt there are now "the latest émigrés / of a spent Commonwealth" crowding the station: "drawn toward what prospect, from what / point of origin?"

What she calls the "old assumptions," based on the idea of the marvellous destination, "of fool's-gold El Dorado," are no longer tenable, indeed never were. As the speaker travels to Iona, first by train, then bus and boat, she ponders "the collapse of distance," a fact of life that no longer requires an imaginative leap:

> Rain seeps in;
> past the streaked, streaming pane,
>
> a fir-fringed, sodden glimpse, the
> verberation of a name: Loch Lomond.
> "Really?" The callow traveler opposite
>
> looks up, goes back to reading — yes,
> it really is Thucydides: hubris,
> brazen entitlements, forepangs of
>
> letting go, all that.

Again for Clampitt, as in "A Procession at Candlemas" and "The Quarry," history is layered, a series of accretions, most of which make the current amnesic epoch seem ironic. In this case, the Greek Thucydides, whom Macaulay judged the greatest historian ever to have lived, provides the ironic backdrop as Loch Lomond is fleetingly glimpsed from the passing train. Of Thucydides, one mid-twentieth-century commentator writes:

> The assumption of the uniformity of history is by all odds the most important assumption in Thucydides' work. But it does not exclude enormous change. And the change is more than technical. Under the benign influence of security, comfort, wealth, freedom, man himself acquires new "turns" or modes of character, becomes complex, versatile, paradoxical, a new and higher kind of human being [MacKendrick and Howe 232].

For Clampitt, the seeds of so-called Western thought can be found everywhere, and they are frequently ironic given their new and critical late-twentieth-century context. Along with Thucydides, Clampitt also imagines Keats and St. Columba, as well as the massive cohort of westward-trekking emigrants of the last three centuries.

Indeed, as Clampitt reaches Iona, she dramatically reverses Anne Bradstreet's backward and eastward gazing. More than three centuries after Bradstreet, Amy Clampitt could be said to return the look, to regard the pioneers who, like Bradstreet herself, both longed for and reviled what they had left behind. "But from this island...," she writes, "the prospect / is to the west." Contemplating the mirror of her own history, Clampitt's poetic vision encompasses what Sacvan Bercovitch has called "that astonishing Westward leap of the imagination" that transformed the original colonial Puritan "vision from a transatlantic to a transcontinental direction" (*Rites* 75–6). From Iona, she sees

the pioneers, the children's
children of the pioneers, look up from

the interior's plowed-under grassland,
the one homeland they know no homeland
but a taken-over turf: no sanction, no cover

but the raveled sleeve of empire: and yearn
for the pristine, the named, the fabulous,
the holy places.

The "backward-looking" poet compares herself to her predecessors whom she imagines yearning for, and gazing back toward, the apparently civilized east. From her vantage point on Iona, Clampitt discovers that what drove these "forward-slogging" wayfarers westward was not so much religious doctrine as the desire for epiphany, the "opening / at the water's edge." Significantly, the form of "Westward" takes it cue from Dante's *Divine Comedy*— the run-on tercet itself resembling the "routes, / the ribbonings and redoublings," all of which "bear witness" to the common desire for an answer, an end, an omega point, an orderly arrival. In the unnamed reaches of the prairie more than a century before, the pioneers whom Clampitt now contemplates stood "at the brim of an illumination" that Anne Bradstreet would have understood, one

that can't be entered, can't be lived in —
you'd either founder, a castaway, or drown —

a well, a source that comprehends, that
supersedes all doctrine: what surety,
what reprieve from drowning, is there,

other than in names?

This she calls "The prairie eyeblink," which she sees "rimmed by the driftwood" of history: "of embarkations, landings, dooms, conquests, / missionary journeys, memorials." Evoking "A Procession at Candlemas," Clampitt again ponders the ramifications of colonizing the New World landscape: how in fact the act of naming helped the heartland settlers, as it did the various other westward-trekking questors, deal with the potential and very threatening "loss of ego" that can accompany the "unfamiliar sense of space" identified by Barry Lopez in his study of Arctic exploration (245).

The longings that propelled Clampitt's forebears into the heartland of North America also moved Columba and his religious brethren, with their woven boats, to travel westward from Britain and found the colony on the island of Iona, which now provides Clampitt's frame. But this in turn had its own progenitor in earlier journeys from the east. Clampitt sees in this persistent westward push "the braided syntax / of a zeal ignited somewhere to the east, / concealed in hovels, quarreled over, / portaged westward." Metaphors for the migratory process stimulated by religious and cultural assumptions seem to pile up in Clampitt's lines. The long push west is "a basket weave, a / fishing net, a weir to catch, to salvage / some tenet, some common intimation for / all flesh." In a review of *West-ward*, Helen Vendler aptly observes that it is here, from this perspective, that Clampitt's imagination finds "an anchor," in contrast (we might add) to the moving perspective she renders as a passenger on a bus, a train, or a boat: "Facing both ways, back to Europe and forward to the New World, Clampitt imagines the dogged wanderings of what one can only call the Western religious imagination" (109). To be sure, with the fact of climate change well established and beyond any serious dispute, James Lovelock reframes this perspective on Iona in ecological if not outright apocalyptic terms:

> Despite all our efforts to retreat sustainably, we may be unable to prevent a global decline into a chaotic world ruled by brutal war lords on a devastated Earth. If this happens we should think of those small groups of monks in mountain fastnesses like Montserrat or on islands like Iona and Lindisfarne who served [a] vital purpose [*TROG* 198].

Indeed, the value that Vendler identifies in this anchoring moment for Clampitt stems in part from the difficulty of the act she is performing — one of cultural and personal recollection, of sifting through previous westward movements and reassessing what those movements now, and in the future, may mean. Barry Lopez writes of how the "[d]ifficulty in evaluating, or even discerning, a particular landscape is related to the distance a culture has traveled from its own ancestral landscape" (12). So it is that Clampitt, in making the journey to Iona, a crucial outpost of Christianity, returns to an ancestral landscape that is, temporally-speaking, a middle ground from which she can evaluate America to the west and continue at the same to gaze eastward and further back in time.

Reaching for the Interior: Western Mythic Metaphor, Part 2

As Clampitt states in "My Cousin Muriel," also found in *Westward,* "it's my function / to imagine scenes, try for connections" (*CPAC* 331). Here she makes the broad historical analysis of "Westward" more specific and personal with a recollection of her cousin Muriel, now dying in a hospital in California. Clampitt recalls their shared childhood from the vantage point of "Manhattan, a glittering shambles." Like the basket weave, fishing net, coracle, and weir visualized in "Westward," "the *punto in aria* / of hybrid pear trees in bloom" in this poem acts as the visual metaphor precipitating the act of recalling the past.[57] Literally a pattern in the air outside her window, the blossoming trees blur Clampitt's view of the city as she reaches out to her cousin "by way of switchboard and satellite."

The fact of their disparate personal histories — with one going west, the other east — prompts Clampitt also to examine the broader context, what she calls "the long-drawn larger movement"

> that lured the Reverend Charles Wadsworth
> to San Francisco, followed in imagination
> from the cupola of the shuttered homestead
> in Amherst where a childless recluse,
> on a spring evening a century ago, A.D.
> (so to speak) 1886, would cease to breathe
> the air of rural Protestant New England —
>
> an atmosphere and a condition which
> by stages, wagon trains, tent meetings,
> the Revival, infused the hinterland
> my cousin Muriel and I both hailed from.

While Clampitt is certainly no recluse, she refers to herself here as the "childless spinner of metaphor," drawing an obvious parallel between her early life with, and feeling for, Muriel, and the relationship a century before between Emily Dickinson and her beloved friend, Charles Wadsworth. Both Wadsworth and Muriel, as well as Muriel's faithless husband, Dorwin, are "part of the larger exodus" pulling the masses inexorably westward. The prairie heartland is "evangel-haunted" just as much as the Old England of Anne Bradstreet's time, restlessly prodding believers to move on, settling and resettling. Clampitt herself, though, heads east to New York and "a Village basement" while "others [are] for California":

> whatever
> Charles Wadsworth, out there, foresaw
> as consolation for anyone at all — attached,
> estranged, or merely marking time — little
> is left, these days, these times, to say
>
> when the unspeakable stirs like a stone.

Here Clampitt's attempted "raid upon the inarticulate" (Heaney 170), with the Yeatsian image of the stone repeated three times throughout "My Cousin Muriel," evokes the mystery of flux and stasis, linking the poem again to "Westward" with its invocation of the unsayable, with whatever might exist outside human experience, language, culture: "There at the brim of an illumination / that can't be entered, can't be lived in" (*CPAC* 300).[58] The poet recalls her youth with Muriel, visiting "the state fair campground" where they witnessed "a man shot from a cannon," constituting a kind of rite of initiation for the two girls. It is a "*punto in aria* of sheer excitement" for the cousins who now, via their telephone call,

> suspend, uprooted from the hinterland,
> this last gray filament across a continent
> where the unspeakable stirs like a stone.

Clampitt's attempt to push the limits of language, history, and the personal experience of being on the move is also strikingly present in "Iola, Kansas," one of the Greyhound bus poems. Like "Gradual Clearing" and "Marine Surface, Low Overcast" (both of which are discussed in the final chapter of this volume), "Iola, Kansas" marks the ongoingness of experience with one elaborate sentence, though here the experience of travel through different mid-western states is partly evoked as well by the poem's quatrains, as opposed to the stitch-like and stichic form of "Gradual Clearing" or the formal ebb and flow of "Marine Surface" (*CPAC* 8 & 13). And as in "A Procession at Candlemas," the flux — "Riding all night, the bus half empty, toward the interior" — provides the context in which a rest stop in Kansas is described:

> we've come to a rest stop, the name of the girl
> on the watertower is Iola: no video, no vending machines,
> but Wonder Bread sandwiches, a pie: "It's boysenberry,

I just baked it today," the woman behind the counter
believably says, the innards a purply glue, and I eat it

with something akin to reverence: free refills from
the Silex on the hot plate, then back to our seats,
the loud suction of air brakes like a thing alive, and
the voices, the sleeping assembly raised, as by an agency

out of the mystery of the interior, to a community —
and through some duct in the rock I feel my heart go out,
out here in the middle of nowhere (the scheme is a mess)
to the waste, to the not knowing who or why, and am happy[59]
[*CPAC* 291].

    The poem examines the at-times false and falsifying dichotomy that appears in perceptions about Westernized landscapes, between exterior and interior, surface and core, in ways that, again, create reverberations with other poems — not just Clampitt's but also Bishop's:

Westward toward the dark,
the undertow of scenes come back to, fright
riddling the structures of interior history.
[AC, "A Procession at Candlemas"].

Here at the raw edge
of Europe — limpet tenacities, the tidal
combings, purplings of kelp and dulse,
the wrack, the blur, the breakup

of every prospect but turmoil, of
upheaval in the west — the retrospect
is once again toward the interior.
[AC, "Westward"].

We leave Santos at once;
we are driving to the interior.
[EB, "Arrival at Santos"].

Just so the Christians, hard as nails,
tiny as nails, and glinting,
in creaking armor, came and found it all....
*   *   *   *   *   *   *

they ripped away into the hanging fabric,
each out to catch an Indian for himself —
those maddening little women who kept calling,
calling to each other (or had the birds waked up?)

and retreating, always retreating, behind it
            [EB, "Brazil, January 1, 1502"].

As Bishop does in "Brazil," Clampitt in "Iola, Kansas" implicates the exploitative greed of transplanted European culture, what she calls the "homunculi swigging at the gut of a continent." Her little men correspond to the conquistadors in Bishop's poem, who hunt "those maddening little women" through layers of tropical forest. Both poets powerfully echo Frantz Fanon's 1961 statement in *The Wretched of the Earth* that "in a very concrete way Europe has stuffed herself inordinately with the gold and raw materials of the colonial countries.... Europe is literally the creation of the Third World" (102).

For Clampitt, the examination of the age-old quest for spiritually-illuminating or treasure-filled interiors constitutes the focus of her poem. The phraseology bears this out: "toward the interior," "the gut of a continent," "*heart like a rock*," "the bandstand in the park at the center, the churches / alight from within," "the middle of nowhere." The interior is a "mystery" sought out by the speaker aboard her bus, even though the vehicle meanders, "the scheme is a mess," and every interior she locates is trivialized, degraded, and altered by layers of history, like the interior lights of the churches filtered by their "perpendicular banalities of glass / candy-streaked purple-green-yellow (who is this Jesus?)." To the parenthetical question, Clampitt gives us her answer in an essay on St. Paul:

> Who was he? A Jew with no plans to found a new religion, who simply *was* what he proclaimed — that the Kingdom of Heaven is here and now. I think of modern Thessalonica, where the authentic residues of a Byzantine past amount to little more than a glimmer of mosaic, defaced, covered over and uncovered, further defacement being the price of salvaging anything at all [*Predecessors* 105].

And what is salvaged, finally, as the bus pulls in to Iola, at the heart of the North American continent, is fresh boysenberry pie, "the innards a purply glue": "I eat it / with something akin to reverence." This sacramental moment is like another Clampitt recalls, also in the essay on St. Paul, in which she experienced an unexpected and "totally unasked-for" moment of serenity that "felt like an intervening flood" (103). With the consumption of the "innards" of something so profane and yet so connected to the proverbial American Dream as pie, "Iola, Kansas" approaches the kind of epiphany found in Bishop's "Filling Station": "Somebody loves us all." Everything for Clampitt becomes transformed by the eating of the boy-senberry glue, the boysenberry itself the fruit of a hybrid bramble bush, like the hybrid pear tree in "My Cousin Muriel."[60] By taking pie and cof-fee, the sleepers on the bus are "raised," an "assembly" now, "to a commu-nity"; and the speaker knows a moment of grace such that "through some duct in the rock I feel my heart go out, / out here in the middle of nowhere."

Hence it turns out that it is Clampitt's own heart that provides the sought-after experience of the interior, one which reaches out specifically "to the waste" and makes of Iola a place. She hints, as she more forth-rightly states in other poems, that it is only through such experience that Westerners can orient themselves, make sense of the environment, whether it's the heartland of De Soto's time or the current period with its "homun-culi [still] swigging at the gut of a continent." Clampitt notably does not remove herself or withdraw from the inane and lost culture she so acutely identifies and even accuses. She is, finally, like both Bishop and Bradstreet, a member of the community, however frightening, fragmented, and wrong-headed it has been all along, and however ambivalent she herself might feel about such a prospect.

The irony of westward transhumance, whose dimensions Clampitt so painstakingly draws, is that it could result in something as glib and cul-turally impoverished as the humanized landscape seen from her seat on a bus, not only in "Iola, Kansas" but also in "A Procession at Candlesmas." One obstinately wonders, though, why the figure of the artist should have to provide what seems like the sole stay against a culture's interior confu-sion, its waste and forgetfulness. In the long poem, *The Prairie*, Clampitt quotes Emerson: "*The country's mind, / aimed low, grows thick and fat*" (*CPAC* 350). And citing another poet, the Russian writer Joseph Brodsky (himself a westward-trekking emigré escaping Soviet Russia), she expands the meaning of *West* into its twentieth-century geo-political sense — "A West that proved ... to be, essentially ... / *Essentially a customer,*" which Brodsky stipulated has nothing to offer. Clampitt makes plain the fact that this is her subject, her "epic theme," this "long-drawn-out / shadow-war against the old ones" with their "places / that go strange, that vanish into something else":

> To be landless, half a nomad, nowhere wholly
> at home, is to discover, now, an epic theme
> in going back.[61] The rootless urge that took
>
> my father's father to Dakota to California,
> impels me there. A settled continent: what
> does it mean?

Here Clampitt echoes, of course, Elizabeth Bishop's sifting questions in "Questions of Travel": "*Should we have stayed at home, / wherever that may be?*" Like Bishop's reference in "Arrival at Santos" to Miss Breen's home, "when she is at home," Clampitt's question suggests that the accepted notion of settlement is really transitory, an interim moment that constitutes the exception to the rule of movement. All the movement, the endless questing, is in this poem with which *Westward* closes, seen finally as a temporary stay against anxiety and uncertainty.

Indeed, Clampitt argues here that the cultural constructs of the West — the memes on which it is built — are erected out of fear: fear of the unknown, the unnamed, and the unmeasured evoked most powerfully by the spaces of the heartland and, ironically, the immense Pacific from which Clampitt's forebears turn away. The great eastern city, New York, where Clampitt resides, is "a propped / vacuity" built on money and profits. Money, cities, sonnets, fences, houses, gardens, property — all are brought under her intense scrutiny as she measures them against the things early North American settlers rejected the most: homelessness, "unfenced spaces," "the shiftless," Native American spiritual practices, untilled land, places without names, biodiversity. As she does in "Westward," Clampitt here takes a perspective that looks both east and west, this time taking in the steppes of Russia during the time of Anton Chekhov, and pursuing this as a doppelgänger narrative running alongside the story of her own grandfather and father and how they found "The settled life" on the American prairie. The two storylines entwine throughout *The Prairie*, implying — as "The Burning Child" implies — that the recent westward coursing of people constitutes a single overarching narrative of empire.

And empire is flawed and easily unraveled. It will, Clampitt argues, come undone. Here she introduces subtexts and characters that reveal the illusions of empire. Early in the poem, readers are introduced to "Chekhov's imagined Jew," Solomon, found in the novella *The Steppe: The Story of a Journey* (1888), whom she reimagines from the point of view of her Manhattan highrise, outside which the "houseless / squinny at us, mumbling." The homeless, like Solomon, like the nomadic aboriginals of North America or "the nomads of Sakhalin," exist outside the construct of Western culture, and their very existence acts as an arbiter against the West's monolithic pretensions, signified more than a century after Chekhov's novella by terms such as Americanization and globalization. Clampitt sees Solomon, who in the story burns his portion of the family inheritance in a stove, "as the muse of what's become / of us." An ironic version of his Old Testament namesake, Solomon judges and undermines the cultural assumptions of the other characters, including his innkeeper brother, Moses, and the group of travelers, led by Father Christopher and the merchant Kuzmichov, who during a business trip make a brief stop at the inn for tea. As Christopher and Kuzmichov count out the latter's money on the table, the Jewish brothers' disparate responses to seeing piles of currency laid out before them underscore the tenuousness of the cultural constructs that both Chekhov and Clampitt examine: "On seeing the money Moses showed embarrassment, stood up, and — a sensitive man not wanting to know others' secrets — tiptoed from the room, balancing with his arms. Solomon stayed where he was" (Chekhov 35). Unlike his brother, who has invested his inheritance in the inn where Solomon now ironically resides, Solomon so eschews the hypocrisies and lies of their culture that he destroys the thing that is valued most. To Father Christopher especially, this "plucked, bird-like figure" is "not human" (32, 38) because Solomon in no way acknowledges the values agreed upon and inherent in a bank note or a journey that has a beginning and an end.

As its subtitle indicates, *The Steppe* tells the story of a journey, but the journey is not simply a commercial one. The business objective is complemented by Kuzmichov's promise to his sister Olga to deliver her nine-year-old son, Yegorushka, to a school so that he can become educated and a gentleman. The poignant, budding perspective of the boy therefore provides a gentler alternative to the fierce nihilism of Solomon. As Yegorushka tearfully leaves his mother and his childhood home, he also turns his back to the rising sun. Thus Chekhov subtly indicates that this is a westward journey, but one that has a complex of objectives: not just the commercial transactions pursued by Christopher and Kuzmichov but the pedagogical development enjoined by Olga on behalf of her son. Yegorushka, of course, is not entirely aware of what he is doing or where he is going, so that his perspective is one of rising consciousness as he encounters the wonders and brutalities of both the natural world of the steppe and the cultural one of his fellow travelers.

If *The Steppe* both questions and celebrates the assumptions that inform the notion of the quest, Clampitt is most interested in the nihilistic Solomon. His very existence reminds those around him, and us, that the culture that so values history as the formative idea linked to the concepts of progress, money, and exploration is in fact almost always in danger, even as it endangers and destroys those who oppose it as well as the natural environment. Solomon represents a subversive counterpoint to the massive changes arrived at between 1500 and 1700, as Carolyn Merchant has pointed out: "A subsistence economy in which resources, goods, money, or labor were exchanged for commodities was replaced in many areas by the open-ended accumulation of profits in an international market. Living animate nature died, while dead inanimate money was endowed with life" (*DON* 288). For Solomon, who speaks to his brother's guests with gruesome directness, money especially represents the big lie that would establish his place in the social order, and he refuses (as Dostoevsky's Ivan in *The Brothers Karamazov* refuses God) to be a part of such a fiction, a fiction that, in the eyes of Gentiles, not only includes but frequently focuses—with destructive consequences—on the Jewish people. As Solomon asserts in his exchange with Christopher: "there's no gentleman or millionaire who wouldn't lick the hand of a dirty Yid to make an extra copeck. As it is I'm a dirty Yid and a beggar, and everyone look at me as if I was a dog.... I don't need moneys or land or sheep, and I don't need people to fear me and take off their hats when I pass" (Chekhov 37–8). In Clampitt's vision of a westward-coursing Empire, aspiring to its various El Dorados, Chekhov's Solomon stands as a powerful and dangerous judge, ruthlessly vivisecting its hypocrisies and lies, exposing its notion of a progressive history moving toward Omega as nonsense. It is, rather, "Monoculture on the heels of slash and burn" (*CPAC* 344).

The "travail" behind such analyses is relentlessly confronted by Clampitt in one of her last poems, "Sed De Correr," appearing in the final volume, *A Silence Opens* (*CPAC* 420). This poem, too, is finally about "coming to terms"—with what America has become, with the exiled ego dwelling within the layered, repelling entity of the city—which Clampitt frankly states has for her personally not been easy, her "shades drawn against being seen, against systems." And indeed, there is apparently much to take in as Clampitt holds the reader's head at the window of her apartment "overlooking the eyesore / of real estate that is Harlem," where earlier in the century the Spanish writer Federico Garcia Lorca also gazed, indignant and angry, spurned into writing *Poet in New York:* "escape, the urge to disjoin, the hunger / to have gone, to be going: *sed de correr.*" Not only Lorca but the Peruvian poet Cesar Vallejo, as well as Virginia Woolf, Franz Kafka, Gregor Samsa, and the painter, Jan Muller, comprise the cadre of predecessors alluded to in this poem. "Sed De Correr," in fact, is constructed as though on staggered linguistic and cultural terraces overlooking the constructed landscape which is the city, inheritance of the West. From each terrace (built on a colon), one of the cadre is invoked until the poem builds to a crescendo of migrations, dispersals, arrivals, and — that twentieth-century phenomenon — refugees:

> Refugees:
> from the songless amputated tree
> Lorca wrote of: leaves fallen, adrift,
> the great trunk lost sight of, the stasis
> of such scattering, such dispersals.

The image of the tree, of such import to Clampitt in "My Cousin Muriel," is one which, in this poem, she shares in a much darker sense with Lorca. With the axe "laid / at the root," it becomes a metaphor for the loss of personal, cultural, and ecological memory inherent in the "westward trekking" that includes Anne Bradstreet, also a refugee in the year 1630.

The poem opens with a passionate straining to recall a moment in childhood that is redolent with Chekhov's Yegorushka and in which Clampitt remembers another tree like the one outside her window: "Caught on the move — no knowing what year it was —/ through the leaves of the ash tree outside the schoolroom." Clampitt sees herself as the poet who answers the call of Chekhov in *The Steppe* for a bard who can speak to "the triumph of beauty" represented by "the night bird" whose "wealth and inspiration are lost to the world" (Chekhov 43). As in Chekhov's story and "A Procession at Candlemas," memory in "Sed de Correr" is evoked by a bird, whose "streakings / and shadings" typify its elusiveness, and with which the child, like Yegorushka, is identified. The Western adult mind, inclined to list and categorize everything, cannot name the species and proceeds to differentiate the bird from the remembered ash tree, which has its own inner chemistry and movement. If the child is "Caught on the move," the bird is

> uncaught by the impeding
> rigors of the vascular, the cambium's moist secrets
> locked between xylem and phloem, the great, growing
> trunk of it hardening, the mass, the circumference,
> the unhurried, implacably already
> *there*, that's to be escaped from.

This is the moment when childhood withers, when "the urge to disjoin" begins: the "running away from what made one."

What Clampitt does here is to put her finger on America's ambivalence toward origins, indeed its very fear of origins as she does in another poem, "Medusa" (*CP* 211). So the personal wish to flee New York becomes one with the cultural wish to disperse, move, "the hunger / to have gone," to migrate. Yet, inevitably, what is found and experienced also compels one to look backward: hence Clampitt refers to "the botch / of being young," just as in the seminal Candlemas poem she calls memory

> that exquisite blunderer, stumbling
>
> like a migrant bird that finds the flyway
> it hardly knew it knew except by instinct,
> down the long-unentered nave of childhood.[62]

As stipulated at the outset of this chapter, the significance of reaching backwards is more than personal for Clampitt: it is a cultural and mythical act, the ancient work of the poet that needs doing despite Auden's dictum that "poetry makes nothing happen" (Auden 82). For Clampitt, the poet *remembers*. Poetry overcomes fear, maps out boundaries of the self, of history, and questions the "systems gone rotten" that have created places such as Harlem. She would have agreed with Seamus Heaney:

> In one sense the efficacy of poetry is nil—no lyric has ever stopped a tank. In another sense, it is unlimited. It is like the writing in the sand in the face of which accusers and accused are left speechless and renewed [*The Government of the Tongue* 107].

The effect of this writing in the sand (an allusion to the gospel story of Christ's response to the woman taken in adultery [John 8] that Heaney carefully explicates) can also be seen in Clampitt's bird, which she waits to witness again in the context of "This arson":

> the lisped *tsip,*
> in a back-garden catalpa, the fluttering fan
> of a warbler on the move: spring or fall,
> that glimpsed inkling of things
> beyond systems, windborne, oblivious.[63]

If there exists here a longing for transcendence, it is qualified by the pre-ceding passage, where Rilke is also invoked: "Not those great wings. / I was too much afraid." The bird and the tree in Clampitt's mythic imag-ination are of this world, of its past, its "backward-ramifying / antecedents" (*CPAC* 23), though they also hint at the possibility of another world, a spiritual reality, in which Clampitt is no less interested. What is here and now, however, is "The moving vehicle. The estrangement." And

> The axe is laid
> at the root of the ash tree. The leaves of dispersal,
> the runaway pages, surround us. Who
> will hear? Who will gather
> them in? Who will read them?

Clampitt alludes at once to her own earlier questions in "A Procession at Candlemas" as well as to Elizabeth Bishop's "fat brown bird" in "Ques-tions of Travel" and the exotic, diverse foliage in "Brazil, January 1, 1502." In the latter poem, too, there are birds, "big symbolic birds" with "beaks agape" that are, however, silent. And if Bishop creates a portrait of the explorers who "ripped away into the hanging fabric," Clampitt describes how their work has fared: how "the tree is dying," how the aboriginal women of Bishop's poem have, in "the breaking / wave of displacement,"

> translated here, to
> the crass miracle of whatever it is that put up
> the South Bronx.

FOUR

Anne Bradstreet: "Contemplations" and the Problem of Nature

Subduing the Wild; Serving the Father

As we have seen in the first chapter, Anne Bradstreet gave priority to the needs of her family and community. "The family," writes Cheryl Walker, "was the unit of political power for the Puritans. Doors to politics opened from the inside" ("Woman Poet" 257–58). Bradstreet's most ardent readers were, in fact, her husband, Simon, and her father, Thomas Dudley, both of whom eventually became governors of their communities, and both of whom, to use Walker's metaphor, opened the door to poetry for Anne and, with that, the gender-biased politics that inevitably ensued and with which Bradstreet would have to contend for the rest of her life.[64] John Winthrop, for one, opposed "the practice of writing by women" (Stanford "Dogmatist and Rebel" 79). Hence it's no surprise that despite writing poetry that was read and appreciated within her family, Bradstreet, like other Puritans in early seventeenth-century Massachusetts, was very careful to "observe in her conduct an exact conformity to the mores of her community" (79). By the time of "Contemplations," which dates several years into the Restoration period when New England would surely be feeling the loss of the Commonwealth, this poet had long set herself a difficult task indeed. Practising dissent by the very act of writing poetry, Anne Bradstreet still managed to acquiesce to the communal requirement for solidarity, creating within her a spiral of the mutually-exacerbating pressures of conformity and subversion in evidence throughout much of her work (77).

As we turn in this chapter to "Contemplations," long regarded as Bradstreet's best poem, we will witness how this vortex of opposing forces makes itself apparent; with that, we will also notice how the issue of audience comes to the fore again, this time in connection to the colonial perception of nature and landscape in New England. This perception is one that, in the words of Raymond Williams, "implies separation and observation" (149); at the same time, and precisely because it is primarily "vision-oriented" (Nash *WATAM* xi), it also implies fear and alienation: "wilderness was construed ... to be in league with devils, demons, and the evil forces of darkness that civilization must overcome" (x).[65] Like "A Dialogue between Old England and New," "Contemplations" sees the speaker's ultimate capitulation to Puritan ideology, but what makes "Contemplations" a more compelling poem than the earlier one is its, at times, anguished attempt to make a passionate lyrical utterance from what W. B. Yeats, in a different century, called "the deep heart's core" (Yeats 44). Because, however, Bradstreet abbreviates her own lyrical impulse in an act of self-censorship, "Contemplations" is also a poem that evokes pathos. It is, in this analysis, pathic because, while there undoubtedly exists in it a "clash of feeling and dogma" (Stanford "Dogmatist and Rebel" 87), this conflict is one in which the former (which is great and stems from the heart and mind of a sensitive individual) is contained and controlled by the latter (which grows out of New World Puritan ideology rather than the ethos of nature).

Pathos and ethos are addressed by biologist Lyall Watson in terms that apply to this reading of "Contemplations": "Pathos is the opposite of ethos, which deals with nature, character and community, giving rise to 'ethics' and 'ethology' ... *pathic* and *pathics* ... identify the study of that in nature which represents a loss of character and community, leading away from rather than towards natural cohesion" (Watson 26). The *Oxford English Dictionary* defines *pathic* in this sense as describing the "person who passively suffers or undergoes something"; likewise, *pathos* is the "[p]hysical or mental suffering; sorrow" that results from or accompanies the pathic state. What we return to is, once again, the conflict between the individual and the community in Puritan New England, this time with a telling ecological twist. Indeed, "Contemplations" derives its very power from the speaker's conflicted state concerning the nature of nature — from her personal aspiration towards integrity with nature coupled with an acute awareness of how this desire must remain curbed. Hence, at certain key points in the poem, the speaker can be accurately described as frustrated, and the poem as a whole can be seen in many ways as a recapitulation of Anne Bradstreet's earlier life narrative, her personal and artistic efforts in the wilds of the New World to find openings for genuine self-expression.

In addressing a patriarchal readership bent on subjugating and reforming the wilderness, Bradstreet's speaker in "Contemplations" becomes "mute, can warble forth no higher layes" than "the merry grashopper" and "black clad Cricket," who "glory in their little Art" and "resound their makers praise." The speaker castigates herself for her inability to lavish melodious praise on God and nature, and denounces herself for what she calls her "imbecility":

> My humble Eyes to lofty Skyes I rear'd
> To sing some Song, my mazed Muse thought meet.
> My great Creator I would magnifie,
> That nature had, thus decked liberally:
> But Ah, and Ah, again, my embecility! [*CW* 169].

Yet the fact of "Contemplations" itself as song contradicts the speaker's avowal of dumbness, leaving readers to wonder perpetually about the extent to which the Puritan ethos compelled Bradstreet to delineate a patriarchal, theocentric world view about which she had misgivings. Cheryl Walker, for one, argues that Bradstreet feels compelled to "express the views of the patriarchy even when such views diminish the status of [her] own sex." Anne Bradstreet, in Walker's estimation, is "caught between her patriarchal text and her sex" ("Woman Poet" 256–57).

Walker's recognition of Bradstreet's precarious position as a female poet who was also a Puritan contrasts with the stance taken at this point by Wendy Martin. Although Martin acknowledges that "The Puritan social order was achieved by subordinating the individual to the community and emphasizing the necessity for traditional definitions of masculinity and femininity" (65), she also maintains: "Unlike the Puritan fathers, Bradstreet does not seem to have felt the need to impose sacred order on the landscape. Instead of trying to reform nature, she appreciates its cyclicity and diversity. Perhaps the tradition of female receptivity and nurturance freed her from the need to rigorously control her environment" (46). In other words, Martin argues that, despite the enormous influence of the Puritan community in general and of her father in particular, Anne Bradstreet was able to write relatively freely about nature from her own perspective as a woman; the fact that she was also a Puritan writing for a Puritan audience is of secondary importance. Certainly this view has merit; just as certain is the complexity this poet continually presents to readers as they try to come to terms with the turbulent, shifting cultural context provided by seventeenth-century New England. An alternative view of "Contemplations" in its mid–1660s post–Restoration context might look something like this: If Anne Bradstreet writes freely in "Contemplations," she writes freely not about the ethos of nature — not about the entropic, cyclical reality of the biosphere apart from Puritan ideology — but rather about her lifelong need to stake out a world view that is true both to her community, her community's view of the environment, and to herself, a difficult task to say the least. Bradstreet accomplishes this in part by positioning herself as "mute" and an embecile — a rhetorical strategy that would immediately make her less threatening to "a readership both of men and women who possess the quality of mind and temperament that in her dedication she ascribed to Thomas Dudley — the ability to judge, prove, try, and sort the work and to distinguish chaff from wheat" (Rosenmeier 61). Simultaneously, Bradstreet encodes within "Contemplations" her innermost feelings and beliefs about Puritan culture in the New World and the place of the individual within that context. On this reading, the poem does not render a realistic, or for that matter feminist, portrait of nature in the New World. Rather, it employs what Leo Marx, in his invaluable analysis of culture and nature in early America, calls "ecological images ... displaying the essence of a system of value" (42); and the poem goes on to interpret these images in terms of the reformed Judeo-Christian myth at the same time as it expresses anguish over the cost of this system to the individual, especially the individual woman writer. Hence, the pathos. In point of fact, "Contemplations" actively demonstrates that cost even as it argues — at times almost in spite of itself — that the Biblical Father God is the source of order, meaning, and history, and that the natural world, whether beneficent or hostile, reflects His presence and omnipotence.

In loyally setting forth a predominantly masculine world view, Bradstreet qualifies her own aspirations as a woman poet at the same time as she enacts them. In other words, she writes about how she cannot, must not, write, and she does so because it is true and because this continues to be the most secure and politically savvy strategy, ensuring her survival as a writer even at this late stage in her career. More than three decades after the landing of the Winthrop Fleet and a decade after the death of Thomas Dudley, the powerful call of the first-generation Puritan community in the New World does not simply evaporate. This contextual truth can be seen most clearly and eloquently in the figure of Philomel in "Contemplations." Although the song of this female bird represents a kind of art that is free from Puritanism's pressures and politics, Bradstreet's speaker cannot, in the end, liberate herself to sing with Philomel. Although she desires it, she cannot combine her voice with the voice of the ethos of nature, compelling as it is and which indeed Anne Bradstreet herself must have heard and taken to heart in the wilds of New England. And while it is undoubtedly significant that Bradstreet powerfully evokes the importance of the personal lyric in "Contemplations," it is equally significant that she appears to recognize its great difficulty, and consequently stifles it for (or disguises it within) a practical poetic craft that will serve — yet again — her struggling, increasingly unsettled patriarchal community.

Wendy Martin's argument constitutes a fairly common twentieth-century critical position regarding Anne Bradstreet, one in which she is seen mainly as an early feminist rebel valiantly trying to subvert Puritan ideology. Those who take this view may also proceed to portray Bradstreet as a predecessor of the Romantic poets vis-à-vis nature. Martin, as we have seen, asserts that Bradstreet felt no "need to impose sacred order on the landscape." Josephine K. Piercy feels that the Romantics must have read "Contemplations," and she goes on to make connections where she can between Bradstreet and Wordsworth, Coleridge, Shelley, and Emerson. "The important thing," writes Piercy, "is that Anne Bradstreet, Puritan poet, felt and wrote as they [the Romantic poets] did about nature and about themselves" (Piercy 101). Robert D. Richardson, Jr., although he views Bradstreet not as an early Romantic but as a Puritan poet with specifically Puritan aims, calls "Contemplations" "a demonstration, in the form of a recorded experience, that nature itself generates belief." According to Richardson, Bradstreet in this poem creates

> a carefully reasoned and emotionally convincing resolution of the problem of how to live in the world without being of it. "Contemplations" spans both worlds. It accepts both worlds, perceives their connection, and acquiesces in that connection [Richardson 114].

Thus, while he also takes note of the uneven quality of the writing, Richardson apparently recognizes no struggle in "Contemplations," nothing of the "clash of feeling and dogma" articulated by Stanford and noted here already. Alvin H. Rosenfeld, on the other hand, after recapitulating much of the controversy surrounding this poem, tries to run the gauntlet between the two conflicting positions, one which sees Bradstreet as a Romantic and a rebel, the other which sees her as a full-fledged Puritan: "if it is finally unfair to throw Anne Bradstreet fully into the camp of the Romantics, so too is it unfair to cast her completely as a traditionally believing 'Puritan' poet." In "Contemplations" in particular, Rosenfeld finds "the war of the contraries everywhere" (128). As will be seen in the next section of this chapter, even though Rosenfeld misses the import of both the sun's masculinity and Philomel's crucial status in "Contemplations," he rightly makes much of Bradstreet's aborted sun worship, stating, "The defeat of Phoebus meant the defeat of Anne Bradstreet's creative imagination in 'Contemplations'" (Rosenfeld 132).

Stylized Nature in the New World

In contrast to the essentially defensive position taken by the speaker in "Contemplations," Elizabeth Bishop's "At the Fishhouses," which will be examined in detail in the following chapter, explicitly relinquishes the patriarchal burden of the past, even though the poem is not a counter-argument specifically directed at Bradstreet. It does however illuminate the longstanding discussion regarding "Contemplations." That Bishop's speaker, facing the Atlantic, sings Martin Luther's "A Mighty Fortress is Our God" to a curious seal is telling in the context of this chapter and needs to be mentioned here, for the hymn also evokes the "ecological images" that both stimulated and rationalized the colonization of New England. These images have been widely discussed,[66] but for the purposes of this study will be referred to as the cultivated garden and the hideous wilderness. As Marx, McKibben, Nash, Merchant, and others have shown, these often contradictory images of order and chaos possessed the Puritan imagination both before and long after initial transplantation to the New World.[67] A line from Robert Frost — "The land was ours before we were the land's" (Frost 348) — suggests how the Puritan colonists could imaginatively appropriate an uncharted territory prior to a solid peopling of and identification with it.[68] It also suggests how, in the post-colonial era, coming to terms with the actual appropriation of a living landscape constitutes a major project.

Unlike "Contemplations," Bishop's poem refuses to exalt or make absolute any sort of construct, even a poetic one. With its ironic, yet delicate handling of the themes of continuity and community, "At the Fishhouses" is typically modernist; but it so qualifies the idea of tradition that it distinguishes Bishop not only from Bradstreet but also from the major male modernists immediately preceding her: Frost, Stevens, Eliot, and Pound.[69] If Bishop's speaker holds on to anything, however provisionally, it is to the minutiae detected by her senses as "flowing and flown" in a setting that is personal. The attempt to gather up details while intimating their impermanence is the only "bulwark" (to use an image from Luther's famous battle-hymn) that "At the Fishhouses" has to offer. Indeed, this poem sees the community as gaining a more genuine sense of unity, of integration with nature, by acknowledging its own mutability and by realizing its origins — and thus its history — in nature itself.[70] In contrast to "Contemplations," "At the Fishhouses" overturns the colonial vision of nature as inviting relentless exploitation.[71]

Luther's hymn would certainly have focused the Puritan colonists' express need to protect themselves from the unbridled, malignant forces perceived by them to be at work in the wilderness. In an essay called "The Idea of the Wilderness of the New World," George H. Williams lists some of the adjectives used by the Puritans to describe their environment: "'dark,' 'desolate,' 'horrible,' 'horrid,' 'howling,' 'mighty,' 'squalid,' 'terrible,' 'vast,' 'waste,' and 'wretched.'"[72] Further adjectives I have found include *raw, roaring, forlorne, poore, remote, mean, vacant,* and *uncouth*; indeed, these qualifiers are so plentiful as to be picked up by any careful reader of seventeenth-century writing about the New World, writing that is, in the words of Roderick Nash, "permeated with the idea of wild country as the environment of evil" (*WATAM* 36). "To be wild," writes John A. Livingston, "is to be ungovernable, which means uncivilized" (5).[73] With the wilderness and its native inhabitants all around them, the early colonists gathered in the crude meeting-houses that Daniel Boorstin tells us "had no artificial light and no heat" (Boorstin 14).[74] Unlike the Plymouth pilgrims, the people of the Winthrop Fleet generally came from middle-class England and "also represented the most literate and educated colonists to settle in the New World in the seventeenth century" (Conforti 44–5). Many of them found the colonial experience much harsher than they had imagined it would be. As Carolyn Merchant tellingly puts it concerning the Winthrop Fleet:

> When the Puritans reached Massachusetts Bay after a two-month voyage, they found the legacy of wilderness terror alive and well in the New England forest. Pilgrim leader William Bradford, who had preceded John Winthrop by ten years, viewed the land as a "hideous and desolate wilderness full of wild beasts and wild men." "Our fathers were Englishmen which came over this great ocean and were ready to perish in this wilderness," he recalled in his account *Of Plimouth Plantation*. Bradford, Winthrop, and their followers set about transforming the eastern forest and its attendant evils into a New World garden [Merchant *RE* 98].

Having camped the first year in crude shacks and earthen dwellings dug out of hillsides, many Winthrop colonists quickly succumbed to the effects of weather, disease, and malnutrition. During their first year in the New World, Thomas Dudley sent word back to England that "we yet enjoy little to be envied, but endure much to be pitied in the sickness and mortality of our people" (Carroll 53). Hence, whether or not the Puritans were familiar with Luther's Reformation hymn, it genuinely expresses their worldview in the face of the wilderness:

> A mighty fortress is our God,
> A bulwark never failing;
> Our helper he amid the flood
> of mortal ills prevailing.[75]

According to Ian Bradley, "Ein' feste Burg" "was first translated into English by Miles Coverdale in 1538 (as 'Oure God is a defence and towre')." But both Bradley and Armin Haeussler emphasize that the hymn remained largely unknown to the English-speaking world until the mid-nineteenth century, when Thomas Carlyle and the American, Frederick H. Hedges (whose translation Bishop uses), produced popular English versions.[76] Saturated with the sense of the demonic, the hymn emphasizes the reality of evil in order to make God, as conqueror, appear omnipotent: "And though this world, with devils filled, / Should threaten to undo us; / We will not fear, for God hath willed / His truth to triumph through us." Indeed, Haeussler states: "The historian Leopold von Ranke speaks of this hymn as 'the production of the moment in which Luther, engaged in a conflict with a world of foes, sought strength in the consciousness that he was defending a divine cause which could never perish.' 'Living dangerously' was not a mere catch-phrase for Luther; he knew what it meant at first hand" (312). In this respect, "Ein' feste Burg" would certainly have been attractive to the people of Bradstreet's community.[77] As Roderick Nash comments concerning the New England Puritans' sense of mission: "[They] conceived of themselves as the latest in a long line of dissenting groups who had braved the wild to advance God's cause" (*WATAM* 34).

As "Bulwark never failing," the Puritans' God would, to use a seventeenth-century metaphor, form a protective hedge around His people to shield them from the forces of evil (Carroll 87–88, 111–112). In fact, hedges, fences, gardens, and orchards served as popular tropes to console homesick pilgrims and to motivate them to reform the environment, to anglicize it, as swiftly as possible. Back in England, these metaphors were employed by pamphleteers to encourage would-be colonists to emigrate to a world where all would be as it was in the beginning. In keeping with the Puritans' interpretation of *Genesis*, "plenty would emerge only from subduing the earth" (Carroll 53). The onus, in other words, would be on the settlers to transform the wilderness into a New England that would be representative of the first garden. Indeed, Carolyn Merchant outlines the phases of the "heroic American Adam ... born in New England" (98) in *Reinventing Eden* (2003): "The story of how the Pilgrims filled and replenished the land launches the recovery of the garden in the New World and creates the American Recovery Narrative" (99).

The 1677 John Foster map of New England helps us to clarify this vision of a civilized New World. According to Cecilia Tichi, the Foster map (the first cut by a colonist) makes remote settlements look as large and populous as those around Boston, while

> the formidably mountainous Berkshires appear as hillocks, and the forest is reduced to a few clusters of shrubs interspersed among the settlements. Only north of the Merrimack in the Maine region ... does the map maker acknowledge the actual wilds. There the verdure is larger, and wild animals (rabbit, bear, wolf) are drawn in, in addition to two Indians, who more resemble sporting nymphs than the satanic agents whose barbarities are set forth endlessly in the volume [William Hubbard's *Narrative of the Troubles with the Indians*] in which the map is bound [Tichi 13–14].

In a very real sense, then, the wilderness in Bradstreet's era was transformed, brought to heel.[78] Garden, in Marx's words, "stands for a state of cultivation, hence a less exalted estimate of nature's beneficence" (42).

Like Foster's map, Bradstreet's "Contemplations" constitutes a highly-wrought portrait of the early New England landscape, one which stylizes the wilderness and thus anticipates (and participates in) its domestication, transforming it into something like an Old World garden:

> Sometime now past in the Autumnal Tide,
> When *Phoebus* wanted but one hour to bed,
> The trees all richly clad, yet void of pride,
> Were gilded o're by his rich golden head.
> Their leaves & fruits seem'd painted, but was true
> Of green, of red, of yellow, mixed hew,
> Rapt were my sences at this delectable view.

To be sure, the hideous wilderness is not altogether concealed. At certain points, "Contemplations" acknowledges the vulnerability of the settlers to the elements: the sun has "scorching force," winter and night must be endured, and "a storm spoils all the sport" of the mariner. More importantly, the garden/wilderness paradox in "Contemplations" falls under the rubric of the Puritan ideal of covenant with God, an ideal which would bind the colonial group together. In similar fashion to Luther's hymn, then, the poem envisions the Christian God as the absolute protective force in the New World. At the same time, He is also the molding and shaping power who works through the Puritans to fashion a landscape that, as Stanford states, "is orderly and clearly divided into its separate parts" (*Worldly Puritan* 103). Like the buildings, orchards, farms, fields, and roads that the Puritans worked to create out of the raw wilderness, "Contemplations" stresses order and utility, and the poem's structure, with its ababccc rhyme scheme and alexandrines, supports such concepts.[79]

Addressing the sun by its classical name, the speaker perceives it as playing a pre-eminent role in the cosmos or *natura*, what the ancients referred to as the order of things; with that, she attributes to the sun certain powers, most notably the power to make the trees appear "gilded o'er" and "painted." Nature is portrayed in Edenic terms as the speaker also finds in "the glistering Sun" an image of the numinous, which she calls "Soul of this world, this Universes Eye." The sun is "as a Bridegroom" or "as a strong man," who

                    joyes to run a race,
The morn doth usher thee, with smiles & blushes,
The Earth reflects her glances in thy face.
Birds, insects, Animals with Vegative,
Thy heat from death and dulness doth revive:
And in the darksome womb of fruitful nature dive.

                         6
Thy swift Annual, and diurnal Course,
Thy daily streight, and yearly oblique path,
Thy pleasing fervor, and thy scorching force,
All mortals here the feeling knowledg hath.
Thy presence makes it day, thy absence night,
Quaternal Seasons caused by thy might:
Hail Creature, full of sweetness, beauty & delight.

Yet, even though the sun plays a considerable role in Bradstreet's stylized
portrait of nature, it also swiftly becomes indicative of less restrained desires
and aspirations associated with wild nature. Rosenfeld's thesis that here
Bradstreet engages in a kind of pagan sun-worship which will be ultimately defeated by the claims of Puritanism is significant and worth noticing. When the speaker says to the sun, "No wonder, some made thee a
Deity: / Had I not better known, (alas) the same had I," she suggests (to
use Thoreau's expression regarding life by Walden Pond) an underlying
desire "to live deep and suck out all the marrow of life" (Thoreau 172).

The parenthetical "alas," countering all the admonitions of a Puritan
upbringing contained in "Had I not better known," seems especially to point
to the pathic in "Contemplations." Eliminating any hint of self-righteousness that this line might otherwise suggest, the speaker's "alas" instead discloses both urgent desire and quiet resignation, which are given expression
in the stanzas that follow (two of which are quoted above). These stanzas
constitute a passionate articulation of the speaker's yearnings, yearnings which
are then neutralized or checked by a conventional didactic apostrophe:

          Art thou so full of glory, that no Eye
          Hath strength, thy shining Rayes once to behold?
          And is thy splendid Throne erect so high?
          As to approach it, can no earthly mould.
          How full of glory then must thy Creator be?
          Who gave this bright light luster unto thee:
          Admir'd, ador'd for ever, be that Majesty.

Here Bradstreet qualifies desire using a common meditative technique which, as Richard Baxter, a Puritan minister, put it, constitutes

> yet another way by which we make our senses serviceable to us; and that is, By comparing the objects of sense with the objects of faith; and so forcing sense to afford us that *Medium*, from whence we may conclude the transcendent worth of Glory, By arguing from sensitive delights as from the lesser to the greater [Stanford *Worldly Christian* 94].

In the light of Baxter's statement, it can be seen how the paean to Phoebus in "Contemplations" reveals a practical motive, and thus we as readers are brought back to the poem's preoccupation with order and utility. The speaker's utterance of delight and desire is used in the end to serve a particular aim that goes beyond the merely personal; or, to use Baxter's words, the speaker's senses are made "serviceable."

The whole argument regarding Bradstreet's sun-worship can be further qualified by the observation that Phoebus also evokes the Old World order, one which the Puritans, with all their classical learning, were keen to impress on the "hideous" wilderness. Thus, even the speaker's desire to break free from the constraints of the Puritan belief system is conditioned and limited by the patriarchal, European establishment out of which that belief system grew. Stanford, in fact, locates a probable source of the image of the sun as "this Universes Eye" in Raleigh's *History of the World*, which "has at the top center of its frontispiece an eye surrounded by flames, labelled 'Providentia,' which hovers just above a globe of the world" ("Emblematic Garden" 240). Indeed, from the perspective of Leo Marx's study of the pastoral ideal and its invasion by a counterforcing machine, the Judeo-Christian myth can be viewed as constituting the machine in Bradstreet's garden, the former having become "the dominant metaphor" by 1700 (Merchant *DON* 288). Marx's claim that the machine "invariably is associated with crude, masculine aggressiveness in contrast with the tender, feminine, and submissive attitudes traditionally attached to the landscape" has particular applicability to the metaphor of "dark-some womb" penetrated and fertilized by "this Universes Eye" (Marx 25 & 29).[80]

Perhaps nowhere in "Contemplations" does the Christian machine, or counterforce, make itself more strikingly apparent than in the reiteration of the *Genesis* account of Cain and Abel. In terms of Bradstreet's personal yearnings as a woman writer, this legend of fratricide and of subsequent division and alienation within the community signifies the

force of her need to avoid subversion.[81] Born of Adam and Eve after their
exile from Eden,

> Here *Cain* and *Abel* come to sacrifice,
> Fruits of the earth, and Fatlings each do bring,
> On *Abels* gift the fire descends from Skies,
> But no such sign on false *Cain's* offering;
> With sullen hateful looks he goes his wayes.
> Hath thousand thoughts to end his brothers dayes,
> Upon whose blood his future good he hopes to raise.

Having murdered his shepherd brother, Cain the farmer is "Branded with
guilt," and wanders the earth until eventually he "A city builds, that wals
might him secure from foes." Robert Graves identifies the Cain and Abel
story as having origins in the Hercules myth in which Hercules is seen as
"an agricultural as well as a pastoral king who specializes in the cultivation of barley ... and reigns alternately with his twin." In this view, the
myth also contains a "matrilinear succession" connected to Artemis
(127–28). Baring and Cashford find the Cain-Abel story in analogous
Sumerian stories that, by contrast to the ancient Hebrew one, are resolved
by reconciliation and marriage between the goddess Inanna and the shepherd Dumuzi. The latter's brother, Enkimdu, who corresponds to the
Hebrew Cain, is rejected as a hirsute wild man; likewise, "In Genesis,
Yahweh always prefers the younger son, the shepherd, to the elder, the
farmer, whose hairiness implies that he is closer to the beasts" (432–33).
In *The Changes of Cain* (1991), Ricardo Quinones points out how this original fraternity—defined as "that which is proper or belonging to brothers"—is "potently and insistently subversive of the ideals of unity and
community" (Quinones 3 & 5). According to Quinones, the legend

> bears in its background the dream of the human family, the pastoralism of
> the heart, a vision of unity and concord and cooperation so basic that it
> can only be summarized in the unconscious innocence of siblings. And yet
> cutting across this unity it brings difference, discord, and division; the Cain-
> Abel story represents a shattering reminder of the fragility of the human
> compact. In fact, the great purpose of the Cain-Abel story has always been—
> whatever its guise—to address a breach in existence, a fracture at the heart
> of things [Quinones 3].

The pattern of self versus community that is central to the Cain myth
was, in fact, constantly being played out in Anne Bradstreet's community.

133

Deviations in behavior threatened the ideal of group unity — and, indeed, community leaders often described such behavior in wilderness terms.[82] Joseph R. McElrath, Jr. and Allan P. Robb, the editors of the 1981 edition of Bradstreet's works, note a pattern throughout her writings of "self-assertiveness or religious 'rebellion' [followed by] reconciliation with God." At the same time, McElrath and Robb reject the pathic image of Brad-street "as both a cultural and religious Job-figure," arguing that "After all, Bradstreet was not censured, disciplined, or in any way ostracized for her art, thought, or personal assertiveness.... Rather, she was praised and encouraged; and there are no indications that the males in her life treated her as 'property'" ("The Introduction," vii-viii & xvi-xvii). This study contradicts the view of McElrath and Robb. Anne Bradstreet was praised and encouraged not because she was an exceptional woman writing poetry in a male-dominated culture but because she successfully avoided becoming a Job or a Cain-figure either by writing on behalf of her community (as she does in "A Dialogue between Old England and New), reconciling herself to her community's God (as she does in "Contemplations"), or by disguising her intermittent need to subvert or contest Puritan ideology (as we have already seen in the elegies for her grandchildren). Had Bradstreet composed poems that articulated outright, without disguise, the doubt and dissent that she obviously at times felt and that are always carefully counterbalanced, she would have at the very least risked embarrassing her family, especially her father and her father's legacy after 1653. Indeed, she would certainly have been acutely conscious of the fact that any such poetic offering would have been rejected, as Cain's is in *Genesis*.

Philomel and the End of History

Throughout "Contemplations," then, the speaker's senses are compelled by the Christian machine to serve its purposes; they are repeatedly turned from delight for its own sake to some kind of ideological conclusion. This pattern is made clear at the outset, when the speaker, having just declared her "Rapt ... sences," states: "I wist not what to wish, yet sure thought I, / If so much excellence abide below; / How excellent is he that dwells on high?" The "stately Oak" whose existence she contemplates prior to Phoebus is, like Phoebus, ultimately interpreted in terms of Christian belief. "Eternity," says the speaker, "doth scorn" the oak's "strength, and stature." Farther on in the poem, although the elements seem "insensible of time," especially in comparision to "Man's" ephemeral earthly existence, the speaker makes sure to qualify her ode to nature by contrasting it with the Reformed Christian concept of eternity. In the twentieth stanza, she asks:

> Shall I then praise the heavens, the trees, the earth
> Because their beauty and their strength last longer
> Shall I wish there, or never to had birth,
> Because they're bigger, & their bodyes stronger?
> Nay, they shall darken, perish, fade and dye,
> And when unmade, so ever shall they lye,
> But man was made for endless immortality.

Like others in the poem, this stanza provides a good structural example of how Bradstreet's speaker persuades herself to lay aside personal desire in favor of a theological idea. The first four lines of the stanza present a question, with an underlying wish, concerning the enormous cyclical power of nature that the speaker herself has witnessed. This desire is then obviated by the concluding triplet in which the natural world is literally put in its place in the Puritan cosmos. Nature is something that will be "unmade," and if it is to be *decreated* by God at some point in the future, then it follows that it can, in the meantime, be seen "as another field for the exercise of power" (Marx 43).[83]

In the four stanzas that follow, the speaker continues to interpret the natural world in terms of Calvinist dogma. Having subordinated the existence of oak and sun to that of the Biblical God, she now sits "by a goodly Rivers side" and sees in it an emblem of life and death:

> Nor is't enough, that thou alone may'st slide,
> But hundred brooks in thy cleer waves do meet,
> So hand in hand along with thee they glide
> To *Thetis* house, where all imbrace and greet:
> Thou Emblem true, of what I count the best,
> O could I lead my Rivolets to rest,
> So may we press to that vast mansion, ever blest.

Marx reminds us that "Among the more effective of the traditional counters to the idyllic dream have been certain stylized tokens of mortality" (Marx 25), and here the speaker certainly prevents her own idyllic desires from taking shape by envisaging natural processes — in this case, a river and its tributaries flowing inexorably to the sea — as symbols of mortality. Indeed, she perceives even the migrating instincts of fish as a kind of metaphor for the human journey from this world to the next: "In Lakes and ponds, you leave your numerous fry, / So nature taught, and yet you know not why, / You watry folk that know not your felicity."

Knowledge and felicity are important tenets of Puritan thought, and clearly the speaker interprets nature with such tenets in mind. Although the fish have no conscious knowledge of their behavior, they are seen as creatures who are instinctively faithful to a divine order of things. At the same time, however, it is not clear that the speaker's knowledge — what nature has taught her — reflects the pure, unwavering felicity that she sees in the fish.[84] To some extent, she does know why things are the way they are, and such knowledge, limited as it is, does not always jibe with belief. Her felicity is therefore qualified, even though she continually reaffirms it and, in the end, nullifies the yearnings that would contradict Puritan belief. The speaker's ambivalence, which is seen throughout the poem in the regular pattern of rejecting and affirming orthodoxy, is thus apparent in the contemplation of the river.

Then, in the twenty-fifth stanza, Bradstreet's speaker appears to set aside her interpretation of nature as death-trope in order to praise it more for its own sake; in order, that is, to express her delight in nature without the pressure of the Puritan belief system:

> Look how the wantons frisk to task the air,
> Then to the colder bottome streight they dive,
> Eftsoon to *Neptun's* glassy Hall repair
> To see what trade they great ones there do drive,
> Who forage o'er the spacious sea-green field,
> And take the trembling prey before it yield,
> Whose armour is their scales, their spreading fins their shield.

Having just described the fish as creatures who are faithful to, and thus determined by, a higher order of things, the speaker now sees them as wild and unrestrained. As "wantons [who] frisk to task the air," the fish are of a separate, aquatic world, and yet have the strength and vigor to make spontaneous momentary forays into the speaker's world. Connoting both abandonment and withdrawal, the word *wanton* primarily evokes sexual instinct, a kind of instinct that would not have a readily acknowledged place in the Puritan world view. The *OED*, in fact, gives an obsolete definition of the noun *wanton* as one who is rebellious and unmanageable. Hence, these "wantons" are organisms that quite literally "task" the speaker's "air" or ethos, as suddenly she recognizes in nature an order of things alien to her own and outside the jurisdiction of New England Puritanism.

But the speaker is not sure how to take this insight, or what to do with it, and so she again projects Old World concepts on to what she otherwise has trouble understanding. To this aquatic *other* world she applies the concepts of "hall" and marketplace: down below are "great ones" who "trade" and barter. More important, perhaps, is the speaker's pastoral vision of life in the depths of the river, as she imagines how the fish "forage o're the spacious sea-green field, / And take the trembling prey before it yield, / Whose armour is their scales, their spreading fins their shield." Here is a place where there is plenty, a submarine cornucopia — in fact, a visionary, paradisal locus free of the encumbrances of Puritan dogma; and it is no surprise that at this point in the poem, the speaker breaks into a climax of revery and liberation as her meditation on the fish is interrupted by the song of a "merry Bird," who

> chanted forth a most melodious strain
> Which rapt me so with wonder and delight,
> I judg'd my hearing better then my sight,
> And wisht me wings with her a while to take my flight.

The speaker now turns her attention away from the aquatic world, which clearly represents her own desire for freedom, to the natural world above, which, as we shall see, rapidly becomes an apotheosis of desire. Indeed, Bradstreet's curbed poetic aspirations are now given obvious expression by the speaker's rapture at what she calls "The sweet-tongu'd Philomel percht ore my head." This is the poet's Acteon moment, one in which she feels she must decide between culture and nature; unlike Acteon, who in the moment of his transformation by Diana can go neither forward into wilderness nor back to the civilization that is his home, and is consequently destroyed, Bradstreet abbreviates her encounter with Philomel and nullifies the risk involved in entering into a transformational, oracular experience. In the twenty-seventh stanza, the speaker quickly perceives and describes Philomel's nature:

> O merry Bird (said I) that fears no snares,
> That neither toyles nor hoards up in thy barn,
> Feels no sad thoughts, nor cruciating cares
> To gain more good, or shun what might thee harm
> Thy cloaths ne're wear, thy meat is every where,
> Thy bed a bough, thy drink the water cleer,
> Reminds not what is past, nor whats to come dost fear.

Free from Puritan *history*, from its constraints of the past and the apocalypse contained in its future, Philomel is identified as female, and undoubtedly, in the speaker's estimation, as representative of true poetic expression (in contrast to a kind of *poesis* that is compelled to represent a certain body of ideas and beliefs). On this reading, the speaker's desire for "wings with her a while to take my flight" indicates Bradstreet's yearning for escape from the pressures and confines of Puritanism, so that it is here more than any other place in "Contemplations" that Bradstreet makes her personal dilemma clear. Lee Oser makes the interesting point that this New World Philomel is distinct from her tragic European predecessors because she is "merry"; Oser also convincingly argues that Bradstreet's speaker interprets the bird in terms of the Sermon on the Mount (Oser 197). On an ecological reading, though, the speaker sees Philomel as sustained by the bounty of nature; she is merry because she is unconstrained by human, specifically Puritan cares and concerns, and lives her life outside history. Philomel is indeed arguably a new kind of bird, hybridizing and adapting the Old World nightingale represented in poetry and myth with a new kind of bird representing the speaker's environmental experience and awareness. That Bradstreet captures this in language suggestive of Christ's words, words which arguably subvert the overriding value placed by Puritans on labour, further underscores Bradstreet's wide reading as well as her ability to apply that reading in the New World. The speaker's classical "said I" itself points to the magnitude of this moment in the poem. Although the parentheses might seem to imply her wariness, her sense of pressure, they also reflect the speaker's need here to insert a personal utterance; she implies, in effect, that now she speaks for herself rather than for her community.

For a moment, then, the speaker can disengage herself from cultural concerns and revel in the bird's wilderness autonomy, in Philomel's ability to sing her own song and not someone else's:

> The dawning morn with songs thou dost prevent,
> Sets hundred notes unto thy feathered crew,
> So each one tunes his pretty instrument,
> And warbling out the old, begin anew,
> And thus they pass their youth in summer season,
> Then follow thee into a better Region,
> Where winter's never felt by that sweet airy legion.

What Bradstreet portrays here is a community of singers that practises a form of natural congress. No divine Governor is described or alluded to in any of the stanzas concerning Philomel; instead, as we see here, each member of the community, acknowledging the cyclical reality of the biosphere, "tunes his pretty instrument / And warbling out the old, begin anew." In the ecological context, John A. Livingston describes what occurs when a cardinal breaks out in song:

> The songbird's existence has miraculously become hugely greater than himself, incorporating as it does plants, animals, micro-organisms, soil, water, and sunlight into his total being. We may take this even farther. The bird has himself become a community of existences, and at the instant when he sings, the momentary (once only) event of that song is numinous. The numen is not, of course, a presiding spirit of that place, external to the songbird; the numen arises from the mutuality or the complementariness of the bird and his co-participants [Livingston 96].

Bradstreet's speaker tells us, however, that much as she might wish to join this group, she is compelled finally to remain a member of her own. In the ancient mythological depiction, Philomela has her tongue cut out by King Tereus, who, wishing to marry her when he has already wed Philomela's sister, Procne, must find a way to silence her. Philomela, however, communicates with her sister by embroidering the truth into a robe which she sends to the banished Procne. When Tereus discovers this, he attempts to kill the sisters, who are transformed, along with the king, into birds. The gods thus intervene on Philomela's behalf and change her into a nightingale before Tereus can murder her. The parallel with Bradstreet herself seems obvious. She will continue to be "Subject to sorrows, losses, sickness, pain" in a world where a struggle exists between an aggressive culture (with its constructs) and things as they are (where winter is felt), but she weaves an underlying message entailing her endeavor to find her tongue into the fabric of her best poem. While the constant struggle serves to protect and preserve a vulnerable New World Puritan community, it also limits Bradstreet to its exclusively masculine language. The speaker cannot, in the end, let loose the "thousand fancies buzzing in [her] brain." Bradstreet's potentially oracular moment, which Robert Graves identifies as central to the purpose of the original "iconotropic myth" of Philomela, is aborted. Ironically, Graves describes the myth as a series of "religious pictures" in which the scene depicting "the cutting out of Philomela's tongue shows a priestess who has induced a prophetic trance by chewing laurel leaves; her face is contorted with ecstasy, not pain, and the tongue that has been cut out is really a laurel leaf that an attendant is handing her to chew" (436).

Bound by her community and culture, Bradstreet's speaker therefore turns to its belief system for orientation, hope, and comfort; and, of course, the most significant hope and comfort offered is the Reformed Christian belief in "divine Translation" from this world to the next, the end of *history* identified by Vine Deloria (in the Introduction of this study) as the Western concept that urgently needs to be reconciled to nature (Deloria 59). Hence Bradstreet loyally returns to the issues found in the first part of her meditation (on the river), and with that she also returns to images of order and chaos in the natural world. Nature ceases to represent freedom, becoming instead a paradoxical image in which wilderness and garden are once again in conflict with one another. "The Mariner that on smooth waves doth glide" is seen as the "great Master of the seas," until

> suddenly a storm spoiles all the sport,
> And makes him long for a more quiet port,
> Which 'gainst all adverse winds may serve for fort.

Nature is viewed as unpredictable and dangerous, as something that therefore needs to be controlled. "Port" and "fort" again signify the speaker's capitulation to metaphors of vigilance against the forces of nature.

In the final two stanzas of "Contemplations," the speaker's reunion with Puritanism becomes complete. What some critics see as resolution is actually a mere articulation of conventional religious wisdom, a major source of which is found in the *Book of Proverbs*. Like stanza seven, where the speaker nullifies her "sun-worship" with a didactic summation, Bradstreet concludes the entire meditation by stating commonly-held Reformed Christian beliefs, all of which amounts to forced resolution at best. In the penultimate stanza, she rails against "this world of pleasure" and against the "Fond fool, [who] takes this earth ev'n for heav'ns bower" even though she herself has just finished savoring the life of fish and the numinous song of Philomel. In keeping with orthodox Puritan thought, the speaker now moralizes on the dangers of worldliness and of trusting too much in the illusion that nature is beneficent: "Here's neither honour, wealth, or safety; / Only above is found all with security."

Finally, Bradstreet's speaker closes "Contemplations" with an apocalyptic eight-line stanza, in which she delineates the Puritan belief in the end of history, when not only nature but New England culture will fall before "Time the fatal wrack of mortal things":

> That draws oblivions curtains over kings,
> Their sumptuous monuments, men know them not,
> Their names without a Record are forgot,
> Their parts, their ports, their pomp's all laid in th' dust
> Nor wit nor gold, nor buildings scape times rust;
> But he whose name is grav'd in the white stone
> Shall last and shine when all of these are gone.

Unlike the fleeting glory of Philomel, however, this promise is inextricably bound up with the patriarchal community and the Judeo-Christian myth. In contrast to the city founded by the exiled Cain, the New Jerusalem comes "down out of heaven from God, prepared as a bride beautifully dressed for her husband" (Rev. 21:4). Moreover, while the notion of flux is found in other bodies of thought, most notably that of the pre–Socratic philosopher Heraclitus, it is here obviously drawn from Biblical sources; i.e., the Old Testament prophets and the *Revelation of St. John*. Although connections have been made between this final stanza and Shakespeare's Sonnet 55, Shakespeare, it must be noted, never resorts to Christian dogma to counter entropic truths.[85] The end of the culture that has so qualified and contained this poet's expression is viewed finally only on its own terms, terms which emphasize a new beginning and the ultimate triumph and glorification of Puritan belief.

141

FIVE
_____

Elizabeth Bishop:
Garden Knowledge;
Wild Knowledge

Facing the Ocean: Origins of Culture, Part 1

If, according to Peter Carroll, the Puritan thinker Thomas Hooker "distinguished between 'a gracious and a sanctifying knowledge, garden knowledge,' ... and 'a wild and common knowledge' which directed the behavior of hypocrites" (Carroll 113), then Elizabeth Bishop's speaker in "At the Fishhouses" has aligned herself with that which is "wild and common." With self-conscious irony, she not only relinquishes the cultural burden of the past but also deflates the colonial tendency towards absolutism by pointing out how all our making — whether of fishhouses or apocalyptic myths — is "flowing and drawn." At the same time, Bishop's poem also reveals a reverence for the exact details of these passing things, and in its attempt to gather up these details it tenuously draws the community together. Bishop accomplishes this without sacrificing her own voice; on the contrary, it is precisely what James Merrill calls her "quirkiness of mind" that enables her to envision the human community as humbly unified in its recognition of itself as yet another incidental part of the ecosystem.[86] In this, indeed, she echoes the voices of twenty-first century ecologists and scientists such as E.O. Wilson who, in an essay called "Manifest Ecology," reminds his American readers that "we need a stronger ethic, one woven in more effective ways from science and poetry. The foundation of it will be the recognition that humanity was born within the biosphere, and that we are a biological species in a biological world" (30).

"At the Fishhouses" is, as Ann Stanford would say of "Contemplations," a "composition of place" and, like Bradstreet's poem, it moves from the evidence supplied by the senses to a kind of resolution, albeit not Bradstreet's forced metaphysical one ("Meditative Writer" 93; *Worldly Puritan* 96). Just as "Contemplations" stresses the autumnal colours, the powers of sun and ocean, or the song of Philomel, Bishop's poem constantly appeals to the senses. In this setting, "it is a cold evening," "the heavy surface of the sea" is silver, and

> The big fish tubs are completely lined
> with layers of beautiful herring scales
> and the wheelbarrows are similarly plastered
> with creamy iridescent coats of mail,
> with small iridescent flies crawling on them [*CP* 64].

Indeed, the title itself suggests a certain powerful aroma associated with fishing and the sea: "The air smells so strong of codfish / it makes one's nose run and one's eyes water."

Unlike Bradstreet's orderly imagistic feast, with its gilded trees and painted "leaves & fruits," Bishop's composition of place clearly tries to ground itself more authentically in the physical world. While Bradstreet's speaker responds to her "delectable view" with rapt senses, in order to argue from the creation to its Creator, Bishop's speaker describes both the beautiful and the repugnant in nature. She describes "beautiful herring scales" as well as "small iridescent flies." Admittedly, "Contemplations" portrays human vulnerability in the face of natural forces, but it does so only to remind the reader that ultimately "man was made for endless immortality." "At the Fishhouses," on the other hand, while it also deals with metaphors of garden and wilderness, order and chaos, stresses the transience of figures and myths and, in fact, implicitly criticizes what Guy Rotella calls the "destructive illusion" of permanent structures (223). John A. Livingston particularly stresses this point, calling the nature/culture paradigm "the most overwhelmingly important myth in our cultural inheritance," and he quotes Northrop Frye: "mythology is not a direct response to the natural environment; it is part of the imaginative insulation that separates us from that environment" (Livingston 141). Hence, to use Hooker's metaphor, garden knowledge must take into account how, in the poem's terms, it is "flowing and drawn, and since / our knowledge is historical, flowing, and flown" (*CP* 66).

"At the Fishhouses" begins by describing and juxtaposing the interacting forces of nature and culture as parts of a single biosphere. The old man who "sits netting, / his net, in the gloaming almost invisible," does so even though "it is a cold evening." "The five fishhouses [with] steeply peaked roofs," "The big fish tubs," "the wheelbarrows," "an ancient wooden capstan," and the old man with his "shuttle worn and polished" are situated between "the heavy surface of the sea" and "the wild jagged rocks." Here is a fragile place of order and industry, where "narrow, cleated gangplanks slant up / to storerooms in the gables / for the wheelbarrows to be pushed up and down on." The old man, we are told, "has scraped the scales, the principal beauty, / from unnumbered fish with that black old knife, / the blade of which is almost worn away."

The wilderness, on the other hand, is also at work: "an emerald moss" grows on the "shoreward walls" of the fishhouses, while the capstan is "cracked," "bleached," and stained with something "like dried blood, / where the ironwork has rusted." With "sequins on his vest and on his thumb," the old man is depicted as weathered and worn, a human scape in a larger environment shared by nonhumans, and as subject to entropy as the artifacts around him. The speaker states: "He was a friend of my grandfather. / We talk of the decline in the population." The local human community, where the speaker has familial roots, has withered. Like the old man's net, it has become "almost invisible."

Yet the speaker's sense of loss in this first part of the poem, her resignation to the inevitable erosion of human patterns of meaning, is qualified by her sense of humor, which Rotella astutely sees as "one of several strategies by which the poet restrains her desire to transform the events she describes into a familiar poetic pattern, a transcendent moment discovering comforting truth" (Rotella 220). Rotella points to the double effect of the "Lucky Strike" line, but does not take his analysis any further. In the midst of so much decomposition, Bishop tells us, "The old man accepts a Lucky Strike." Sandwiched between descriptions of rusting ironwork and "the decline in the population," the brand-name of a cigarette not only acts as a kind of benediction on the old man, it also resonates with the crass ethos of a commercial society. The structure and wording of "The old man accepts a Lucky Strike" accentuates his passive relationship to the outside world — he accepts what happens to him, whether it is the offer of a smoke or the swelling over of the sea. What the speaker sees in the scene before her — not to mention what she cannot see — constantly subjects any sense of loss to the kind of tough-minded-ness that is also apparent in her comic moments. There is something unmistakably arbitrary about "the benches, / the lobster pots, and masts, scattered / among the wild jagged rocks." The scene is disheveled — or better yet, messy — like the dirty, oily scene in "Filling Station." The absence of a clear, ordered distinction between nature and culture is part of what Tom Paulin sees as

> Bishop's gay refusal to take the idea of natural purity seriously. That refusal is a form of radical camp, which unpicks the cultural complacencies that produce images of "embroidered nature" in European painting and poetry. By dissenting from this manner of viewing the natural world, Bishop refuses to align [herself] with a dominating acquisitiveness. Very subtly, she questions the power politics that the Western aesthetic tradition so often conceals.[87]

Bradstreet's "darksome womb of nature" and Bishop's "opaque" sea do not envision nature as concealing and relinquishing meaning in the same way. Bradstreet's passive, orderly landscape is penetrated, illuminated, and fertilized by the masculine sun, that symbol of a pagan sky god transformed into an omnipotent, patriarchal deity. Bishop's wilderness, on the other hand, is both more and less threatening as the personified sea swells "slowly as if considering spilling over."[88] Further on in the poem, the sea becomes "absolutely clear," not because of some transcendent agency but because of the poet's understanding of its essential indifference to the human enterprise. Here is the clarity Bishop offers: nature is neither God's nor the devil's, and as such it stands apart from concepts of good and evil.

"At the Fishhouses" is similar in this respect to the characteristic work of Eliot and Stevens, who describe our alienation from nature and expose the fictions that we create to alleviate that sense of alienation. Stevens in particular is preoccupied with the fictions that we create vis-à-vis what he calls "The poem of pure reality, untouched / By trope or deviation" (Stevens 471). But Stevens probably would not say, "The old man accepts a Lucky Strike. / He was a friend of my grandfather." "Anecdote of the Jar," for instance, describes the placing of "a jar in Tennessee" to demonstrate the transformative power of Western culture: set on a hill, the jar (like a Celtic tower) "[makes] the slovenly wilderness / Surround that hill" (Stevens 76).

But "Anecdote of the Jar" does not evoke the personal details that Bishop's poem does. Stevens is more like his Professor Eucalyptus—"[standing] / On his balcony, outsensing distances" (483). This distinction does not make Bishop's a better poem; it merely serves to point out her own poetic strategy.

In a vitriolic essay entitled "A Wrong Turning in American Poetry," Robert Bly criticizes "At the Fishhouses" because "The facts of the outer world push out the imagination and occupy the poem themselves. The lines become inflexible. The poem becomes heavy and stolid, like a toad that has eaten ball bearings" (Bly 26). Bly's simile is revealing but true to only part of the poem, to what Seamus Heaney calls its "Fastidious notations which log the progress of the physical world, degree by degree, into the world of the poet's own lucid but unemphatic awareness" (Heaney 102). Bishop does not merely bog the poem down in details either. She is preparing, on the contrary, "to dare a big leap" (105). And, in point of fact, the details of the physical world operating in the poem are viewed as fleeting, so much so that the poem itself seems bird-like, preoccupied at points with surface details and, at others, with the elusive oceanic depths.

The "thin silver / tree trunks [that] are laid horizontally / across the gray stones, down and down / at intervals of four or five feet" describe gestures towards connection that ultimately disappear in that "Cold dark deep ... element bearable to no mortal, / to fish and to seals." The speaker goes on:

> One seal particularly
> I have seen here evening after evening.
> He was curious about me. He was interested in music;
> like me a believer in total immersion,
> so I used to sing him Baptist hymns.
> I also sang "A Mighty Fortress Is Our God."

Comic pathos again precludes epiphany, putting it off for the time being. As Heaney has noted, observation trumps any sort of romantic vision: "Yet here it is, a rhythmic heave which suggests that something other is about to happen—although not immediately" (Heaney 105). The lines of Luther's hymn that portray God as "bulwark never failing" and "helper he amidst the flood" become particularly ironic here, where there is so much dilapidation and decline. The Puritan legacy itself appears to have dwindled into a parody of the *Genesis*-based mandate to subdue the earth and replenish it, as the speaker describes how she has turned her back on "a million Christmas trees [that] stand / waiting for Christmas."

In contrast to Bradstreet's Philomel, the seal signifies no potential escape from the world, with its hardships and oppressive cultural paradigms. Instead, the speaker knowingly invests this creature with human qualities; the seal examines her "with a sort of shrug / as if it were against his better judgment": "He was interested in music; / like me a believer in total immersion." Tongue-in-cheek, the speaker projects her own cultural heritage (which seeks and celebrates transformation in rites like baptism) on to the seal; but in doing so she also playfully implies a subtle distinction between herself and the wilderness. Although she obviously alludes to the New Testament tradition of baptism into the Kingdom of God,[89] she is also simultaneously referring to a total immersion in that "element bearable to no mortal." So she teasingly gestures towards identification with the seal but at the same time suggests that this is a difficult, though not impossible, task. Barry Lopez recounts his own meeting with a seal in the Arctic: "To contemplate what people are doing out here and ignore the universe of the seal, to consider human quest and plight and not know the land, I thought, to not listen to it, seemed fatal" (13). Likewise, Bishop realizes the apparent otherness of nature and yet accepts that fact cheerfully and without fear. The speaker's stance therefore encompasses both difference and tenuous correspondence, evoking the kind of paradox often felt by distant relatives on meeting one another. Indeed, it is the speaker herself who becomes the meeting point, the pastoral "middle landscape," between wild nature and Western civilization. Again, the passive syntax of "element bearable to no mortal"—like "The old man accepts a Lucky Strike"—simply promotes a wise and humble acquiescence to the limits of the human condition. The fact that the sea is so stark, alien, and almost untouchable suggests, however, that it is bearable to one who is immortal—to the God who is a mighty fortress. But, Bishop implies, we can know nothing for certain about this God. We have no evidence that He exists or intervenes on our behalf. There are only traces of our own now decadent traditions—"a million Christmas trees stand / waiting for Christmas."

The speaker believes in "total immersion" in the often unforgiving, harsh details of the world because they are real, and so she says of the sea: "If you should dip your hand in, / your wrist would ache immediately, /

your bones would begin to ache and your hand would burn." In fact, there is no revelation offered here, but rather the results of repeated experience: "I have seen it over and over, the same sea, the same, / slightly, indifferently swinging above the stones, ... / above the stones and then the world." Increasingly, the speaker appeals to the senses to attempt to evoke raw physicality; and, yet, even the language of sensory experience seems too limited. The more she refers to the senses, the more she uses conditional language, until, in the penultimate section of the poem, the ability of language to describe the details of experience appears finally limited: "If you tasted it [the sea], it would first taste bitter, / then briny, then surely burn your tongue." Whether we are makers of fishing nets, gardens, or poems, we draw patterns that are impositions on nature — and if we should touch or taste or in any way immerse ourselves in the wilderness itself, we will come up against both the transience and origins of our patterns. "The ocean mother of 'At the Fishhouses,'" writes Marilyn May Lombardi, "is coolly indifferent to our sufferings" (Lombardi 98).[90]

Bly again criticizes poets like Eliot and Pound for their puritanic fear of "All animal life and sexual life," and he accuses them of transmitting this disdain to the poets of Bishop's generation (Bly 21–22). Certainly Alan Watts would agree with the notion that this "unparalleled cultural imperialism" (Watts 53), largely under the aegis of Christianity, has resulted in a widespread sense of the body "as territory captured by the Devil" (3). Yet Bly's criticism is one that in Bishop's case simply does not stick. "At the Fishhouses" is, if nothing else, a discarding of the old puritanical fears of the hideous wilderness; although, as Heaney points out, this last part of "At the Fishhouses" recognizes "a knowledge-need which sets human beings apart from seals and herrings,... Her scientific impulse is suddenly jumped back to its root in pre–Socratic awe, and water stares her in the face as the original solution" (106). Further to that, it is not only the recent Darwinian, empirical impulse but also the Puritanical, religious fear which Bishop bypasses in the moment of lyrical truth that Heaney justly and eloquently finds here, although it must be noted too that it is debatable whether "knowledge-need" really distinguishes humans from nonhumans. The seal's curiosity could be seen as evidence of seal knowledge-need, despite Bishop's playful, self-conscious projections.

Facing old fears, however, may be painful and threatening. We still live in a culture that has aggressive designs on nature and that takes its own constructs as absolute mandates preordained by God. With the onset of global warming, and our agonizingly slow acknowledgement of it as a reality, we are forced finally to face the subconscious world views we carry around with us, world views that have a profoundly real impact on the environment. As Al Gore has written, "Our capacity for analysis sometimes leads us to an arrogant illusion: that we're so special and unique that nature isn't connected to us" (Gore 160). Bishop shows us otherwise. In the final passage of "At the Fishhouses," the ungovernable, constantly moving sea itself becomes an emblem of the community's store of knowledge and of its traditional ways of building and making. Her tentative likening of the sea to "what we imagine knowledge to be"—"derived from the rocky breasts / forever"—would have been anathema to the Puritan colonists. Indeed, the sea was to them a spiritual metaphor for the "disorder and unrestraint ... of unregenerate man," that is, a type of the wilderness, where, as Thomas Hooker states, "curiosity is not studied" (Carroll 83). To study curiosity would entail accepting the wilderness on its own terms, which is exactly what the Puritans, with their divine mandate for land reform, could not do.[91] As Guy Rotella says of the final section of "At the Fishhouses": "It recalls religious and transcendental poems in which reconciling and mediating truths are discovered in a natural world originally inscribed by God. But it denies the analogy on which such discoveries are made" (223).

Unlike Bradstreet's malleable landscape, Bishop's is hard and rocky, offering sustenance but not yielding to relentlessly exploitative ideas and ideals. In "At the Fishhouses," it is the all-too-human realm of knowledge—or what we imagine is knowledge—that, like the sea, is in constant flux above the world and that, again like the sea, must be approached with caution. By deflating some of our cultural paradigms, the poem reverses the traditional Western deployment of power in the relationship between nature and culture. Recognizing that culture originates in nature, it obviates a destructive and erroneous polarizing of the two and rightly insists that we pay closer attention to what nature is constantly telling us. As Bishop says in a different context in "North Haven," her elegy for Robert Lowell:

> the White-throated Sparrow's five-note song,
> pleading and pleading, brings tears to the eyes.
> Nature repeats herself, or almost does:
> *repeat, repeat, repeat; revise, revise, revise.*

"At the Fishhouses" envisions a community that, attending to the voices of nature and acknowledging its own limitations and uncertain status, comes together to reiterate its history and traditions, and "revise, revise, revise."

Facing the Ocean: Origins of Culture, Part 2

As we have seen in the first chapter of this study, Anne Bradstreet's "A Dialogue between Old England and New" constituted a poetic shrinking of the 3,000 miles separating England and its colony. As such, this poem became an analogue for a map, doing what Barry Lopez has aptly argued maps in fact do: acting as "an evaluation of what is important" (279). Orienting its readers to their new place in the world, Bradstreet's poem salved homesickness and dispelled uncertainty; like a map, it "masquerade[d] as an authority" (Lopez 280) that colonial Puritans in the seventeenth century wilderness of the New World would have accepted and welcomed. Similarly, in the chapter preceding this one, we have seen how "Contemplations" became the textual site on which Bradstreet tried to come to terms with nature in the New World. The Puritan community of which she was a part was motivated to anglicize — to domesticate and develop what it defined as — untouched wilderness as quickly as possible, perhaps as a consequence of its acute need to overcome the distance between itself and England. Read in this context, Elizabeth Bishop's early poem "The Map" illuminates the similarities between poetry and cartography as well as the false binaries of culture and nature. Reading "Dialogue," for instance, Bradstreet's fellow colonists might, in Bishop's words, "take the water between thumb and finger / like women feeling for the smoothness of yard-goods" (*CP* 3). That poem, in other words, conferred a recognizable value on the relationship between the Old and New Worlds in 1642. Like Bishop's "Fishhouses," "The Map" describes how we decide the relationship between land and sea, and thus how we attempt to make ourselves at home in a particular landscape. In this analysis, the act of reading a map — which is what this poem describes — becomes a metaphor for setting forth a world view. Or as Anne Colwell remarks, in a statement that also recalls this study's earlier discussion of Bishop's "Santarém":

both mapmaker and historian, as human individuals, possess the same gift and curse as the poet: whatever they look at wears the mark of their looks. Both delicately transform and give human meaning to apparent chaos, and both cannot help but distort and limit, and perhaps make accurate knowing impossible [38].

Here Bishop's questions of travel, like Bradstreet's, are about managing distance and difference so that "North's as near as West." But in contrast to the Puritan poet's endeavor to negotiate a relationship with England as well as with a strange new landscape, Bishop is more interested in describing how maps make such negotiations possible in the first place. Since "Topography displays no favorites," it permits any number of perspectives and is essentially wide open to interpretation by way of names, colours, boundaries, and so on. Hence "The Map" begins with basic aspects of cartography by outlining the relationship between land and sea — "Land lies in water; it is shadowed green" — but it also quickly proceeds to reveal ambiguities in "the simple blue from green" by asking questions that point to the equivocal nature of map-making and -reading and, finally, of Western acculturation itself. Increasingly, "The Map" moves from geographic to political cartography and, as it does so, begins to disclose greater complexity. Like the wasps' nest in "Santarém," a map can be approached and described from various, and even opposing, vantage points: "We can stroke these lovely bays, / under a glass as if they were expected to blossom, / or as if to provide a clean cage for invisible fish."

A map also invites the reader to see the familiar in the strange and thus to domesticate it; or, as Eric J. Leed states, "Travel in general, and 'exploration' in particular, may be motivated not by love of the strange and unfamiliar but by the desire to reduce, by active and aggressive means, the uncertainty implicit in the strange and unfamiliar" (Leed 68). Having been placed behind glass or in "a clean cage," the bays lose their wildness and can be touched by the domesticated human hand. Bishop's lines at this point strike two distinctly culturative chords — one horticulture and the other aquaculture — that again emphasize the controlling and containing nature of cartography. Likewise, in other lines already mentioned here, "These peninsulas take the water between thumb and finger / like women feeling for the smoothness of yard-goods." Once land has been possessed, its contours begin to reflect the ideological contours of the makers and readers of maps. Through naming, maps permit further familiarization with terrain that might otherwise remain unknown, and Bishop's poem reveals how place-names appear to subdue territory and how the act of naming confers a creative power that is liable to become inflated:

> The names of seashore towns run out to sea,
> the names of cities cross the neighboring mountains
> — the printer here experiencing the same excitement
> as when emotion too far exceeds its cause.

According to "The Map," colours also allow the reader to order and rationalize the world. Yet the poem's last (rather teasing) question — "Are they assigned, or can the countries pick their colors?" — is concerned with agency, which underscores the existence of various, possibly conflicting interpretations of land and sea. Maps, says Bishop, necessarily reflect decisions and compromises about relationships between global constituents, because otherwise they could not do their job: to render a reading of the world as tamed and ordered.

In the much later poem, "Crusoe in England" (*CP* 162), Bishop again comes to grips with the relationship between culture and nature. In many respects like the speaker of "At the Fishhouses," "Crusoe's" speaker is a solitary observer who meditates for twenty-eight years on the sea- and landscapes of the island where he had formerly been shipwrecked. Bonnie Costello calls him "a desperate Darwin, trailing off into the unknown. Perhaps the ultimate breakdown of empiricism and its legacy of logical positivism occurs in Crusoe's temporal displacement" (Costello 203). Using Daniel Defoe's retrospective narrative technique in *Robinson Crusoe*, Bishop explores the themes of regret and longing for home as these are found in the novel itself. While *Crusoe* sees its narrator splitting his perspective between England, which represents the domesticated past, and the wild, unnamed island where he has been shipwrecked alone, Bishop's speaker emphasizes — in ways that are remarkably analogous to Bradstreet — how his island eventually became home even as England gradually became an alien place. After his long solitude, Bishop's Crusoe now finds himself dislocated in England, "another island, / that doesn't seem like one, but who decides?" As in "The Map," the question evokes the poem's central issue of how culture and nature intersect in the mind of one whose very sense of self has been both shaped and threatened by solitude.

This issue is evoked in the title of the poem as Crusoe, Defoe's famous character, is thrown back into English society after having been changed by the natural circumstances of his exile. Consequently, the sense of home that is so important to the novel is turned upside down in the poem as Crusoe becomes nostalgic about his "poor old island." And when he juxtaposes newspapers with the birth of volcanoes in the opening lines, emblems of nature and culture become readily apparent. Having lived so long in the natural world, Crusoe now disconcertingly gains his perspective through the opaque medium, and media, of English civilization. The first pair of lines in this poem seems to separate for a moment the disparate worlds of Crusoe's experience. He knows that "A new volcano has erupted," but his knowing stems from his reading of what "the papers say" and the reference to "last week" places him firmly in the frame of Western culture and linear time. Yet the first line also brilliantly evokes the creative power found in nature, and the fact that Crusoe immediately sees this power in the context of a containing and naming culture is ironic. Like "The Map," "Crusoe in England" views the act of naming as potentially both arrogant and naively playful, and like the earlier poem it explores the relativity of scale. As Lorrie Goldensohn writes concerning scale in "The Map": "Bishop exploits the distortion of scale, the slippage between mediums of representation" (106). Indeed, Crusoe himself has "time enough to play with names" and, of course, this pastime stems from his cultural background. Hence the "island being born" is witnessed via "the mate's binoculars" just as the new volcano is also reported by a newspaper. Seen from the binoculars, the birth of an island is objectified: it is "a black fleck" that is "caught on the horizon like a fly" and then quickly named.

A sense of loss, not so much the loss of his wild island home as that of uninterrupted propinquity to raw nature, pervades the viewpoint of Bishop's Crusoe as he begins his monologue, which in no way spares his tortuous coming to terms with wilderness. Although he misses his island, Crusoe remains firmly European and is thus divided at points over what to make of his own experience, one which involved the earlier loss of civilized English society. That his island home remains "un-rediscovered, un-renamable" implies satisfaction as well as loss: satisfaction because his island has been spared the attention of an objectifying, cataloguing culture; but also loss because Crusoe himself discovered, named, and possessed the island, and "None of the books has ever got it right." Unlike what "the papers say," Crusoe knows from experience that the tomes written about his island are erroneous; he suspects, therefore, that a disjunction exists between his culture's view of the world and what the world constitutes in his own experience. Hence, what "the papers say" is also subject to doubt, especially since there are no alternative sources of information besides Crusoe's memory. To be sure, "None of the books has ever got it right" could also allude to Defoe's novel (itself based partly on the life of Alexander Selkirk), thus of course placing *Robinson Crusoe* (appropriately) among the propagators of the Western myth of exploration and possession.

Certainly this myth is one in which Bishop's Crusoe finds himself entangled, but "Crusoe in England" is, in large part, about such entanglement, and the narrator evinces an acute awareness of his predicament. His awareness is revealed throughout the poem as Crusoe describes the evolution of his life in the island from a raw, confusing existence in nature to a gradual, albeit incomplete, re-orientation in a self-made culture taken roughly from his English upbringing. So in the second verse paragraph of the poem, Crusoe returns to his volcanic imagery to evoke the wilderness where he struggled to retain his sense of self:

> Well, I had fifty-two
> miserable, small volcanoes I could climb
> with a few slithery strides —
> volcanoes dead as ash heaps.

In contrast to the containment of nature found in England, Crusoe finds himself, like the colonial Puritans of Anne Bradstreet's era, overwhelmed by the scale of things on his island. Here nature seems at first totally out of his control, although he tries vainly to counter this by counting volcanoes.

At this juncture especially, Bishop makes one important result of shipwreck on a deserted isle much starker than Defoe does — that is, the near decimation of the self, a cultural artifact in its own right. "The concept of 'self,'" writes John A. Livingston,

> is an expression of dualism. It dichotomizes our world by requiring the additional concept of "other." The twin notions are mutually reinforcing. They are analogous if not identical to the conceptual human/Nature dichotomy [Livingston 100].

If culture and its accompanying artifact *self*—what Alan Watts calls "the separated ego" whose "fate" (7) eventually takes up much of the obsession and energy of Western culture — provide a sense of proportion and place, Bishop's Crusoe reveals their catastrophic loss. In fact, if "The Map" ana-lyzes the manipulation of scale and perspective for the purpose of orien-tation (personal, cultural, ideological), Daniel Defoe's Crusoe describes a sense of *dis*orientation from which Bishop's character can never fully recover. Defoe's Crusoe puts it this way at one point early in the novel: "so I ventured to make to the coast, and come to an anchor in the mouth of a little river, I knew not what, or where; neither what latitude, what country, what nations, or what river" (Defoe 46). Similarly, the great unhappiness of Bishop's speaker stems from the sudden loss of distance between nature and himself. Eventually, through his experience, Bishop's Crusoe becomes aware of how human culture is essentially chimeric, how it distorts land and sea with its own myths and values. Eventually he loses what Bradstreet retains, however ambivalently, in "Contemplations," the ability to examine nature from a distant, culturally-anchored vantage point.

There is a connection to be made at this juncture to the Acteon myth discussed in the Introduction. Crusoe's loss of belief in human culture cre-ates his Acteon moment, threatening his sense of himself as human and set apart from other animals. Consequently, having nearly lost his human-ity, Bishop's Crusoe "with a few slithery strides" climbs the volcanoes' sides. Yet, like some kind of half-wild Pythagorean, he also counts volca-noes in what seems like a losing attempt to retain a familiar sense of scale. Bishop's language reveals how unacceptable this loss of proportion is, as Crusoe describes "volcanoes dead as ash heaps" that are "naked and leaden, with their heads blown off." Like Swift's Gulliver as well, Crusoe cannot place himself in his new surroundings without becoming overwhelmed: if the volcanoes seem too small, the goats, turtles, and gulls seem too big, just as Crusoe himself seems out of proportion. From his perch on the highest volcano, he is uncomfortably besieged by "a glittering hexagon of rollers / closing and closing in." Like the "absolutely clear" sea in "At the Fishhouses," the ocean here provides a continual reminder of the ephemer-ality of culture, relative only to its moment in time and in need of con-stant revision. Land meets sea as it does in both "Fishhouses" and "The Map," yet in "Crusoe" it evokes none of the solidity and stability gained through naming. Rather, land on the island reflects a primal world of flux in which "folds of lava, running out to sea, / would hiss." Such "running out to sea" differs from that found in "The Map," where "The names of seashore towns run out to sea." If the earlier poem describes how culture displays and exhibits itself to the point of seeming to run roughshod over nature, "Crusoe" describes a very different interaction between land and sea, one in which land represents neither control nor containment, but rather loss of control, suffocation, and eventual dissolution of the ego.

However, like Defoe's character, Bishop's alleviates homesickness by making and naming things — in short, by creating his own rough culture proximate to the only one he knows, replete with "home-brew":

> I'd drink
> the awful, fizzy, stinging stuff
> that went straight to my head
> and play my home-made flute
> (I think it had the weirdest scale on earth)
> and, dizzy, whoop and dance among the goats.
> Home-made, home-made! But aren't we all?

Here Crusoe describes a nascent pastoral that parallels, albeit less soberly, Bradstreet's "Contemplations." Like the Puritans, he is driven by loneliness and alienation to try to replicate his own culture even though he admittedly suffers from a lack of knowledge, which results not just in bad beer and idiosyncratic flutes but in "a miserable philosophy" as well. Crusoe's question about being "home-made" points to the fact that all culture is taken from the raw stuff of nature; likewise, every scale is weird in the beginning. This truth becomes obscure over time, however, and is replaced by the erroneous notion that culture is *ipso facto* something unto itself which exists separate from nature and, indeed, has a claim over it. Thus Crusoe's ignorance in the face of the wilderness, his lack of a cultural standard held up by community, is exposed by his complete isolation and becomes in the end his central dilemma:

> Why didn't I know enough of something?
> Greek drama or astronomy? The books
> I'd read were full of blanks;
> the poems — well, I tried
> reciting to my iris-beds,
> "They flash upon the inward eye,
> which is the bliss..." The bliss of what?
> One of the first things that I did
> when I got back was look it up.

The quotation, taken from Wordsworth's "I Wandered Lonely as a Cloud," rivals Bishop's opening lines in its indication of the contrast between illusion and reality in the mind of the speaker. While Crusoe's experience in nature is anything but romantic, his educated mind nonetheless recalls a fragment of a poem that celebrates solitude and apparent union with nature. Yet if Wordsworth makes, even in the title of his poem, a virtue of wandering by oneself, he does so in the context of the English countryside, which as we have already outlined in the Introduction constitutes a humanized, groomed nature. As Aldous Huxley states, Wordsworth "asks us to make [a] falsification of experience" by assuming that nature is "that chaste, mild deity who presides over the *Gemüthlichkeit*, the prettiness, the cozy sublimities of the Lake District":

> A few weeks in Malaya or Borneo would have undeceived him. Wandering in the hothouse darkness of the jungle, he would not have felt so serenely certain of those "Presences of Nature," those "Souls of Lonely Places," which he was in the habit of worshipping on the shores of Windermere and Rydal [Huxley 1–3].

To use Huxley's terms, Bishop's Crusoe has been "undeceived" by his experience of shipwreck and exile, and his expression of disillusionment clearly contrasts with Wordsworth's cultivation of communion with a seemingly benevolent nature. In contrast to Wordsworth's daffodils, Crusoe's "iris-beds" are actually snail shells whose occupants "crept over everything, / over the one variety of tree, / a sooty, scrub affair." Reciting to these "flowers," of course, calls forth the fragment of Wordsworth's verse as well as the question, "The bliss of what?," which Crusoe cannot remember until he investigates on his return to England.

Although Bishop playfully withholds the sought-after missing word, "solitude," the context of the poem provides an incisive critique of the Wordsworthian viewpoint, a viewpoint which constitutes an epistemological and cultural claim: that the individual contains within him- or herself a visionary essence that steps forth to creatively interpret objective reality so that human being is ultimately a kind of marriage between the perceiving, fashioning person and the world. Hence, if Wordsworth is right, English culture is the result of a creative co-conspiracy between temperate nature and a long array of god-like, visionary humans over time. Bishop's Crusoe, however, living in his solitude, does not demonstrate anything like Wordsworthian optimism. Juxtaposing his "flowers" with

Wordsworth's bears this out. Next to Crusoe's snails creeping over and lying under the island's "one variety of tree ... in drifts," Wordsworth's daffodils are "A host" that are "Continuous as the stars that shine / and twinkle on the milky way":

> Ten thousand saw I at a glance,
> Tossing their heads in sprightly dance.
> The waves beside them danced; but they
> Out-did the sparkling waves in glee:
> A poet could not but be gay,
> In such a jocund company [Wordsworth 191].

For Wordsworth's speaker, this "jocund company" will later "flash upon that inward eye" as he recollects his experience, so that the poem ends with an affirmative recollection of solitude in nature: "And then my heart with pleasure fills, / And dances with the daffodils." Here land and sea, in the Wordsworthian view, affably compete to celebrate their co-existence. Yet while Wordsworth's speaker recounts experience from his comfortable couch, Crusoe recalls grappling with his alienation from nature "With [his] legs dangling down familiarly / over a crater's edge."

What, then, is this fragment of Wordsworth's poem doing in Bishop's, besides acting as a Romantic foil to her Crusoe's experience? Besides that, which is much, Wordsworth evokes yet another cultural representation of nature that is opaque, yet another form of media, in the face of Crusoe's difficult and undeniably real experience. According to Bishop's Crusoe, solitude in nature is not pleasurable but arduous, harsh, almost impossible to endure, resulting in what he calls "a miserable philosophy." This philosophy stems, it seems, from his not knowing enough — that is, from the fact that Crusoe as a cultural creation largely falls apart, becomes undone, once he is alone in the wilderness: "The books / I'd read were full of blanks." The question, "Why didn't I know enough of something? / Greek drama or astronomy?," obviously points to the identity crisis in which Crusoe finds himself, yet on another level it sidesteps what he really does know: that nature itself cannot be accurately described by words such as "fluttering" or "twinkle" (Wordsworth 191) when it also requires terms like "erupted" and "naked" and "hissing." Likewise, the sea does not — as Wordsworth would have us believe — "sparkle," it "glitters," like something hard and impenetrable; and clouds do not "float on high o'er hills and dales," they hang "above the craters — their parched throats / ... hot to touch." More importantly perhaps, Crusoe the writer and poet learns to see himself for what he is: not a cultivator of words and landscape — not, in other words, a creature of culture — so much as an animal among other animals, an organism in a frightening and complex world of other organisms: "The goats were white, so were the gulls, / and both too tame, or else they thought / I was a goat, too, or a gull."

But the goats and gulls are not tame; Crusoe has become half-wild, and the new knowledge and consciousness he has acquired are of so-called wildness. He has become, therefore, unmade. As he comes to realize, such knowledge, difficult as it is to come by, does not wither or erode once he returns to England. On the contrary, it drives him to write, not only about his experience in exile but also about his inability to reabsorb things English. The act of writing for Crusoe, however, is completely unlike Wordsworth's "recollection in tranquillity." If Wordsworth expresses a cultural wish about the nature of nature, Crusoe exposes it by describing his very real experience *in* nature. Unlike both Bradstreet and Wordsworth, Elizabeth Bishop has, through the character of Crusoe, evoked experience in the natural world that is as free as possible from the insularity provided by anthropocentrism, by Western culture and myth-making, even while it is so clearly embedded in all of these.

Obviously Anne Bradstreet encountered real wilderness but, as has been noted already, she was part of a community that feared and rejected such encounters; and Bradstreet's "Contemplations" reveals just how important culture became to the New England pilgrims as they attempted to counter the threat posed by uncultivated nature. Although fishes and birds tempt Bradstreet to stray from the tenets of Puritanism, they do not, in the end, cause her to backslide or become a writer living in exile. Her version of the landscape in seventeenth-century New England is, finally, ornate and controlled. Bishop, on the other hand, as we have already witnessed in "At the Fishhouses," simply describes the intersection of culture and nature as it, in fact, is. As a poet, she sidesteps the task of becoming a verbal landscaper or gardener; instead, she takes the role of acute observer, one who recounts the relationship between humans and their environments. Hence the seal in "Fishhouses" is seen as mysterious and inhuman at the same time as the speaker realizes her position between land and sea and that, moreover, she truly shares the world with both the seal and the old fisherman mending his nets.

Bishop's Crusoe, likewise, describes his encounters with the animals he meets on the island. As has already been indicated, these creatures — goats, turtles, gulls — seem out of proportion because Crusoe has lost his bearings. The animals he meets are, even more than the seal in "Fish-houses," baffling and unapproachable: "The turtles lumbered by, high-domed, / hissing like teakettles. / (And I'd have given years, or taken a few, / for any sort of kettle, of course)." The simile highlights Crusoe's long-ing for cultural reminders of his sense of humanity, and it is ironic that an animal that so threatens his humanity should also remind him of it. Indeed, after a time, Crusoe makes a point of projecting his longings and cultural repertoire on to the goats, even though he finds them alienating:

> One billy-goat would stand on the volcano
> I'd christened *Mont d'Espoir* or *Mount Despair*
> (I'd time enough to play with names),
> and bleat and bleat, and sniff the air.
> I'd grab his beard and look at him.
> His pupils, horizontal, narrowed up
> and expressed nothing, or a little malice.
> I got so tired of the very colours!
> One day I dyed a baby goat bright red
> with my red berries, just to see
> something a little different.

Crusoe's need to project extends also to Friday, the human animal whose very name indicates scales and standards of measurement. Contra-dicting Defoe, whose Crusoe discovers the presence of other humans on the island with great trepidation, Bishop's character claims, "Just when I thought I couldn't stand it / another minute longer, Friday came." The "nightmares of other islands" that have come to plague Crusoe's imagina-tion are placed in a time-frame in which he counts minutes as though they were volcanoes, until the welcome arrival of Friday: "Friday was nice." The sexual interest in Friday — "he had a pretty body" — also contrasts with Defoe's fictionalized account, but this too manifests Crusoe's need to repli-cate the culture he has left behind: "I wanted to propagate my kind, / and so did he, I think, poor boy." Crusoe takes this, perhaps, from the *Gen-esis* mandate to "be fruitful and multiply," although he simultaneously clusters Friday together with the baby goats: "He'd pet the baby goats sometimes, / and race with them, or carry one around."

Once Crusoe and Friday are returned to England, Crusoe finds himself "bored." Ironically, the nightmare of monotony that compelled him to paint a baby goat red, for instance, clings to Crusoe as he finds himself "surrounded by uninteresting lumber." The poem's implication, that the drive to make and live in culture is finally inescapable, is made clearest in terms not so much of created things — utensils, lumber, trousers, and so on — as of concepts such as scale and standard. Daniel Dennett calls these concepts "memes," "distinct memorable units," such as wheel, calendar, alphabet, and calculus, through which a culture evolves out of nature (344):

> the evolution of memes could not get started until the evolution of animals had paved the way by creating a species — *Homo sapiens* — with brains that could provide shelter, and habits of communication that could provide transmission media, for memes [345].

Friday's name constitutes one important indication of what is meant here, in terms of the measurement of time, as does history, which can be seen in the retrospective view that the poem's narrative structure adopts. Crusoe's monologue demonstrates how kinds of measurement, whether of minutes or musical notes or volcanoes' heads, are the inherent bases of Western culture out of which material things are made. Hence he constantly measures time and, consequently, locates meaning in the past where he has come close to experiencing firsthand the natural origins of culture:

> The knife there on the shelf—
> it reeked of meaning, like a crucifix.
> It lived. How many years did I
> beg it, implore it, not to break?
> I knew each nick and scratch by heart,
> the bluish blade, the broken tip,
> the lines of wood-grain on the handle...
> Now it won't look at me at all.
> The living soul has dribbled away.
> My eyes rest on it and pass on.

Only in the context of wilderness does the knife "[reek] of meaning." In that world, Crusoe's eyes intimately know and count "each nick and scratch ... / the bluish blade, the broken tip, / the lines of wood-grain." In a real sense, he turns to animism, which biologist Lyall Watson describes as "a

161

time in both personal and human history when we are closest to nature, most easily touched by mystical experience, most accessible to a connection that provides a real sense of the presence of power around us" (Watson 241). Morris Berman, like Carolyn Merchant (*DON* 288), identifies tremendous changes in Western culture after 1500, changes that include the "gradual elimination from Western thought" (58) of animism and the "shift from Hermeticism to mechanism" (117):

> the forces that triumphed in the second half of the seventeenth century were those of bourgeois ideology and laissez-faire capitalism. Not only was the idea of living matter heresy to such groups; it was also economically inconvenient. A dead earth ruptures the delicate ecological balance that was maintained in the alchemical tradition, but if nature is dead, there are no restraints on exploiting it for profit.

As though he himself had just read Defoe's novel, Berman adds to this "the triumph of the Puritan view of life, which concomitantly repressed sexual energy and sublimated it into brutalizing labor" (117). On the domesticated English island of Bishop's poem, Crusoe's "eyes rest on [the knife] and pass on," indicating not only loss of meaning and consequent boredom but also the loss of life itself. As Crusoe himself states, "I'm old.... And Friday, my dear Friday, died of measles / seventeen years ago come March."

This last pair of lines, where "Crusoe in England" ends, have caustic implications for the culture in which, after nearly three decades of longing, Crusoe finds himself dying almost literally of boredom. A culture that categorizes, names, and measures everything wants, of course, "the flute, the knife, the shrivelled shoes, / my shedding goatskin trousers" as museum pieces. And Crusoe's final question, "How can anyone want such things?," implicates the compulsion to count even as Crusoe himself counts the years since Friday's death. Western culture appears, in the final analysis, to be a disease as surely as the measles that have killed Friday.

"Crusoe's" view of Western culture vis-à-vis nature appears in a less developed form in "Florida" (*CP* 32), where "the careless, corrupt state" is viewed in the context of the ecosystem, represented metaphorically as "the Indian Princess." Nature, in this early poem, is constituted by a swirling cycle of life and death that proceeds in spite of the state, which is alienated from that cycle. Over the course of the poem, the term *state* begins to reflect not only the political entity called Florida, which the speaker calls "the poorest / post-card of itself," but the general human condition itself, set against what is seen as a rampant natural *dis*order requiring containment. Here, at the outset of her career-long interest in geography, Bishop describes the counterfeit relationship between European interpretations of culture and nature:

> The state with the prettiest name,
> the state that floats in brackish water,
> held together by mangrove roots
> that bear while living oysters in clusters,
> and when dead strew white swamps with skeletons,
> dotted as if bombarded, with green hummocks
> like ancient cannon-balls sprouting grass.

Like "Crusoe in England" and "The Map," the act of naming — with its supposedly original mandate in *Genesis* — is central to the cultural agenda. In this case, "Florida," derived from the Spanish *la flor*, indicates the European acknowledgement of the area's lush beauty; but seen in the context of the rest of the poem, which actually describes nature rather than the state, the name evokes both cynicism and loss. Moreover, against the historical backdrop of Spanish exploitation and decimation of the aboriginal population, signaled by the references to "ancient cannon-balls" and Pocahontas' death (also represented by "buried Indian Princess"), *The Flowery Land*, "held together by mangrove roots," takes on a bitter irony.

Such irony is apparent in even a cursory glance at Spanish action in Florida in the sixteenth and seventeenth centuries. Ronald Wright, for instance, like Amy Clampitt, chronicles the deeds of Hernand De Soto, described as "the last outsider to see this part of North America in anything like its pre–Columbian state." Wright states further that:

> Soto's men had little interest in nature; it is hard to reconstruct the landscape in front of their hungry eyes. Their vocabulary for the Appalachians is the same as for the Andes — "very high," "difficult," "very cold," and so forth — like the jottings of a dull schoolchild on holiday. One hardly knows whether they are marching across hot savannas or beneath the shade of mossy oaks.... Their accounts come to life only when they mention something of material value — temples and storehouses, caskets of pearls, a whiff of gold [Wright 86].

Obviously, aboriginal culture, particularly the Cherokee nation, thrived in this part of the continent prior to European contact. As Wright puts it, De Soto found "a landscape profoundly changed by culture" (86), but this culture was one that converged with nature rather than conquered it, and that existed in syncopation with the ecosystem.

Bishop's "Florida" makes explicit the aboriginals' relationship to nature in its references to the Indian Princess, whose skirt, "a gray rag of rotted calico," holds the "fading shells" that ornament the Floridian coastline. Although she employs the pathetic fallacy perhaps partly in order to reveal the grievous loss of habitat, Bishop also humanizes nature by conjoining its existence with that of the buried Princess, whose remains have mingled with earth and swamp and the attendant life-and-death cycle which proceeds endlessly. Thus the oysters "while living" are borne "in clusters / and when dead" are strewn in the swamps and "Enormous turtles ... die and leave their barnacled shells on the beaches," all of this together with "the buried Indian Princess." The Princess is mentioned again at the end of the poem, where "The alligator, ... whimpers and speaks in the throat / of the Indian Princess." If the landscape here is ornamented, it is done in such a way as to complement nature, achieving what Livingston calls "a human/Nature Camelot" that prevailed in this part of North America prior to "the era of the intercontinental warlords":

> up until this time some human races had achieved at least a modest equilibrium with what remained of the prehuman natural communities of the world. The intercontinentalists changed everything forever [Livingston 54].

Montaigne, in his essay "On the Cannibals" written in the sixteenth century, says of the putative barbarians of the New World that "They are still governed by the laws of Nature and are only very slightly bastardized by ours," and he wishes they could have "been discovered earlier, in times when there were men who could have appreciated them better than we do."

> They could not even imagine a state of nature so simple and so pure as the one we have learned about from experience; they could not even believe that societies of men could be maintained with so little artifice, so little in the way of human solder [Montaigne 10].

Reaching for the Interior: Western Mythic Metaphor, Part 3

That the legacy of the "intercontinentalists" constitutes much of the matter of current experience is subtly narrated by the speaker of "The Moose," where the orderly world of modern travel is witnessed and celebrated until a moose, representing a creature apparently untamed and totally other, intrudes on the poem and literally ends it. Here Bishop anticipates the "westward-trekking" and "transhumance" that make up Amy Clampitt's "epic theme," moving westward "From narrow provinces / of fish and bread and tea" on the eastern seaboard (*CP* 169). The poem's literal driving movement towards the interior repeats not only Bishop's earlier "Arrival at Santos" and "Brazil, January 1, 1502," but also recalls the historical pattern of mass migration westward, the Manifest Destiny of the early European explorers and pioneers set forth in the opening chapter of Frederick Jackson Turner's *The Frontier in American History* (1920). The first six stanzas, constituting a single, ballad-like sentence, set up the relationship between land and sea that Bishop delineates in other poems examined here, such as "Florida," "The Map," "The End of March," "At the Fishhouses," and "Crusoe in England." The subject of the sentence, "a bus journeys west," is qualified by the natural forces of tide and river that have their own rhythms and interact with each other, described by way of a tripartite structure of "wheres" that evokes the daily tidal swing and its relation to fish, river, and sun. From the primordial sea and its endless cycles, the bus (with its "dented flank / of blue, beat-up enamel") leaves "on red, gravelly roads," setting up the cultural dynamic of sugar maples, farmhouses, and churches, past which the moving community travels intact within the bus. As Victoria Harrison puts it so well:

> The bus meets the well-prepared scene, teeming with the life of nature's cycles and with human beings' civilizing structures. But as the bus gathers the people, who, we assume, fill the houses, cook the fish, and serve the bread and tea, it resets them, including them in its own small, traveling world, removed just enough from home that they can reflect on it [199].

In contrast to the long, complex interactions built into nature, the bus's stops and starts are abrupt and simple, occurring within and explained by the teleology of the road, and what the road means to a culture firmly built on the ideas of quest and conquest: "Goodbye to the elms, / to the farm, to the dog. / The bus starts." The prosaic language employed to describe the banality of stopping and starting, as well as the mundane activities — the goodbyes and the greetings —, is juxtaposed with a lyricism that hints at the mysterious otherness of nature, the fog, the changing light, "the cabbage roses," and "the sweet peas [that] cling / to their wet white string." Against this is the litany of place names: Bass River, the

Tantramar marshes, Boston, the New Brunswick woods. These and the fences and garden string, as well as "a ship's port lantern," make the passing landscape, the flux, more recognizable, secure, and connected.

As the road, string, and garden fences all do their jobs, and as the light of day fades and gives way to moonlight, the passengers feel safe and oriented, moving forward on their journey on the familiar road. Even the bus's entry into the woods of New Brunswick, now dominated by moonlight, is assuring, although the forest is "hairy, scratchy, splintery," alluding vaguely to ancient human fears, the memory of the wilds on this eastern coastline, or what Simon Schama calls one kind of arcadia, "a place of primitive panic" (517). Nevertheless, the woods catch both "moonlight and mist," and the simile is comforting: "like lamb's wool / on bushes in a pasture." The passengers can "lie back" and take their rest, sleep the sleep of the innocent like characters in *The Tempest.*

> A dreamy divagation
> begins in the night,
> a gentle, auditory,
> slow hallucination....
>
> In the creakings and noises,
> an old conversation
> — not concerning us,
> but recognizable, somewhere,
> back in the bus.

Bishop's use of *divagation* signals the dream-like bucolic state identified by Schama as the antonym of "primitive panic," with its "gentle, auditory" spell reminiscent of Caliban's admonition to his disoriented and drunken captors, Trinculo and Stephano: "Be not afeard: the isle is full of noises, / Sounds and sweet airs that give delight and hurt not" (Shakespeare III.ii.131–2). The voices that alternately wake and lull Caliban on Prospero's enchanted isle are evoked by the "Grandparents' voices / uninterruptedly / talking, in Eternity," waking and lulling the speaker and other passengers aboard the dented bus whose schedule and route along the road operates in a different time than the dream time within. Although there are no "thousand twangling instruments" here (III.ii.133), there are "creakings and noises." And as in the play, the quotidian gives way to hints of the supernatural, the ancestral world:

"Yes..." that peculiar
affirmative. "Yes..."
A sharp, indrawn breath,
half groan, half acceptance,
that means "Life's like that.
We know *it* (also death)."

Talking the way they talked
in the old featherbed,
peacefully, on and on,
dim lamplight in the hall,
down in the kitchen, the dog,
tucked in her shawl.

Now, it's all right now
even to fall asleep
just as on all those nights.
— Suddenly the bus driver
stops with a jolt,
turns off his lights.

Like "At the Fishhouses," where the seal interrupts and transforms the narrative, precipitating the speaker's delving beyond the surface world of appearances which she heretofore has hesitated to do, a moose jarringly intrudes on the dream-state of the community aboard the moving bus. As the bus stops and the lights are turned off, bringing the occupants into the relative darkness of the moose's moonlit world, the flux that has so far dominated the poem is replaced by a momentary stasis: "A moose has come out of / the impenetrable wood / and stands there, looms, rather, / in the middle of the road." In the moment of interaction, if we can call it that, between moose and machine — that is, as the animal "approaches" and "sniffs at / the bus's hot hood" — the poem portrays a direct meeting of mechanized Western culture and nature, which, according to the poem's dictum, are seen as separate yet entwined and sharing in the same realm of existence in this one moment. The moose is "grand, otherworldly" as "she looks the bus over"; she is "Taking her time"; yet she is also "homely as a house / (or, safe as houses)." And the moment — the shared time of moose and humans — is epiphanic for the passengers, who "exclaim in whispers, / childishly, softly, / 'Sure are big creatures.' / 'It's awful plain.' / 'Look! It's a she!'" Like the numinous moment of encounter between Bradstreet and the bird she calls Philomel, this *time* brings a fleeting clarity to both individual and group: an "Awareness of self [that] is emotional, not rational. It is an event, not a construction. It is experienced, not known. It is lived, not abstracted. It is received, not perceived. It is a gift, not an accomplishment" (Livingston 117). Hence, the poem asks a question that encompasses the communal and alludes to the inarticulate, that which cannot be said but can be addressed with a question, which Bishop's speaker poignantly asks: "Why, why do we feel / (we all feel) this sweet / sensation of joy?" The poet carefully repeats the first-person plural pronoun and adds "all," to stake out the "civilized" human response to such moments.

And yet there is a problem here: following the question so typical of Bishop is a remark by "our quiet driver," "Curious creatures," about which Lorrie Goldensohn uncovers a striking — and, it could be added, disconcerting — gloss in a letter by Bishop to Marianne Moore describing "a dreadful trip" by bus:

> ...just as it was getting light, the driver had to stop suddenly for a big cow moose who was wandering down the road. She walked away very slowly into the woods, looking at us over her shoulder. The driver said that one foggy night he had to stop while a huge bull moose came right up and smelled the engine. "Very curious beasts," he said [*Letters* 141].

What Goldensohn puts a finger on here is Bishop's "early decision" (the poem took twenty-six years to complete) "to elide the driver's mention of the bull moose encounter and to take his 'curious beasts' to refer only to the cow moose at hand, ... making explicit the poem's embrace of a benevolent female Nature" (253). While the word *curious* recalls the seal gazing at the speaker of "At the Fishhouses," it also invokes Thomas Hooker's injunction against "the study of curiosity." The decision on Bishop's part to leave out the fact of the potentially malevolent bull in order to focus solely on the apparently gentler female contradicts the view of nature given at the close of "At the Fishhouses." If it was the more aggressive male of the species that, in point of fact, sniffed at the engine, why change it? Readers familiar with this animal could wonder whether the fact of the male, known to charge and be potentially dangerous, would preclude the experience of "joy" that "we all feel," whether the question the poem asks would not therefore be rendered specious by the overwhelming feeling, rather, of impending threat and brutal animal power. Bishop here wants, it seems obvious, to have it both ways: to be able at once to trigger the experience of awe and domestication, and to be sane and civilized about it, even about the mingled "smell of moose" and "acrid / smell of gasoline." James Longenbach, in "Answer to a Question," a poem published in *The Yale Review,* pointedly addresses the problems apparent in Bishop's question (which conspicuously reappears as his poem's epigraph):

> Because our being in the world is not
> A busride through darkest night unless
> We stall midway with our ambivalence.

There is also, says Longenbach, "a longing / To revoke the question posed" (62).

In Act IV of *The Tempest,* to return to that play for a moment, it is Caliban who causes the rupture as he interrupts Prospero's masque, suddenly dispelling the romantic illusion, which in turn precipitates Prospero's well-known speech to Ferdinand. Bishop's moose constitutes a device that likewise functions to interrupt the masque-like journey of the passengers on the bus and vex their minds; but this moose, unlike Caliban, does not in any way threaten the civilized, domesticated passengers with disorder and death. Reality of some kind is implied, but Bishop evades total accuracy, the complete truth about nature addressed in the questions posed by Northrop Frye that are discussed in the Introduction to this study: "Are there two natures, and if so are they separable?" Bishop's question, by contrast, quite arguably amounts to a capitulation to an urge to order like the one found in Bradstreet's "Contemplations," surrendering to the opaque cultural media that her own Crusoe looks through, giving way to the bliss that, in fact, her other poems interrogate. In this poem, at any rate, she wants, in the words of Simon Schama regarding the intention behind his *Landscape and Memory,* "to show ... that the cultural habits of humanity have always made room for the sacredness of nature. All our landscapes, from the city park to the mountain hike, are imprinted with our tenacious, inescapable obsessions" (Schama 18). So too this oft-read and commented-on poem by Elizabeth Bishop appears imprinted with like-minded obsessions. But it bends the knee to its own artifice, like a park, like the moose it asks us to revere. It creates an intersection between culture and nature but on the former's terms, something that Bishop manages so admirably to avoid in, say, "Crusoe in England." Even though the battered bus wends its way inland from the sea, there is a puzzling absence of the recognition that culture originates *in* nature, and that nature is indifferent, cool to that fact. Here, instead, is a nature that is gentler, more approachable, precipitating joy, *for* us, for *all* of us — assuming, in fact, what the human response will be, ignoring the fact that some humans would prefer to shoot the moose and would find their joy in that. The poem and its question imply, as Schama seriously argues regarding humanized landscapes, that we do not have "to trade in our cultural legacy or its posterity," which, given the ecological crisis at hand in the form of a rapidly overheating planet, at the very least recognizes that this one-sided view of the human/nature relationship might, as Schama himself admits, entail a "facile consolation" (18).

Getting Below the Boat

"The Fish," by contrast, does not give way to consolation. This poem, indeed, provides a coming to terms with nature and the human impact on nature that can stand alongside the masterful "At the Fishhouses" discussed earlier in this chapter. An early poem published in *North & South* with "The Map" and "Florida," "The Fish" admirably portrays the complexities and contradictions found in the very human relationship with nature. In this tale recounting the capture of a large, old fish, Bishop is as true as any Western, civilized person can be both to wild nature and to the civilized tendency to scape it. The fish in this poem is a kind of scape, both of land and sea; and Bishop's similes indicate the need to find ways to describe undomesticated animal life, scarred by human contact. But unlike "The Moose," where the cow moose is related to by way of tropes that compare her "otherworldly" presence to human structures like house and church, the fish is seen more fully and equitably in terms of both the human and nonhuman. Although its skin is "like wallpaper" and its bottom lip "weaponlike," and while the hooks trailing from its mouth are "Like medals with their ribbons / frayed and wavering," the poem's other similes are drawn from nature: the wallpaper contains "shapes like full-blown roses," the flesh is "packed in like feathers," and the swim-bladder is "like a big peony" (*CP* 42). To be sure, each of the latter similes stretches to imply the human as well — the roses are on the wallpaper; the flesh is by extension a comforter; and the bladder looks like a favored botanical denizen of almost any European or North American garden.[92] The human

and natural worlds mingle and mesh here almost without the reader noticing. Neither world counterpoints the other; neither is idealized. Although
the fish is "tremendous," he is also "battered" and, like the moose,
"homely"—by which the reader could understand not just the current
meaning (plain, almost ugly) but also more archaic definitions such as
"belonging to the home" and "at home with" (*OED*). Evoking the natural world that the speaker is directly connected to by her fishing line, which
holds the fish temporarily against the side of her boat, the fish's body is
representative of nature itself: ancient, diseased, entropic, beautiful. It is
"infested / with tiny white sea-lice" and strives for "the terrible oxygen";
the gills are "frightening" because they "can cut so badly." The eyes are
bigger than the speaker's but, like the goats on Crusoe's island, do not
return her "stare," and as she examines the fish she uses yet another simile in her genuine and time-limited attempt to connect beyond the material line that holds him in her part of the world they both share:

> — It was more like the tipping
> of an object toward the light.
> I admired his sullen face,
> the mechanism of his jaw.

While he is to the speaker an object, like a piece of art or something
mechanical — in other words, nonhuman — she cannot help but let slip a
personifier as she describes his face as "sullen." Likewise, the bevy of hooks,
leaders, and lines that trail from the fish's mouth are "a five-haired beard
of wisdom." Hence, very human values are ascribed to the fish (he *is* valu-
able) to get at his history of interaction with and escape from humans.

The fish *is* humanized, groomed nature, nature imposed on by culture and carrying in its contours and geography the human imprint, a history of contact. The speaker's "victory" is poignant and ambiguous. Is the
speaker's "victory" a victory over the fish or is it over the previous five
humans who have tried and failed to catch this, their prey? Can triumph,
for a poet of the modernist era, be invoked other than ironically, as the
fish who "didn't fight" lies in "the pool of bilge / where oil had spread"?
The "little rented boat," too, is battered and homely in its way, rusted and
"sun-cracked." And, of course, the speaker tells us in the last line that she
"let the fish go," presumably removing her own, the sixth, hook from the
mouth of the fish before she did so. This is her "rainbow" moment, which
is also clearly elegiac, as she captures not just a fish but the nuanced and

ultimately estranged relationship of humanity to nature, all of it swirling with oxygen, blood, water, and oil, this last component in particular the one on which the global human enterprise perilously operates.

It is in "The Riverman," however, that Elizabeth Bishop succeeds in evoking a relationship with nature that is non–Western. Found in the *Questions of Travel* volume with its Amazonian quest for interiority, the poem conjures a human voice that speaks from the interior and the bottom, "that magic mud" of the Amazon River. The inquisitive, Western, outsider voice is gone, replaced here by one that seeks another, much older kind of knowledge, the lore of the shaman who can shapeshift like nature itself already does. If the first-person speaker of "The Fish" tells her angling tale from the vantage point of the lone angler sitting in her boat (who brings up a nonhuman creature of the deep to share the — to him — caustic air with her before she gives him back again), the first-person narrator of "The Riverman" goes *below the boat* to speak to his human family: "your canoes are over my head; / I hear your voices talking" (*CP* 109).

This is a transformation narrative to rival anything in Ovid. In fact, here we encounter another form of the Acteon myth in which a lone male is changed by the goddess into a lifeform that retains human consciousness and memory. Unlike Acteon, however, the Riverman goes willingly into the metamorphosis experience, entering the river to meet the Brazilian serpent goddess Luandinha and her consort, the Dolphin, who initiate the Riverman into a new kind of consciousness and being, "in a language I didn't know / ... [but] understood, like a dog, / although I can't speak it yet." A "tall, beautiful serpent / in elegant white satin," Luandinha invites this man into her river world where she is having a party. She meets with her human visitor three times until he (in contrast to Bradstreet) begins to change both physically and ethically: "the river smells in my hair," his extremities are cold, and, he tells us, "I don't eat fish any more." As he returns to the human world, he begins to reassess what it means to be human, to have a house, wife, family, village, to live in counterpoint to nature. He knows now that there are nonhuman beings "under my canoe" as well as a spirit world around him. He also wishes he could find "a virgin mirror / no one's ever looked at" that will reflect back at him not the human world with its vanities and ego constructs but the invisible spiritual reality about which he is newly conscious. By the close of the poem, the Riverman has joined that nonhuman world within the river:

You can peer down and down
or dredge the river bottom
but never, never catch me.
When the moon shines and the river
lies across the earth
and sucks it like a child,
then I will go to work
to get you health and money.

The Riverman's below-the-boat point of view with its discovery of ancient knowledge rooted in the mud and silt of the Amazon contrasts with Crusoe's tormented question as his ego fragments: "Why didn't I know enough of something?" Once Crusoe's transformation has been established, he cannot return to his native English perspective, even though he physically returns to his homeland. Crusoe is permanently caught between his experience in nature and his cultural conditioning.

The Riverman, however, speaks to and for his community. He reminds them that "everything we need / can be obtained from the river" and that he will "be there below" working on behalf of his kinship network to improve their lives. Implicit in the connection between the speaker and his audience is his audience's understanding and acceptance of his metamorphosis. As Debra Picchi writes concerning the Bakairí of Brazil:

> The Bakairí believe in the existence of a sacred realm that is inhabited by supernatural beings who live inside such things as animals and plants.... These beings can be seen by people, but they typically stay hidden.... Spirits sometimes can be contacted and even manipulated by *shamans*, who are religious semispecialists. These individuals, through long and arduous periods of training, learn to contact and direct specific spirits with whom they have special personal relationships. Through the intercession of these supernatural beings, shamans are able to cure diseases and to perform sorcery against their enemies.... The power of these spirits is very strong and ultimately derives from the river [Picchi 134].

The speaker's culture retains its ties to nature, represented here by the serpent, making his initiation possible so that he can go back and forth between his village and the river. The Riverman is following what Anne Baring and Jules Cashford call "The coiling path of the serpent, like the great rivers of the earth winding from mountain to sea, [that] traces the spiralling of the life energy as it travels from one dimension to another" (64). Luandinha is one form of "the Goddess of the Lower Waters" who "appears in many different mythologies as the creative source or generator of the universe" (64). Likewise, the Amazon River Dolphin or Boto, held sacred by indigenous peoples in the Amazon and Orinoco basins can be seen in terms of the Fish Goddess, "the Mistress of Life and Death, a generative womb" (Gimbutas 260). The point of view rendered by "The Riverman" stands in stark contrast not just to "The Fish" but also to many Western texts, from *Beowulf,* in which the eponymous Christianized hero descends into the realm of the Goddess, Grendel's mother, to kill her, to *Moby-Dick,* in which Ahab makes war on the White Whale. Western culture cannot accept, in the words of Paul Shepard, "the ambiguity of life living on death," which is absolutely central to nature, and it therefore cannot fully recognize "the spiritual nature of nonhuman life," losing what "The Riverman" celebrates: "traditions of human membership in natural communities embedded in place and ancestry" (*Others* 506).

SIX

Amy Clampitt:
"Let There Be Sundews"

Dark Water

In her essay on St. Paul, Amy Clampitt describes her embrace of Christianity, the way having been "prepared by exposure to music and painting, as well as to the writing of the likes of Dante, Donne, Hopkins, and (I dare say) T.S. Eliot" (*Predecessors* 103). For Clampitt, this conversion was not merely a gesture, but rather a confirmation of what she had already begun by tracing and plumbing "the sorrow / of things moving back to where they came from" (*CPAC* 25). Simply to look behind her was not enough, however; as we have seen in "Westward," she wanted also to *be there* as far as she could, to write from the point of view of the "landscapes of untended memory" (*CPAC* 43). Christianity, she conceded, had "its institutional horrors" but it nonetheless bore witness to what for Clampitt was fact: "that what is most real is the incorporeal," which is "here and now" (*Predecessors* 106). She took note of the modern physicists bearing this out in science (106), even as she was translating Canto IX of Dante's *Inferno* and, in the same volume, which would be her last, wondering about the "uncodifed," her term in one late poem, "Bayou Afternoon," for the metaphysical reality that at times seems to glimmer at the edge of nature (*CPAC* 393).[93]

For an established American poet of the postmodern era to be persistently curious about such things is, one would think, both unusual and risky. Yet Clampitt followed her instinct, not just to wade into the natural world but to delve "beyond / the surf-roar on the other side of silence / we should die of (George Eliot / declared) were we to hear it," cognizant of the fact that "Many / have already died of it" and that, on top of this,

175

nature itself contains puzzling horrors (*CPAC* 108). In various places in her poems, Clampitt makes this latter fact abundantly clear, from the "Serengeti lions" of "Good Friday" looking up from their bloody kill, to the "forked lightning's / split-second disaster" found in "Meridian" (*CPAC* 68 & 18), both early poems that are true to Clampitt's willingness to artic- ulate what E.O. Wilson calls "[t]he reverse side of nature's green-and-gold, ... the black-and-scarlet of disease and death" (*TFOL* 141). Amy Clampitt knew this. She also knew full well that a morality commensurate with Chris- tianity cannot be found in nature, that, as she writes in "A Hermit Thrush,"

> Whatever moral lesson might commend itself,
> there's no use drawing one,
> there's nothing here
> to seize on as exemplifying any so-called virtue [*CPAC* 272].

All this being the case, transcending nature — forging into and beyond it — is a central task for Clampitt, and in the aftermath of her death in 1994 a critical discussion of this aspect of her project has just begun. Her search for the "uncodified" is ubiquitous in her poetry, and in her medi- tative forays into the American wilderness she evinces an eco-theological sensibility unique among her contemporaries. Certainly she does not use her excursions to convert others to her religious stance. What, instead, she consistently displays, in lyrics that are at once grand and devotional, is the quality Robert Bly admires in Federico Garcia Lorca, and what Lorca called *duende*, "the sense of the presence of death":

> Duende involves a kind of elation when death is present in the room. It is associated with "dark" sounds; and when a poet has duende inside him, he brushes past death with each step, and in the presence associates fast ... [Bly 49].

Clearly this is what Clampitt does as well, perhaps in part because of her advancing age at the time her poems began to appear in public,[94] but also because she recognized that what nature offers (if not guarantees) to the solitary pilgrim in its midst is death. And by the time Clampitt was writ- ing "Sed de Correr," the poem discussed at the end of Chapter Three of this volume, her own death was imminent and Lorca was weighing on her imagination, Lorca who (as Bly quotes him) remarked, "The magical qual- ity of a poem consists in its being always possessed by the duende, so that whoever beholds it is baptized with dark water" (Bly 50).

This is an apt image for what Clampitt does, especially in her final volume, *A Silence Opens* (1994), where at least half of the twenty-eight poems attempt the depths of nature's dark water, invoking *duende*. Death, writes J.D. McClatchy, is "the subject that has consistently animated [Clampitt's] work" (McClatchy 312). If in an earlier piece like "Savannah," she could write of "A stillness / out there" (*CPAC* 318), she would in her last work return fearlessly to this theme. In "Bayou Afternoon," watching a bird "called the spoonbill, back from / a rim known as extinction," she also sees

> the rim we
> necessarily inhabit, a happenstance
> still brimming, still uncodified [*CPAC* 393].

In "'Eighty-Nine," she has "inklings / of undoing ... having made one's peace with / whatever the elements can do."

> Or almost.
> For beyond that peace is the shape of
> calamity nobody is ever
> ready for [*CPAC* 408].

And in "Homeland," a remembered storm cellar called "the Cave" was "witness ... to unmitigated terror," brought on by the howling gale outside (418).

Attempting forthrightly to investigate nature alongside — paradoxically — the Christian hope of transcendence, Clampitt also delineates the parameters of human culture and history, consistently finding their roots in the very mystery she sets out to explore. "[A] / wilderness swallows you up," she writes in an early poem about the carnivorous plant, the sundew, although she does not, like Bradstreet, try to control the experience via poetic form or ideology (*CPAC* 15). Instead, Clampitt allows such experience to shape form and encounter faith, without throwing away either.[95] Simultaneously, she neither overturns the old creeds of the Church or attempts to revise what she finds in nature, making it acceptable to her, her audience, or the creeds she has embraced. What she does do, however, is to uncover questions about how things specifically human — things as various as remorse, barbed wire, landfill, and syntax — are related to, rather than separate from, nature, and how this fact needs to be *remembered*. History does not exist in some absolute textbook; it is, rather, "the shadowy predatory tentshow" (*CPAC* 375) that has risen within us, and which we conjure out of our botched memories and imaginings of the past, our predilection for telling stories.

In this chapter, then, the project is threefold: first, to set forth Clampitt's unique approach to the biosphere, particularly in the poems with which she opens *The Kingfisher,* poems that constitute not only approach, but reapproach and walking in, and that announce a pattern found throughout her body of work; second, to notice the human arti-facts that, for Clampitt, find both their source and end in nature, under-mining the erroneous and destructive notion that the human world, with its "winking imaginary map that leaps / from the minds of the computer programmers" (*CPAC* 137), is an unrelated entity "fabricated through accumulating tradition to stand in the place of natural, biological, inher-ent ways of being" (Livingston 10); and, finally, to observe and analyze Clampitt's theology, what J.D. McClatchy calls "Her religious tempera-ment, which seeks both to accommodate the world and transcend it" (312), noticing how she brings both God and nature to the poetic table, and hence closes in on the problems faced by Anne Bradstreet and Eliz-abeth Bishop.

Facing the Ocean: Origins of Culture, Part 3

Approach to nature is central to "The Cove," the first poem in *The Kingfisher* (*CPAC* 5). Here Clampitt acknowledges her predecessors and proclaims her major themes: westward human movement and the dynamic, non–dualistic relationship between nature and culture. If the import of Mozart and Marianne Moore is made explicit in the opening lines of this poem, the influence of Elizabeth Bishop is made hardly less unequivocal in the portrayal of setting: "the snug house" next to "a pavement of ocean, at times / wrinkling like tinfoil, at others / all isinglass flakes." These are lines that clearly acknowledge poems such as "At the Fishhouses," "The End of March," and "The Fish." The setting is, however, all Clampitt's. She begins the poem, and hence the whole of her *oeuvre,* inside a house much like that which Bishop, in "The End of March," imagines retiring; and it is from this place that Clampitt studies the natural world, working outwards from the civilized interior:

> Inside the snug house, blue willow-ware
> plates go round the dado, cross-stitch
> domesticates the guest room, whole nutmegs
> inhabit the spice rack, and when there's fog
> or a gale we get a fire going, listen
> to Mozart, read Marianne Moore, or
> sit looking out at the eiders, trig
> in their white-over-black as they tip
> and tuck themselves into the swell, almost
> as though diving under the eiderdown
> in a *gemütlich* hotel room at Innsbruck.

This is no "crypto-dream house," boarded-up and viewed wistfully from the outside, its interior a matter for dreamy conjecture, but a real one where Clampitt the poet already resides and where she and her company project the details of domesticity, cheerful and cozy as an Austrian hotel room. The opening stanza is replete with the civilized, with the modern, established urbanity of the eastern seaboard that extends the *gemütlich* of the Old World. Clampitt here uses almost the same term Aldous Huxley does in his scathing criticism of Wordsworth's view of nature ("that chaste, mild deity who presides over the *Gemüthlichkeit*, the prettiness, the cozy sublimities of the Lake District"), except that Clampitt employs the word to describe the view projected from the cultured interior of a New World house. Every object and action within the house has its niche, from the plates encircling the top of the wall to the activities scheduled during inclement weather.

The second stanza, however — and also the second sentence — turns this world to the presumed vertical perspective of a nonhuman organism living immediately outside the house, alongside the eiders:

> At dusk we watch a porcupine, hoary
> quadruped, emerge from under the spruce trees,
> needle-tined paddle tail held out straight
> behind, as though the ground were negotiable
> only by climbing, to examine the premises,
> and then withdraw from the (we presume)
> alarming realm of the horizontal into
> the up-and-down underbrush of normality.

Here Clampitt signals her deft ability to take herself out of the house, to realign the sensual and civilized human perspective, suddenly and without warning, with what she perceives in nature. Indeed, this realignment, which is really a paradigm shift, takes place in a way that strikingly recalls the character of Sylvia in Sarah Orne Jewett's "A White Heron," when the girl climbs a massive old-growth pine tree to the very top and finds as a result that her orientation to nonhuman life — in this case a pair of white herons nesting in a nearby marsh — is revolutionized. Clampitt's field of vision relative to the civilized human world she inhabits, the relative normality that she ushers us into quite comfortably in the first stanza, undergoes supple, unassuming suspension as it is replaced with the porcupine's prickly, vertical world view that exists at a right angle with the speaker's, whose frame then rights itself in the third stanza as it turns to a turtle "as it hove eastward, a covered / wagon intent on the wrong direction." Immersing herself in the nonhuman biotic world outside her door, Clampitt begins, in the terms of the ecologist Aldo Leopold, "thinking like a mountain" (Nash, *RON* 64). The reader can almost feel the speaker's neck and head momentarily assume the vertical perspective of the porcupine, only to return to the horizontal in order to observe the turtle. The turtle, seen now "From the sundeck, overhung by a gale- / hugged mountain ash, limbs blotched / and tufted with lichen," reinforces the nonhuman perspective as Clampitt playfully projects on to it the common American image of the westering covered wagon.

The poem's four stanzas, each one a single sentence, transfer spatial and visual perspective from house to spruce trees to sundeck and then, finally, to the rocks on the shore at low tide. The outward thrust into the cove itself brings point of view to bear on the sea, presaging the poet's "epic theme," her backward and eastward gaze at westward-migrating humanity, what she calls *transhumance*.[96] The language also indicates that nature has its own culture: that indeed nature is always organizing itself into patterns, albeit patterns on which humans project the designs with which they themselves are most familiar. Hence, says "The Cove," when we look, we also tend to domesticate; we "bring [nature] into our house" (Livingston 15), or vice-versa — we bring our interior, domesticated world with us into nature. So, in the final stanza, we see "a pavement of ocean, at times / wrinkling like tinfoil." But then Clampitt carefully proceeds beyond the Bishopian imagery to something that "can't be looked at," though the sea is still initially likened to the familiar: "a curtain wall just frescoed / indigo." The indigo, however, becomes "so immense a hue" it surpasses description and almost cannot be observed, while the lighthouse that "pulses, even / in daylight," can nonetheless, it is implied, still be seen. The final two lines, "in daylight, a lighthouse, light- / pierced like a needle's eye," emphasize the brightness of the lighthouse standing over the cove; but even this condensation of light and its disparate sources, with *light* repeated pulse-like in the penultimate line, does not preclude observation.

Three more sentences make up the respective three stanzas of "Fog," the poem which follows "The Cove" and whose subject literally envelopes the former light and "immense" blue down by the rocks: "A vagueness comes over everything, / as though proving color and contour / alike dispensable." The lighthouse is now "extinct," the human dwellings "reverting into the lost / and forgotten." The fog is "the / universal emulsion" that takes everything into itself, changing even the ocean, formerly "like tinfoil" or "all isinglass flakes, or sun-pounded / gritty glitter of mica," to a different order of sensory experience: an Emersonian "mumble." Again Clampitt disorients the reader by revealing how the usual markers of human experience get obviated or confused, much like Melville does in the Masthead chapter in *Moby-Dick* or as Bishop does in the dizzying dream reported at the close of "The Unbeliever": "The spangled sea below wants me to fall. / It is hard as diamonds; it wants to destroy us all" (Bishop *CP* 22).

Here Clampitt not only reverts to the tactile and auditory, she grafts vision on to them, creating out of fog a form of synaesthesia, uniting in her consciousness her sensory experience with the apparent objective reality into which she forages. Next to the ocean's "mumble" are "panicled / foxtail and needlegrass, / dropseed, furred hawkweed." Far from limiting experience, fog "opens up rooms," providing a "showcase" in the now figurative inner house of experience that has been subtly transposed from the "snug" one of the previous poem. The moment approaches the hallucinatory, the poet imagining how Georgia O'Keefe might paint the sound of foghorn as the inner whorl of a flower without hue, replacing the immensity that "can't be looked at." Associating fast, Clampitt couples "nodding" with "campanula," "ticking" with "filigree," and thus also condenses not only sense experience but nature and culture: bell buoys become bell-shaped flowers; bird voices evoke the delicate tracery of gold and silver. Ecological writers such as Al Gore and E.O. Wilson have urgently asserted that it is on just such altered perceptions of the world that human survival hinges. "It is in human mental development," writes Wilson, "that the perceptions of living Nature and human nature unite" (*Creation* 63). Similarly, Gore argues that "Our capacity for consciousness and abstract thought in no way separates us from nature" (Gore 160).

If "Opacity / opens up rooms" in "Fog," the return of light in "Gradual Clearing" reveals "a texture / not to be spoken of above a whisper." In a single sentence, Clampitt completes the opening trilogy of poems about facing eastward toward the Atlantic, each with its own outward-thrusting movement from the known to the unknown. Point of view in this poem is towards "the half-invisible / cove" as "the fog / wrung itself out like a sponge." As the fog gradually lifts, and vision is restored, perspective, signaled by the use of metaphor grounded in the human world, is also regained, but only to be removed again. The fog lifts in "wisps and scarves." Using syntax that mimics the pucker and "tatting" of experience, Clampitt relies on exotic textile metaphors to correlate to restored vision: "plissé," "peau-de-soie," and "percale" provide an alliterative trio of materials that evoke a slow smoothing out caught by the human eye. Ironically, however, this moment in which vision is regained is also one where the tactility invoked in "Fog" is absorbed by the inarticulate.

The end of "Gradual Clearing" and the beginning of "The Outer Bar," which immediately follows, naturally merge with one another. As the former poem closes with an opening into both the unknown beheld in nature and the historically-known found on the eastern horizon, it also constitutes a natural segue into the poet's account of an offshore foray. The image of "the lip of a cave" found at the end of "Gradual Clearing" anticipates exploration of the unknown just as the alternative lip "of a cavernous, / single, pearl- / engendering seashell" recalls the line with which Bishop paradoxically closes "Over 2,000 Illustrations and a Complete Concordance": " — and looked and looked our infant sight away." And indeed, the act of entering, of stepping into, the unknown is what "The Outer Bar" begins with:

> When through some lacuna, chink, or interstice
> in the unlicensed free-for-all that goes
> on without a halt out there all day, all night,
> all through the winter,
>
> one morning at low tide you walk dry-shod across
> a shadow isthmus to the outer bar.

As Clampitt observes in a note on the poem, the bar refers to "a bar island off the coast of Maine" precariously attached by a reef to another, inner bar. She quotes Louise Dickinson Rich: "But you can't stay very long. The minute the tide turns you have to start back" (*CPAC* 435). Hence, "lacuna [the empty spot in bone or tissue], chink, or interstice" constitute the figurative, transient portals for the poet's venture beyond shoreline and inner bar, and into "the unlicensed free-for-all," the oceanic ditch that so troubled and entranced the settlers of Anne Bradstreet's era.

With its second-person point of view, this is a poem replete with Lorca's *duende,* as well as with, it should be added, the ominous side of American Transcendentalism found in Herman Melville. Crossing the "shadow isthmus to the outer bar," the poet becomes a pilgrim who, on entering the wilderness, knows that, except for a few artifacts, she leaves the human world "Back in the village."[97] The speaker's world is relinquished at the "shadow isthmus" with its "dry-shod" crossing, after which "you find yourself, once over, sinking at every step / into a luscious mess —"

> a vegetation of unbarbered, virgin, foot-thick
> velvet, the air you breathe an aromatic
> thicket, odors in confusion starting up,
> at every step like partridges,
> or schools of fishes.

The poet/pilgrim now finds herself in the thrice-repeated "out there": "an element you swim through / as to an unplanned, headily illicit / interview." This is an order of things utterly other than, and indifferent to, the civilized human one, as evidenced by the fate of the made objects found by the speaker: the "familiar portents" that constitute an alien "rim" of reminders, reminders of death and of just how fragile human culture is.

So the scene becomes one in which the human is incidental and its history is easily obliterated. The "silhouetted shipwreck" foregrounds "The light out there, gashed / by the surf's scimitar," which "is blinding, a rebuke — Go back! Go back!" The warning, of course, is also entirely human, a projection of panic buttressed by the fact that the shipwreck's history is unknown and the speaker's queries in the nearby village go unanswered. Likewise, a bellbuoy the speaker observes is "a blood-red-painted harbinger" of the "lawless" cosmos "out there." The irony for Clampitt is that both ship and buoy are transfigured by the forces of nature into horrifying signifiers of that order. Established thus in a kind of natural hell, they are "chain-gang archangels" damned to eternal repetition. Borrowing almost directly from Hopkins' "The Windhover," Clampitt describes the "prismatic / frenzy" of human artifacts as they "fall, gall and gash the daylight / out there, all through the winter."

The destiny of human culture is stressed again in "Beach Glass" (*CPAC* 11), a present-tense account of a walk on the beach that not only extends Clampitt's exploration of the limen between land and sea but reflects Elizabeth Bishop's concerns in poems such as "At the Fishhouses" and "The End of March" (not to mention "The Map" and "Crusoe in England"). Both poets stress nature's indifference to human existence using oceanic imagery. If the sea in "Fishhouses" is "icily free above the stones, / above the stones and then the world," in "Beach Glass" it "goes on shuffling its millenniums / of quartz, granite, and basalt." For Bishop the "indifferently swinging" sea becomes a metaphor for "what we imagine knowledge to be," while in similar fashion Clampitt sees the ocean's "random / impartiality" as signifying

> an intellect
> engaged in the hazardous
> redefinition of structures
> no one has yet looked at.

And both poets discover the flotsam and jetsam of human culture — the "lengths and lengths, endless, of wet white string" in Bishop's case in "The End of March"; and, in Clampitt's, a wider array of what she calls "the permutations of novelty —/ driftwood and shipwreck, last night's / beer cans, spilt oil, the coughed-up / residue of plastic." Bishop's "over and over" phrase, describing the action of water on these vestiges of civilization, which she uses in both "Fishhouses" and "The End of March," is itself repeated by Clampitt: "turning the same thing over and over, / over and over." The territory is so obviously Bishop's that, like the plethora of empty "mussels and periwinkles / ... abandoned" on the beach Clampitt walks, "it's hopeless / to know which to salvage." She takes her cue from the ocean, however, for whom "nothing / is beneath consideration," and finds her motif in what she calls "beach glass" —

> amber of Budweiser, chrysoprase
> of Almadén and Gallo, lapis
> by way of (no getting around it,

184

I'm afraid) Phillips'
Milk of Magnesia.

This passage gives Clampitt her tack, allowing her to move into her own territory, away from the ironic Romanticism created by Bishop — and apparent in a poem like "The End of March" with its cold wind, fickle "lion sun," and boarded-up "crypto-dream-house" whose bare interior she can only imagine. It is the "process" that Clampitt, by contrast, wants to get to, the thing that "goes on forever," washing, eroding, grinding the artifacts of human history:

> they came from sand,
> they go back to gravel,
> along with the treasuries
> of Murano, the buttressed
> astonishments of Chartres,
> which even now are readying
> for being turned over and over.

The "process" of finding what Arctic explorer Barry Lopez in another but similar context calls "the odd but ubiquitous piece of plastic, a strict reminder against romance" (Lopez 310) constitutes Amy Clampitt's agenda as well, her "hazardous / redefinition of structures": her willingness to tread and sift through the same sand Bishop has, yet go beyond the "thick white snarl" of string, the "sodden ghost," to explore and delineate the ways in which nature works things over particle by particle. Like the story behind the worn, animistic knife in "Crusoe" or the hymns sung in "Fish-houses," both of which Bishop more readily and powerfully develops, Clampitt's beach glass connotes the origins and destiny of culture, and at the same time manifests her own poetic voice and thematic concerns. She is, in a real sense, serving notice: she will follow the wire Bishop sees attaching her dream house on the beach "to something off behind the dunes."[98]

Nature Holds the Mirror

For Amy Clampitt, this "something off behind the dunes" is God, a God not wholly unlike the transcendent entity worshipped by the settlers of Anne Bradstreet's era.[99] The "hideous wilderness" that the seventeenth-

185

century Puritans maintained was in moral opposition to their deity, and that in Bradstreet's best-known poem, "Contemplations," has pattern and embroidery imposed on it from without, is unflinchingly examined by Clampitt. And much like Elizabeth Bishop, Clampitt finds in nature evidence not only of beauty but of the repugnant, the indifferent, even the malevolent—in other words, "the twin oceans of horror and beauty" described by Clampitt's contemporary, Annie Dillard (Dillard 69). Yet Clampitt goes beyond overturning the nature/culture dichotomy, daring to bring the whole problem of wilderness and culture, which so reverberates throughout American history and literature, full circle, back to the "inklings of an omnipresence" (*CPAC* 292) cast out, lost, or (by some) sorely missed in the twentieth and twenty-first centuries.

Hence, the two poems that follow "Beach Glass" constitute the endgame of Clampitt's opening announcement of her own *poesis,* replete with predecessors, which she achieves by portraying her pilgrimage into the elemental stuff of nature itself. After the prognosis for civilization given in "Beach Glass," she turns to describing the ocean, attending solely to its surface. "Marine Surface, Low Overcast" is another poem comprised of one sentence—one where appearance is reality or, rather, a series of realities, and surface (which continually reflects, refracts, and filters light) becomes depth. The surface of the sea is "a stuff so single / it might almost be lifted." But it is also multivarious in form and texture: among other things, a reflection of living sky ("this / herringbone of albatross") as well as "a suede of meadow" and "laminae of living tissue." Still, the first six stanzas, tour-de-force that they are, are no mere celebration of the sea, or of its mystery, but an argument with a single point whose force gathers with the momentum of the poem/sentence, and is then released. The ever-changing oceanic qualities are those which, finally,

> no loom, no spinneret, no forge, no factor,
> no process whatsoever, patent
> applied or not applied for,
> no five-year formula, no fabric
> for which pure imagining,
> except thus prompted,
> can invent the equal.

Clampitt again uses the word *process,* but this is a different kind of process than the natural one described in the preceding poem. The marine process "goes on forever," while the human one of manufacturing — of making things — is of another, imitative, and thus limited order, although Clampitt excepts the *artistic* process, making a high claim for its reach and origins. If humans come from nature, as Charles Darwin hypothesized, then they come as art-making creatures, as the caves of Altamira, for instance, demonstrate. Only this late in the "process," humans having traveled a great distance — figuratively speaking — from nature, do the arts seem "full of what is profoundly unnatural" (Frye 240).[100] E. O. Wilson comments directly on this when he asks, "[H]ow did natural selection prepare the mind for civilization before civilization existed? That is the great mystery of human evolution: how to account for calculus and Mozart" (*Consilience* 52).

Its opening lines hinging on the close of "Marine Surface, Low Overcast," "The Sun Underfoot Among the Sundews," which follows, completes the former poem's argument regarding the creative and destructive forces found in nature, but only to take the reader into what seems a new problem and yet another argument. Instead of surface that becomes depth, this poem details depth with millions of interior, reflective surfaces as the speaker employs the second person to narrate the experience of wading into a bog filled with the carnivorous sundew:

> A step
> down and you're into it; a
> wilderness swallows you up:
> ankle-, then knee-, then midriff-
> to-shoulder-deep in wetfooted
> understory, an overhead
> spruce-tamarack horizon hinting
> you'll never get out of here.

The insoluble problem — "you'll never get out of here" — is not new. It amounts, rather, to the old Puritan dilemma over what to do about wilderness, what to make of nature at its rawest and most unconstrained and all-encompassing, how best to account for it and yet maintain — or in Clampitt's case, regain — a God worth believing in: "a not-yet-imaginable solstice / past that footstone (O terror) / the unsupported senses cannot cross" (*CPAC* 292). In the poem "Medusa," the problem of wild nature for the Puritans is represented by the figure of the Gorgon, who strikes such a note of fear — of "Terror of origins" — that they revise her, giving her "a new / and siren sliminess. John Milton / put her at the gate of hell" (*CPAC* 211). Like "Marine Surface, Low Overcast," "Medusa" searches for origins, "the sea's heave, the cold mother / of us all."

The Thoreauvian Annie Dillard, writing about Tinker Creek, also puts a finger precisely on what has been (and is) for America the problematic issue of human origins:

> Look: Cock Robin may die the most gruesome of slow deaths, and nature is no less pleased; the sun comes up, the creek rolls on, the survivors still sing. I cannot feel that way about your death, nor you about mine, nor either of us about the robin's — or even the barnacles'. We value the individual supremely, and nature values him not a whit. It looks for the moment as though I might have to reject this creek life unless I want to be utterly brutalized. Is human culture with its values my only real home after all? Can it possibly be that I should move my anchor-hold to the side of a library? This direction of thought brings me abruptly to a fork in the road where I stand paralyzed, unwilling to go on, for both ways lead to madness.
> Either this world, my mother, is a monster, or I myself am a freak [Dillard 176–77].

Dillard, not wanting to choose the first option, ambiguously settles for the second: "I must go to the creek again. It is where I belong" (179).[101] The problem here is that Dillard, like the Puritans, cannot entirely escape the first alternative, that the world is a monster — "I bring human values to the creek, and so save myself from being brutalized" (179) — and this inevitably brings her right back to all the potential for destruction (for the madness she herself identifies at the heart of this dilemma) inherent in the West's attitude towards nature.

This is an ancient and vicious circle for Western culture, and Amy Clampitt clearly knows it and agonizes over it. She tries to avoid it, even as she gets further into "this bog full of sundews, sphagnum- / lined and shaped like a teacup," finding in it an ominous reflection of the world above, a reversal of the convention that art holds the mirror up to nature, as Perseus holds the mirror up to Medusa in order to slay her. Indeed, in "Perseus," which follows "Medusa," Clampitt makes clear that the "intervening mirror" Perseus uses is the gift of the masculinized Athena, and that this mirror is "above all indispensable," allowing this early Western hero to look "at one remove at what he'd vowed to take." If in "Perseus" Clampitt finds a myth to delineate the fatal gap between a patriarchal cul-

ture and the nature it observes and exploits, she removes that gap (or tries
to) in "The Sun Underfoot." Here nature holds the mirror (actually "a
million / of them") up to the artist; Clampitt sees herself in the "webwork
of carnivorous rubies" that she discovers at her feet:

> either
> a First Cause said once, "Let there
> be sundews," and there were, or they've
> made their way here unaided
> other than by that backhand, round-
> about refusal to assume responsibility
> known as Natural Selection.

This "trap set to / unhand unbelieving" also catches gnats; the cock-
leburs are "double-faced." The either/or, like Dillard's, is not straightforward, although the diction reveals which alternative Clampitt tends
towards. Her theistic choice, indeed, is found where "The Sun Underfoot"
begins: "An ingenuity too astonishing / to be quite fortuitous." But it ends
with the reflected world above the poet's head, a reflection in which the
human world is necessarily included, and which therefore obviates alienation. We are part of this "understory," says Clampitt; indeed, we come
from it and are swallowed up by it if we step in this or that direction. In
the words of Paul Shepard (in his formidable essay on the Puritans and
their schizoid relationship to wetlands), "There is an undeniable unconscious substrate in which this muckiness is also the landscape of human
origin" (*Nature and* Madness 83). The poem reminds readers, in an age
when wilderness is threatened with obliteration, that, as E.O. Wilson
writes, "Every person deserves the option to travel easily in and out of the
complex and primal world that gave us birth" (*Creation* 12). Clampitt here
succeeds in evoking the complexity of the natural world of which Wilson
speaks.

Nonetheless, from the dual action of rejecting what she calls the
"impassivity"[102] of Natural Selection and falling upward into the light-filled
cup of the world at her feet, it follows that Clampitt also accepts that the
First Cause, from which both nature and culture would (in this argument)
derive their existence, must also "assume responsibility" for the horrors
found in nature. The phrase necessarily entails more than making a case
against arbitrariness. And this, in a real sense, constitutes part of the "trap"
set by the sundew's millions of mirrors, where the either/or is found —

which helps to explain why Dillard calls these alternatives "The Horns of the Altar": "The creator is no puritan. A creature need not work for a living; creatures may simply steal and suck and be blessed for all that with a share — an enormous share — of the sunlight and air" (233–34). Clampitt shares this uneasiness about the nature of the creation. "[S]he is not," as one early reviewer observes, "merely a 'nature poet'.... [Her] voice is at once that of a frail creature buffeted by natural forces and that of a scientist trying to analyze and transcend those forces" (Morrisroe 45).

In "Good Friday," Clampitt ruminates more thoroughly on the problem of depravity built into nature itself, and thus, inevitably, into culture as well:

> Think of the Serengeti lions looking up,
> their bloody faces no more culpable
> than the acacia's claw on the horizon
> of those yellow plains [*CPAC* 68].

The mystery, then, also lies in the just-as-real fact of human remorse: How did remorse grow out of all this? Indeed, she wonders, "what barbed whimper, what embryo / of compunction, first unsealed the long / compact with a limb-from-limb outrage"? In her extensive endnote to the poem, Clampitt explains her preoccupation with both Christianity and Darwin's theory of Natural Selection, "which for many nowadays has acquired an almost theological authority" (*CPAC* 439). Despite — or perhaps because of— the flaws inherent in both systems of thought, Clampitt gravitates towards the claims of both: they take "suffering seriously," attempting to grapple with the question of evil precipitated by nature, where "silence / still hands down the final statement."

Yet both ideologies also demonstrate the "limb-from-limb outrage" that they try to explain and resolve: what Clampitt calls "the evolving ordonnance of murder" seems to be as imbedded in systems of thought and belief as it is in the food chain. Religion (capitulating to the state's penchant for war) and science (silent about such matters) are vulnerable to becoming tools for inflicting the very evils they claim to want to understand: hence Darwin's "more-than-inkling of the usages / disinterested perception would be put to" as well as Good Friday's role, two thousand years after the death of Christ, as a complex, ritualized means to inoculate that mysterious thing called conscience. So one mystery, the "remorse in the design of the things," leads to another, "the iron / of a righteousness officially exempt / from self-dismay." "Good Friday" begins and ends as *The Kingfisher* as a whole begins and ends: on one side with a portrait of nature and, on the other, with the tangled, horrific fact of human society gone awry, which in the poem's portrayal is first instigated by some prehistoric "innovator ... unsatisfied perhaps with even a lion's / entitlement."

Reading into Amy Clampitt's poetry about nature necessarily involves running headlong into the enigma of human culture. Repeatedly she puzzles over its existence in the face of nature, finding some emblem of the human that begs definition no less than the emblems of nature — to name a few, "a lighthouse" ("The Cove," "A Baroque Sunburst"), "bell buoys" ("Fog" and "The Outer Bar"), broken glass ("Beach Glass"), garbage ("Salvage," "The Reedbeds of the Hackensack"), grief ("Camouflage"), "this grid of homesteads" ("The Quarry"), "a chipped flint" ("Imago"), "hydrocarbon" ("Or Consider Prometheus," "The Dahlia Gardens"), a town ("What the Light Was Like"), shopping malls ("Urn-Burial"), language ("Losing Track of Language," "Syrinx").

In "The Woodlot," barbed wire fencing is examined as a human imposition on the prairie landscape, although it proves no barrier to storms "swigging up whole farmsteads" (*CPAC* 57). Reaching back to a time prior to the extension of barbed wire across North America, Clampitt finds in the cellarholes that gave shelter in such storms "the earliest memory," a vestigial trace of early humans huddling against elemental forces. This she calls "a blue cellarhole / of pure astonishment" that precedes not only barbed wire but "I/you, whatever that conundrum may yet / prove to be."

The human scene becomes much darker in other poems found in the first volume, such as "Or Consider Prometheus," "Berceuse," and "The Dahlia Gardens" (*CPAC* 89, 95–96), where Clampitt meditates more explicitly on the horrors of culture in the twentieth century, extensions, it seems, of barbed wire. Using Jonathan Swift's Yahoo/Houyhnhnm template for human and nonhuman intelligence in the first of these poems, she contemplates "the great cetaceans, Houyhnhnm / intelligences sans limbs," asking herself and the reader what they might think of the human drive to consume their flesh for fuel, what their response might be to "the trypots / readied for their rendering." From the posited whale point of view, even in the post-whaling era the Western project with its "hunger for the sun" is imagined as unrelentingly destructive. Humans are "fire-drinking vampires of hydrocarbon." In "Berceuse," Clampitt sardonically ponders the role of art after the Nazi concentration camps, coupling the act of listening to a cradle-song by Chopin with the now-extinguished "furnaces of Auschwitz," which tourists now visit: "The purest art has slept with turpitude." The berceuse becomes apocalyptic, and sleep synonymous with moral decay. In "The Dahlia Gardens," commemorating the self-immolation of Norman Morrison in front of the Pentagon in 1965 (endnote, *CPAC* 441), Clampitt juxtaposes the two concepts of nature and culture erroneously separated in and by a society whose existence absurdly hinges on petroleum. The flowers in the garden, what E.O. Wilson would call a microwilderness (*Creation* 18), are "parts of a system that seems, on the face of it, / to be all waste, entropy, dismemberment," but which is

>   enjambed
> without audible clash, with no more than a whiplash
> incident, to its counterpart, a system
> shod in concrete.

Nature, argues Clampitt, will continue on completely indifferent to whatever enterprises humans care to carry on: it will "continue neither / to own nor altogether to refuse the burning filament / that runs through all our chronicles, uniting / system with system one terrible mandala."

Facing the Ocean: Beyond Western Culture

In the seminal "What the Light Was Like" (*CPAC* 119), an elegy for lobsterman Ernest Woodward, Clampitt extends her reach even farther out beyond the shore — the "out there" envisioned in the opening poems of *The Kingfisher*— imagining the lobster grounds as a place outside the pale of human existence represented by "the Baptist spire / shrunk to a compass- / point":

>   for all the labor
> it took to put it there, it's finding, out in that ungirdled
>   wallowing and glitter,
> finally, that what you love most is the same as what you're
>   most afraid of— God.

The overwhelming moment described here constitutes the farthest point out in Woodward's daily quest, the poem having already chronicled the journey "past first the inner and then the outer bar." The lobstermen are portrayed as mystics of the deep who work in "the core of that / day-after-day amazement," described at the core of the poem itself. It is only from this far-flung point of view, where Lorca's *duende* reigns supreme, that the fragility and limitations of Western culture become most obvious. Here, indeed, Clampitt implicitly reaffirms the Puritan settlers' anxieties, their fearsome sense of dislocation, as well as the practical desire to return to the created place called *home*: "Out there, from that wallowing perspective, all comparisons / amount to nothing." The homeward journey towards comfort and order creates an emotional reversal to the outward one (which the lobstermen know so well) into the unknown, where the onset of panic is never far off.

The "out there" takes on greater intensity and depth as the narrator of "What the Light Was Like" reveals how Woodward fails one day to return with the other boats that "had chugged back through the inlet." As the poem marks the death of this lobsterman who is finally found, Christ-like, "on the third day" in a "restricted area, off limits for / all purposes but puffins'," it simultaneously establishes and fulfills Clampitt's metaphor for poetry's purpose and destiny: "to imagine what"

> the light out there was like, that's always shifting — from
>   a nimbus gone beserk
> to a single gorget, a cathedral train of blinking, or
>   the fogbound shroud
>
> that can turn anywhere into a nowhere. But it's useless.

The singularly (for Clampitt) simple statement — "But it's useless" — emphasizes both the futility and impracticality of trying to imagine what it is like to die, that ultimate "out there" that all must one day come to know.

As Clampitt cites Emily Dickinson in an epigraph for *A Silence Opens,* "The Outer — from the Inner / Derives its Magnitude —." "Syrinx," the first poem in this last volume, re-establishes Clampitt's attempt to understand and come to terms with *duende* precognitively (*CPAC* 363). The term *syrinx* itself, defined by the *OED* as "1. An ancient musical instrument.... 2. *Archæol. Pl.* Narrow rock-cut channels or tunnels, esp. in the burial

vaults of ancient Egypt ... [and] 3. *Ornith*. The organ of voice in birds,"
evokes the inarticulate, the magnitude of the "out there," as Clampitt compares it in all three of its denotations to the grammatical, describable order
apparent in syntax:

> Syntax comes last, there can be
> no doubt of it: came last,
> can be thought of (is
> thought of by some) as a
> higher form of expression:
> is, in extremity, first to
> be jettisoned: as the diva
> onstage, all soaring
> pectoral breathwork,
> takes off, pure vowel
> breaking free of the dry,
> the merely fricative
> husk of the particular, rises
> past saying anything.

Like poetry at its best, the aria constitutes the exception to the rule of
human culture — the ability to reach "above the threshold, the all- / but
dispossessed of breath." In Homer, it is the "gibbering / *Thespesiae iach-
ē*," which Clampitt glosses in an endnote as a quotation from A.T. Murray's translation of *The Odyssey* (XI: 34–43) where Odysseus invokes the
dead, "thronging in crowds about the pit from every side, with a wondrous cry."[103] Clampitt also finds traces of the numinous in nature, especially (as she demonstrates repeatedly) "in the throat of a bird." Here is
"air / in a terrible fret," as Clampitt invokes the widespread, ancient asso-
ciation of both wind and bird with death. What precisely the archetypal
bird sings becomes a cultural construct, an imposition of structure, a reading:

> Is it *o-ka-lee*
> or *con-ka-ree,* is it really *jug jug,*
> is it *cuckoo* for that matter? —
> much less whether a bird's call
> means anything in
> particular, or at all.

Apart from the obvious avian influences of Keats, Eliot, and Bishop,
Clampitt for our purposes also recalls Bradstreet's yearning for escape rep-

resented by Philomel in "Contemplations," unconsciously acknowledging
how birdsong precedes and presages language (and thus culture with all
its contraints and agendas); how language (and with that, again, all things
cultural) originates in the inarticulate, which may or may not mean "anything in / particular, or at all." In Clampitt's earlier poem, "Notes on the
State of Virginia," the mockingbird "sings in all weathers" and is

> ignorant of royal grants, crests,
> charters, sea power, mercantile
> expansion, the imperative to
> find an opening, explore, exploit,
> and in so doing begin to alter,
>
> with its straking smudge and smear,
> little by little, this opening in
> the foliage, wet brink of all our
> enterprise [*CPAC* 282].

Earlier still, in "A Hermit Thrush," Clampitt, having characteristically
visited an isthmus at low tide, ponders a thrush's "unbroken music":

> From what source (beyond us, or
> the wells within?) such links perceived arrive —
> diminished sequences so uninsistingly
> not even human — there's
> hardly a vocabulary left to wonder, uncertain
> as we are of so much in this existence [*CPAC* 274].

Perhaps, as Annie Dillard suggests, it is not so much what birdsong "means"
as what it invites us to ask that is important:

> The real and proper question is: Why is it beautiful?... Beauty itself is the
> language to which we have no key; it is the mute cipher, the cryptogram,
> the uncracked, unbroken code. And it could be that for beauty, as it turned
> out to be for French, that there is no key, that "oui" will never make sense
> in our language but only in its own, and that we need to start all over again,
> on a new continent, learning the strange syllables one by one [106–07].

A new continent of beauty is, indeed, the subject of Clampitt's "Discovery" which, following "Syrinx," sees her continuing to reach into the
"out there" — "the actual going invisible" — and juxtaposing that with the
familiar, "the cozy mythologies we've / swindled ourselves with" (*CPAC*
364). The juxtaposition here is between Disney and manatees that have
"come upriver / to Blue Spring," but it is complicated by both the pres-

ent and the past: by the liftoff of the space shuttle *Discovery* as well as by Juan Ponce de León's much earlier "discovery" of Florida in 1513. Like the seal in Bishop's "At the Fishhouses," which the speaker half-jokingly perceives as enjoying old hymns, Clampitt's manatees, inevitably it seems, invoke old stories and images:

> As they came up for air,
>
> one by one, they seemed numb,
> torpid, quite incurious. No
> imagining these sirenians
> dangerously singing. Or
> gazing up yearningly. (So much
> for the Little Mermaid.) True,
> the long-lashed little ones
> might have been trademarked
> Cute by the likes of Walt Disney.

The speaker's voice here bristles with anger and amazement at the literal world "over that way," the amusement park whose images (outlining what is attractive and what is not) have been stamped on much of nature, and whose myth of "taking things easy" has a lineage going back to Ponce de León, Columbus's comrade, who found the Floridian coastline by way of searching for the fountain of youth.

The poet also wonders, though, whether the technology of an aggressive, expansionist culture might still make "the cozy mythologies" come true: "sun-kissed nakedness / on the beach, year-round, guilt-free / hibiscus and oranges." "[W]e keep / looking up" to what the celebrated spaceshuttle astronauts might find, just as Renaissance Europe harbored myths of exploration and colonization — El Dorado, the Fountain of Youth, the Northwest Passage. Clampitt wonders whether these are placebos or part of reality. The astronauts — "out of their / element, jacketed, lolling / and treading" — are analogous to the manatees, "lolling, jacketed, elephantine." The implication, again, is that culture extends from nature rather than stands over against it. Like the lobstermen in "What the Light Was Like," the astronauts are priestly and mystic, venturing into the ocean of space in a craft Clampitt calls "the fabulous itself," which

> could be seen
> unwieldily, jacket by jacket,
> in the act of shedding, as

a snake does its husk, or
a celebrant his vestments.

Clampitt's question — "What are we anyhow, we warmth- / hungry, breast-
seeking animals?" — seems to discard the fallacy that humans are somehow
different, or above, the natural order,[104] even as she describes yet another
act of extension into the unknown on behalf of an acquisitive culture.
Here again is the familiar narrative of westward-trekking humanity, only
this time it is the colonization of the outer atmospheric envelope of the
planet, buttressing Barry Lopez's comment that "the history of Western
exploration of the New World in every quarter is a confrontation with an
image of distant wealth" (Lopez 312). Clampitt's poem ends with another
kind of image, however: of one of the manatees reaching out "across the
wet, warm, / dimly imaginable tightrope" to "let itself be touched," suggesting perhaps a unified cosmos ("one terrible mandala") and not some
bifurcated order of things or a hierarchy with humans at the top. Her
image holds out a measure of hope, but without the danger of a "facile
consolation" (Schama 18) implicit in the end of Bishop's "The Moose."
Besides the fact that here Clampitt is careful to note that it is a single
manatee who reaches out to "discover" the canoe, the poem resonates with
enough disturbing truth about nature and culture to obviate any easy con-
clusions.

"Matoaka," the fifth poem in the collection, continues Clampitt's
meditation on Western technological culture, this time casting an eye
backwards to the now legendary Matoaka: "A woman's name, though /
not the one we know her by, / or imagine we do.... Pocahuntus, well formed
but / wanton, still a child" (*CPAC* 369). Clampitt's use of the word *wanton*, like her use of both aboriginal and English place names, highlights
again America's genesis in cultural imperialism and genocide (Horowitz
94–95); but it also recalls Bradstreet's subversive use of the same word in
"Contemplations" to describe the lives of fish as wild and ungovernable.
The names and stories surrounding and attached to Matoaka, argues
Clampitt, "keep changing": from "A king's / daughter as advocate ... from
which / we've since recoiled / (we being history) in favor of / the hidden,
discreditable motive, / the flagrant fib." The fib is found in John Rolfe's
marriage to Matoaka, which David Horowitz describes as "a political stroke
for the colony": "The wedding was followed by a series of treaties between
the colony and the Powhatan tribes, signifying their submission to King

James and his Virginia deputy" (Horowitz 95). The marriage was, in fact, a "nonaggression treaty" (Mann 45). It is no coincidence, Clampitt implies, that John Rolfe "planted the golden weed that one day / would amount to money." Intensive tobacco farming, together with the introduction of the European honey bee and domesticated farm animals, constituted "a multilevel ecological assault on North America" (Mann 44). Taken to England, Matoaka, "renamed in Christ, / Rebecca," was the "chief show-piece / of colonial bravado."

Beyond this tracing of events, however, Clampitt finds silence in the place names of Virginia and England: and "There in London / a silence opens," this the silence of Matoaka "brought face / to face with majesty, / with empire," acknowledging only Captain Smith, "and Jamestown":

> as for his countrymen (in what tone
> and with what gesture?), they were a people
> that often lied.

> Details are few. At Gravesend, readying
> for the crossing, aged twenty-one,
> she seemingly abruptly
> sickened and died.

Clampitt's unmistakable sarcasm finds its height in her indictment of "the shadowy predatory tentshow / we know as history," against which she finds only "Awe," which "is finally / what's durable." Whoever Matoaka was, finally, cannot be recovered: her true character is as buried in the accreted layers of "the stories / we tell ourselves" as are her bones in a tomb at Gravesend.

Clampitt's final poem, "A Silence," appropriately completes her brooding over *duende* and the possibility of transcendence (*CPAC* 432). The "out there" experienced at the moment of death, as she imagines it in "What the Light Was Like," is here given the sole focus. The speaker herself stands at the edge of the "uncodified," ready to describe what she has heretofore merely pointed towards: "a limitless / interiority" that she associates with T.S. Eliot's epiphanic experience at the age of twenty-one (see Clampitt's endnote to the poem, *CPAC* 458) and that Harold Bloom says "seems to have arisen from Clampitt's impulse to converse with T.S. Eliot at his poetic origins" (Bloom 182). Bloom, in fact, points out how "a limitless / interiority" "engages the Western trope of the ever-growing inner self" and sees the poem "locat[ing] itself in the blank between '(we shall be changed)' and 'a silence opens'" (Bloom 181–82).

The poem, lacking Clampitt's usual deployment of the conventions of syntax and rhetoric, reaches intensely for a way to articulate what is "past parentage or gender / beyond sung vocables." Hence it begins with an utterance like the Homeric one Clampitt refers to in "Syrinx," like the underworld she translates in "The Underworld of Dante," or like the "fabrications" interrogated in "Brought From Beyond," where the poet asks the magpie and the bowerbird, "O Marco Polo and Coronado," where the shapes and forms of existence originate:

> where do
> these things, these
> fabrications, come from — the holy places,
> ark and altarpiece, the aureoles,
> the seraphim — and underneath it all
> the howling? [*CPAC* 377].

As she also asks in "A Procession at Candlemas," "What is real except / what's fabricated?" Such questions, for Clampitt, indicate rhetorical openings, gestures implying her willingness to believe in the transcendence that her last poem explicitly embraces:

> beyond the woven
> unicorn   the maiden
> (man-carved   worm-eaten)
> God at her hip
> incipient
> the untransfigured
> cottontail
> bluebell and primrose
> growing wild   a strawberry
> chagrin   night terrors
> past the earthlit
> unearthly masquerade
>
> (we shall be changed)
>
> a silence opens

This unusual — for Clampitt — open form contains within it a parenthetical text that complements and questions the metamorphosis observed in nature, the "transient / greed to reinvest":

(man-carved   worm-eaten)
*   *   *   *   *
(we shall be changed)
*   *   *   *   *
                    (revelation
kif   nirvana
syncope)
*   *   *   *   *
(George Fox
was one)

The parenthetical evokes the interior reality already noted in several of Clampitt's other important poems. It acts here as a spiritual analogue to the biological transformation of "the larval feeder / naked hairy ravenous," while the familiar nod to Bishop via the word *isinglass* signals another vital — this time literary — subtext, first introduced in "The Cove," which Clampitt is saying, here at the end of her life's work, has not been forgotten. Her use of the word *kif,* as Bloom explains, "mean[s] either Indian hemp or the pleasure caused by smoking it" and is conjoined with "revelation," "nirvana," and "syncope" to try to evoke what Clampitt anticipates in her own death.

If change in nature now becomes a tell, an emblem for transcending nature, the legacy of Elizabeth Bishop remains firmly in place, even though Clampitt entirely discards the modernist irony found in "Over 2,000 Illustrations."[105] Indeed, in her last poetic utterance Amy Clampitt returns full circle to what Helen Vendler, in connection to this poem, calls the "pursuit of the absolute," which so preoccupied and perplexed the fiercely insecure community of Anne Bradstreet and the Winthrop Fleet, looking for a "bulwark against the ultimate insufficiency of beauty and history alike" (Vendler 111).

Notes

1. Now a common concept in Post-Colonial studies, "westward expansion" as it is employed in this book comes from the opening chapter of Frederick Jackson Turner's *The Frontier in American History* (1920); also Roderick Nash's 1973 revised publication, *Wilderness and the American Mind* (24).

2. As Carolyn Merchant puts it in *The Death of Nature* (1989), "Nature-culture dualism is a key factor in Western civilization's advance at the expense of nature" (143).

3. The ecological stakes, in my view, transcend questions about the American canon nicely raised by Timothy Morris. See *Becoming Canonical in American Poetry* (1995), 165. My purpose in this study is to read Bishop and Clampitt not just against one another but in terms of Bradstreet. The cultural, religious, and ecological connections (to name a few) between these three poets are telling. Examining them together can, it is hoped, provide an instructive, critical North American narrative of where we are in terms of where we have been.

4. See page xxi.

5. "Green to very door," however, could also be viewed as describing precisely what is needed on a global scale; what is being questioned here is the Romantic view of nature.

6. See, for instance, Wilson's *The Future of Life* (2002), 106–07; John A. Livingston's *Rogue Primate* (1995); also James Lovelock's *The Revenge of Gaia* (2006).

7. See Robert Pogue Harrison, *Forests: The Shadow of Civilization* (1992); Max Oelschlaeger, *The Idea of Wilderness: From*

Prehistory to the Age of Ecology (1991); and Clive Ponting, *A Green History of the World* (1991).

8. Paul Shepard supports the view that animal rights "patronizes life" (*Others* Shepard 505).

9. Carolyn Merchant notes "the Renaissance philosophy of the nurturing earth as well as those philosophies and social movements resistant to mainstream economic change" (*DON* 29).

10. A notable example of this occurred on May 31, 2007, when Senator Sam Brownback published an op-ed piece in the *New York Times* entitled "What I Think About Evolution."

11. Although he could also be — like the man who is an animal — an uncontrollable "outlaw" male living within a community.

12. See Joseph Conforti, *Saints and Strangers* (2006).

13. See Lynn White, "The Historical Roots of Our Ecological Crisis," *This Sacred Earth: Religion, Nature, Environment*, second ed. (2004); Peter Singer, *Animal Liberation*, second ed. (1990).

14. Chapters Four and Six of this study explore how both Bradstreet and Clampitt come to terms with this problem.

15. The term "*Grizzly Man* moment" is interchangeable with "Acteon moment." As I argue here, Timothy Treadwell is a kind of Acteon figure in his violent transformation by Diana in the form of a Kodiak bear. Later in this study, the term "Acteon moment" is used to refer to similar transformative or potentially transformative points in Bradstreet, Bishop, and Clampitt.

16. See page 36 as well as chapter 11 of E.O. Wilson's *Consilience* (1998) for an

overview of the problematic relationship between human systems of morality and nature.

17. I am indebted to Harrison for his eco-literary analysis of this myth.

18. Benyus's nine ways are, as she acknowledges, gleaned from the notebooks of ecologists:

Nature runs on sunlight.
Nature uses only the energy it needs.
Nature fits form to function.
Nature recycles everything.
Nature rewards cooperation.
Nature banks on diversity.
Nature demands local expertise.
Nature curbs excesses from within.
Nature taps the power of limits [7].

19. Winthrop was Governor of New England from 1630 to 1649, "[e]xcept for three years when he was not elected" (Conforti 55).

20. See William Bradford, *Of Plymouth Plantation 1620–164,* ed. Samuel Eliot Morison, (New York: Alfred A. Knopf, 1959).

21. A gloss on the chart states: "Very likely it is a tracing of a larger chart made by Governor Endecott's orders, and sent back to England as an aid to the *Arbella's* navigation" (Winthrop 281).

22. On page 4, Martin adds: "But she ultimately learned to control her agonizing skepticism by committing herself to the religious values of her culture."

23. The conflict between individual and communal values in Puritan New England has been the subject of much discussion; as such, it has a bearing on this and other chapters concerning Anne Bradstreet in this study. See Michael Zuckerman, "Identity in British America," *Colonial Identity in the Atlantic World, 1500–1800,* ed. Nicholas Canny and Anthony Pagden, (Princeton: Princeton University Press, 1987), 130–31, 140–43; Michael Kammen, *People of Paradox: An Inquiry Concerning the Origins of American Civilization,* (1972; rpt. New York: Oxford University Press, 1980), 23–30, 112–116, 169–204; Virginia Dejohn Anderson, *New England's Generation: The Great Migration and the Formation of Society and Culture in the Seventeenth Century,* (New York: Cambridge University Press, 1991), 89–121; and Martin, 26–7 and 65.

24. Scholarship increasingly emphasizes the heterogeneity of community life in seventeenth-century New England, against which Puritans posited a monolithic ideal (Conforti 3).

25. The masculine pronoun is used here only because a woman was not expected to assert herself— which was Anne Bradstreet's lifelong challenge.

26. Wendy Martin writes that "Thomas Dudley was so angered by his daughter's [Sarah Keanye] conduct that he disinherited her" (59). Concerning dissidence in general, see Dudley's "Letter to the Countess of Lincoln," *Chronicles of the First Planters of the Colony of Massachusetts Bay,* ed. Alexander Young (Boston: Charles C. Little & James Brown, 1846), 315 & 331; also Stannard, 132–33; Martin, 16–17; Anderson, 118. Regarding the Hutchinson scandal, see Conforti 93.

27. Bercovitch quotes here from a text called *The Ancient Bounds* (1645).

28. I am indebted to Peggy Samuels for her fascinating article, "Imagining Distance: Spanish Explorers in America," *Early American Literature* (Vol. 25, No. 3, 1990), 233–252.

29. See Cressy 193–244; Anderson 18; Stannard 123; Ziff 80–82; White 157–169; and Kammen 125–132.

30. Anne Bradstreet's brother-in-law, John Woodbridge, arranged the publication of *The Tenth Muse* in England in 1650 without Bradstreet's knowledge (White 252–57).

31. As Kenneth Requa states: "It is no surprise in a poem by an American Puritan that Old England acknowledges New England to be the current source of truth and knowledge" (Requa 155). See also Conforti 60–64 for a portrait of gender relations in early seventeenth-century New England.

32. See Cressy 74–81, 100–102, 140; Stannard 96; and Zuckerman 143–44.

33. C.V. Wedgewood states: "The supporters of each side in the political struggle recognized the need for propaganda that would strike home quickly to men's minds.... From the outbreak of the war even some poets who were highly skilled in the fashionable manner of the 1630s adopted a simple, even a crude, form of writing when

their intention was to defend the cause ... to as wide a public as possible" (White 165).

34. How much Anne Bradstreet willingly participates in the ideological warfare waged by Puritans is a question that will be discussed further on.

35. Controversy exists over the nature and extent of post-Restoration retribution against the Fifth Monarchy plotters. B.S. Capp devotes a whole chapter to the subject, extensively delineating "severe persecution under Charles II and James II": "Strict censorship and a ban on religious meetings outside the Established Church returned not far behind the king" (195). Wilfrid Prest notes executions, purges, espionage, censorship, and show trials, but qualifies the notion of a "general reign of terror" after 1661 (37).

36. Simon Bradstreet's transcription of his mother's "Meditations Diuine and morall" provides the chronology for most of her later poems. "Bradstreet ... documents — with dates, happily, in many cases — the highs and lows of her life throughout the manuscript book" (McElrath, Jr. & Robb xxx–xxii).

37. Stannard: "Edmund S. Morgan has shown how this 'due distance' worked in both directions, as when Benjamin Colman's daughter Jane wrote to her father requesting forgiveness for the 'flow of affections' evident in some of her recent letters. Colman ... commended her" (57–58).

38. Stannard sees this instability beginning with the eruption of civil war in England, which "brought in its wake an offical doctrine of religious toleration" (123). This was further exacerbated by migration back to England, the deaths of the leaders of the first generation, the failure of Christ to return by mid-century, and the growing material wealth of New Englanders. William J. Scheick supports this view in his intriguing "Tombless Virtue and Hidden Text: New England Puritan Funeral Elegies." He sees growing instability especially after 1660 (see 289–291), when New England Puritan elegies "plumb the depths of the collective self" (290). By comparison, "Extant English funeral elegies do not depict society as a collective self" (291).

39. I am indebted to Mawer for his thorough analysis of Bradstreet's elegy for Elizabeth as well as for his insightful exposition of the wide array of critical viewpoints. See "'Farewel Dear Babe': Bradstreet's Elegy for Elizabeth," in *Critical Essays on Anne Bradstreet*, ed. Pattie Cowell and Ann Stanford (Boston: G.K. Hall & Co., 1983), 205–218.

40. Wendy Martin also draws a parallel between Bradstreet's elegy for Elizabeth and Jonson's "On My First Son," although without making my point that Bradstreet's poem more than merely "[resembles] Elizabethan elegies such as Ben Jonson's"; instead, I argue that we are invited to interpret her elegy as subverting the Puritan convention on one's attitude to the death of a loved one (Martin 70–71).

41. Randall Mawer supports such a reading with his very careful analysis of Bradstreet's use of "his" in this line (Mawer 214).

42. The term "rogue primate" is taken from the title of John A. Livingston's 1994 book, *Rogue Primate: An Exploration of Human Domestication*, which won the Canadian Governor General's Award for nonfiction in 1995.

43. See also Guy Rotella, *Reading and Writing Nature* (1991); Thomas J. Travisano, *Her Artistic Devlopment* (1988); and Cheryl Walker, *God and Elizabeth Bishop* (2005).

44. Including her mother's nervous breakdown and committment to a sanitorium, and Bishop's traumatic removal at the age of six from the home of her maternal grandparents in Great Village, Nova Scotia, to that of her staid paternal grandparents in Massachussetts.

45. Bishop would also visit the Galapogas Islands and Darwin's house in Kent, England. See also Peter Matthiessen's notable account of his journey through South America, *The Cloud Forest* (1961).

46. To be sure, these accounts also recall Bishop's aborted trip to the Straits of Magellan.

47. Susan McCabe takes a slightly different angle: "[Bishop] laments the repetition of the conjunction 'and' and its lack of signifying power, but then proceeds to rejuvenate it.... We must make do with our linking 'ands'" (McCabe 132–33).

48. Simon Schama makes an intriguing point about how his book *Landscape and*

Memory is made of "good wood pulp." He goes on to describe the wood-books created by Germans in the eighteenth century: "By paying homage to the vegetable matter from which it, and all literature, was constituted, the wooden library made a dazzling statement about the necessary union of culture and nature" (Schama 19). Obviously, for Schama the gap between text and site does not need to be there.

49. This was identified by Professor Richard Morton, who also sees the poem as comic: "Cortez puts up a cross and kills everyone in sight — the Misses Bishop and Breen worry about smuggling whiskey!" (letter to the writer, 9 September 1994).

50. In conversation with the writer, July 1990, Nistowiak Falls, Saskatchewan.

51. See "A Procession at Candlemas" (*CPAC* 21), "A Hairline Fracture" (45), "Exmoor" (46), "Beethoven, Opus III" (50), "The Quarry" (55), "Imago" (59), "The Reservoirs of Mount Helicon" (77), "Letters from Jerusalem" (93), "The Burning Child" (101), "What the Light Was Like" (119), "Witness" (128), "Urn-Burial and the Butterfly Migration" (132), "Voyages" (160), "Losing Track of Language" (180), "The Sacred Hearth Fire" (186), "Ano Prinios" (200), "Babel Aboard the Hellas International Express" (255), "John Donne in California" (279), "Dallas-Fort Worth: Redbud and Mistletoe" (286), "At a Rest Stop in Ohio" (290), "Iola, Kansas" (291), "Westward" (297), "My Cousin Muriel" (331), "Nothing Stays Put" (339), *The Prairie* (343), "Manhattan" (402), "Homeland" (418), and "Sed de Correr" (420).

52. See, for example, "A Procession at Candlemas" (*CPAC* 21), "Witness" (128), "At a Rest Stop in Ohio" (290), and "Iola, Kansas" (291). Bishop's "The Moose" is discussed in Chapter Five of this volume.

53. See Connelly 61: "At the festival called the Chalkeia, the priestess of Athena Polias was among those who set the warp for the weaving of Athena's new peplos."

54. Joan Breton Connelly argues that "The process through which Christianity distanced itself from Greco-Roman cult practice, and the conspicuous leadership of women within it, attests to the very potency of Greek feminine priesthoods. They seem

to have posed a real threat in the eyes of the early church fathers" (264). See *Portrait of a Priestess* (2007).

55. Just how crucial Clampitt's project is is underscored by Carolyn Merchant in *The Death of Nature* (1989), when she states: [I]n America the nature-culture dichotomy was basic to the tension between civilization and the frontier in westward expansion and helped to justify the continuing exploitation of nature's resources. Much of American literature is founded on the underlying assumption of the superiority of culture to nature. If nature and women, Indians and blacks are to be liberated from the strictures of this ideology, a radical critique of the very categories *nature* and *culture*, as organizing concepts in all disciplines, must be undertaken [144].

56. Of the former, Blake Morrison, writes: "*Westward*, like her earlier three books, is forever turning up connections and continuities [between the Old and New Worlds]" (Morrison 30).

57. Clampitt herself glosses *punto in aria:* "The needlepoint lace known as *punto in aria*— literally, 'a stitch in the air'— originated in Venice, according to the *Columbia Encyclopedia*, as laceworkers ventured beyond purely geometric designs on a ground of netting to freer ones with no ground at all" (*CPAC* 455).

58. In the long poem *The Prairie*, at the end of *Westward*, Clampitt writes of her father's father "alone in the vast stammer of the inarticulate" (*CPAC* 348).

59. See also "Witness" (*CPAC* 128) for an earlier minor poem treating the theme of travel by bus in a single sentence.

60. *The Concise Oxford Dictionary* calls the boysenberry "a hybrid of several species of bramble" named after a 20th-century American horticulturist.

61. Livingston describes what may be viewed as the "settled continent" (*Rogue Primate* 33).

62. Writing about the connection between memory and migration, biologist Lyall Watson remarks: "No individual zebra or wildebeest inherits a route map for the awesome annual migration across the plains of Serengeti. The movement to ancestral

feeding grounds along traditional paths is a pattern of group behaviour, a kind of social memory that gets passed on down through all the generations. This is cultural inheritance, which has nothing to do with the genes, though it may serve their purpose by enhancing chances of survival" (Watson 236).

63. There is also something akin here to James Merrill's "A Tenancy," in which he recalls waiting

In my old clothes, in the first of several
Furnished rooms, head cocked for the
kind of sound
That is recognized only when heard
[Merrill 116].

64. See the Introduction to *The Complete Works of Anne Bradstreet*, xi–xxii.

65. See also Carolyn Merchant, *The Death of Nature*, 131, for her analysis of the impact of Old Testament perceptions of nature on reformers such as Calvin and the New World Puritans.

66. See John Canup's *Out of the Wilderness: The Emergence of an American Identity in Colonial New England* (1991); also Carolyn Merchant's *Reinventing Eden: The Fate of Nature in Western Culture* (2003).

67. See Marx 42; McKibben 49; Nash *WATAM* 9–24; Merchant *DON* 131; R.P. Harrison 61.

68. The rest of this well-known poem confirms the sense of the first line, i.e., "She was ours / In Massachusetts, in Virginia, / But we were England's, still colonials...."

69. Marianne Moore is quite arguably one of the great modernists immediately preceding Bishop; it is, however, crucial to my argument in the next chapter to show how Bishop writes against the tradition represented by these male poets. "At the Fishhouses" certainly constitutes a departure from the more detached perspective on nature and culture offered, say, by Wallace Stevens in "Anecdote of the Jar" or part two of "The Auroras of Autumn."

70. "Contemplations," to be sure, does give prominence to the theme of impermanence, but it does so in order to highlight the Christian concept of the immortality of the human soul. I am indebted to Guy Rotella's suggestive reading of "At the Fishhouses." Rotella, however, goes no further

than to demonstrate that the poem — in terms of a religious tradition — is ambiguously mystical and that it "recalls" an older order of "religious and transcendental poems" (223). To be sure, Rotella's reading of "At the Fishhouses" invites just this kind of analysis (Rotella 220–223).

71. And by drawing on "A Mighty Fortress is Our God" as an especially important link between these two poems, I am attempting to clarify just how we might read not only Bishop but Clampitt as well in terms of the religious ethos of Bradstreet's time.

72. Taken from the preface to *Magnalia Christi Americana*, ed. Kenneth B. Murdock (Cambridge, Mass.: Harvard UP, 1977), 50.

73. The meanings of terms like *wild* and *wilderness* are discussed in the introduction to this book. Note also that Lyall Watson has written a book about the dark side of nature. One statement in particular echoes that of Puritan clergyman, Thomas Hooker, who advised against the "study of curiosity," pitting "garden knowlege" against "wild knowledge," which is where the next chapter begins. Watson writes: "Nothing is necessary to study such things but curiosity and a willingness to concede that nature has a dark side that deserves as much attention as we already lavish on wildflowers, butterflies, rainbows and sunsets" (Watson 4).

74. Boorstin's description of what the 17th-century New England landscape must have been like contrasts with the ornate character of "Contemplations": "To reach these inhospitable meeting-houses, the early New Englander often had to pick his way, sometimes for miles, across landscape without anything that could be dignified as a road. In winter he went plunging through drifts; in the spring and fall he was deep in mud" (15). See also Conforti 58.

75. See The Harvard University Hymn Book (Cambridge, Mass.: Harvard UP, 1964), #190 for Frederick H. Hedge's 1852 translation. "Ein' feste Burg ist unser Gott" conveniently follows Hedge's version in the hymnal.

76. See Ian Bradley, *The Penguin Book of Hymns* (London: Penguin, 1989), 5–8; and Armin Haeussler, *The Story of Our Hymns: The Handbook to the Hymnal of the Evangel-*

ical and Reformed Church (St. Louis: Eden Publishing House, 1952), 312–316.

77. See Sacvan Bercovitch's analysis of the important links between Luther and Puritanism (*The Puritan Origins of the American Self* 9–11).

78. Writing about the domestication of wild animals, John A. Livingston makes a statement that could also be applied to the landscape: "To domesticate some nonhuman being, literally, is to bring it into our house" (Livingston 15).

79. Stanford argues that even certain suggestions of wilderness — such as stanza eight's "pathless paths" — are part of the garden paradigm ("Emblematic Garden" 245).

80. See also Merchant *DON* 18–20.

81. Lyall Watson sees the Biblical Cain as a signature for evil within nature itself (see his Chapter Six, "The Mark of Cain: The Identity of Evil" in *Dark Nature*).

82. Like Cain, transgressors were often branded, and certainly, in contradistinction to the Massachusetts Law Code of 1648, based on "humanitie, civilitie and christianity" (Canup 46), they were made outcast and looked on as beast-like. See Canup's chapter two, "The Disafforestation of the Mind." This is also intricately related to Livingston's description of pseudospeciation (Livingston 55–56).

83. Marx makes this point while discussing the "hideous wilderness." The term *decreation* is coined and used by Simone Weil in her essays on God and suffering (Weil 92).

84. Whose purely instinctive nature anticipates Amy Clampitt's bird in the last chapter, and Elizabeth Bishop's seal in the succeeding one.

85. See Stanford, *Worldly Puritan,* 143; Oser, 199.

86. Merrill writes: "I was talking about Elizabeth Bishop and wondering what sets her apart from the male giants — Eliot, Pound, Wallace Stevens — who seem in their life's work to transcend human dimensions: somehow wondering whether the light that philosophy casts made a greater shadow on the wall behind them. I kept clinging to the idea of Elizabeth with her sanity and level-headedness and quirkiness of mind" (Merrill 9).

87. "Dwelling Without Roots: Elizabeth Bishop," *Grand Street,* Fall (1990), 102. The essay can also be found in *Minotaur: Poetry and the Nation State* (London: Faber, 1992), 190–203.

88. As Rotella points out, the speaker "gives the sea consciousness and takes it away with 'as if,' [suggesting] a swelling to significance that may be nothing more than an indifferent tidal swing" (220). It may also be a recognition of the "other" in nature.

89. The poem arguably distinguishes between the Baptist and Lutheran traditions in the "total immersion" section. As Bishop herself notes in in one of her letters (*Letters* 307), "A Mighty Fortress" is not a Baptist hymn, and neither Protestant tradition is strictly aligned with Puritanism, although all three have strong theological ties to each other. Admittedly, I am passing over this distinction as my interest here is to read "At the Fishhouses" in the context of early American Puritanism.

90. And she goes on to remark, "the poet knows better than to believe in the uncomplicated vision of women and nature promoted by the romantic tradition" (Lombardi 98–9).

91. Cecilia Tichi discusses John Winthrop's distinction between "carnal naturalism and cultivated civility": "Puritan planters [justified] appropriation of New World lands on the basis of aboriginal failure to improve it.... Failure to make a civilizing impress upon the land they claimed would cancel their self-defined, biblically interpreted rights to those lands" (9 & 11).

92. Gimbutas sees the fish bladder as synonymous with uteri in goddess cultures (81, 234, 273).

93. I use the term *nature* here in the classical sense of the word *natura,* meaning (as I have indicated in the Introduction) cosmos, this world, existence as we know it.

94. And as she told Patricia Morrisroe in 1984, "Younger poets have several decades to produce their life's work. I don't" (Morrisroe 47).

95. In this, J.D. McClatchy is right when he states: "she is not, strictly speaking, an overly 'formal' poet.... One gets the sense from Clampitt's poems of both attention paid and amplitude given" (McClatchy 314).

96. Transhumance is discussed in Chapter Three.

97. It would be well for readers to recall at this point the etymology of the word *wilderness* discussed in the Introduction to of this volume.

98. J.D. McClatchy sees a strong connection also to Marianne Moore's "A Grave," arguing that Clampitt's use of the word *gravely* is not an accident either (McClatchy 318).

99. But also just as obviously connected to, and influenced by, nineteenth-century Transcendentalism.

100. In making the statement that the arts are "full of what is profoundly unnatural," Northrop Frye is alluding to Edmund Burke's difficulty with finding a source in nature for the powerful human urge to create art.

101. Like the Puritans, Lyall Watson clearly chooses the first option in his book, *Dark Nature*.

102. See Clampitt's endnote to "Good Friday" (439).

103. (*CPAC* 456). Ennis Rees translates "wondrous cry" as "the weirdest of wails and shrieks, and I turned / A ghastly pale olive with fear" (Rees 174), while E.V. Rieu renders it "a moaning that was horrible to hear. Panic drained the blood from my cheeks" (Rieu 172). Virgil describes the entrance to the underworld as "a cleft in the flank of the Euboean Rock forming a vast cavern. A hundred mouthways and a hundred broad tunnels lead into, and through them the Sibyl's answer comes forth in a hundred rushing streams of sound" (Virgil 148).

104. See also "A Whippoorwill in the Woods" (*CPAC* 313) where Clampitt compares human and bird behaviors.

105. "A Silence" also recalls Bishop's last Poem, "Sonnet," with its "creature divided" (*Complete Poems* 192).

Bibliography

Anderson, Virginia Dejohn. *New England's Generation: The Great Migration and the Formation of Society and Culture in the Seventeenth Century.* New York: Cambridge University Press, 1991.

Auden, W.H. *Selected Poems.* Ed. Edward Mendelson. London: Faber, 1979.

Banks, Charles Edward. *The Winthrop Fleet of 1630.* Baltimore: Genealogical Publishing, 1968.

Baring, Anne, and Jules Cashford. *The Myth of the Goddess: Evolution of an Image.* London: Penguin, 1991.

Benyus, Janine M. *Biomimicry: Innovation Inspired by Nature.* New York: HarperCollins, 1997.

Bercovitch, Sacvan. *The Puritan Origins of the American Self.* New Haven: Yale University Press, 1975.

_____. *The Rites of Assent: Transformations in the Symbolic Construction of America.* New York: Routledge, 1993.

Berman, Morris. *The Reenchantment of the World.* 1981; rpt. New York: Cornell University Press, 1984.

Bishop, Elizabeth. *The Collected Prose.* New York: Farrar, Straus, Giroux, 1984.

_____. *The Complete Poems: 1927–1979.* 1979; rpt. New York: Farrar, Straus, Giroux, 1989.

_____. *One Art: Letters, Selected and Edited.* Ed. Robert Giroux. New York: Farrar, Straus, Giroux, 1994.

Bloom, Harold. "Poetry in Review." *The Yale Review.* Vol. 86, No. 1, January 1998, 179–184.

Bly, Robert. *American Poetry: Wildness and Domesticity.* New York: Harper & Row, 1991.

Boorstin, Daniel. *The Americans: The Colonial Experience.* New York: Vintage Books, 1958.

Bradford, William. *Of Plymouth Plantation 1620–1647.* Ed. Samuel Eliot Morison. New York: Alfred A. Knopf, 1959.

Bradley, Ian. *The Penguin Book of Hymns.* London: Penguin, 1989.

Bradstreet, Anne. *The Complete Works of Anne Bradstreet.* Ed. Joseph R. McElrath, Jr. and Allan P. Robb. Boston: Twayne, 1981.

Breen, T.H. *Puritans and Adventurers: Change and Persistence in Early America.* New York: Oxford University Press, 1980.

Canup, John. *Out of the Wilderness: The Emergence of an American Identity in Colonial New England.* Wesleyan University Press, 1990.

Capp, B.S. *The Fifth Monarchy Men: A Study in Seventeenth-century English Millenarianism.* London: Faber & Faber, 1972.

Carroll, Peter. *Puritanism and the Wilderness: The Intellectual Significance of the New England Frontier, 1629–1700.* New York: Columbia University Press, 1969.

Carson, Rachel. *Silent Spring.* 1962; rpt. Boston: Houghton Mifflin, 1987.

Chekhov, Anton. *The Steppe: The Story of a Journey. The Oxford Chekhov: Stories, 1888–1889.* Vol. IV. Trans. and ed. Ronald Hingley. Oxford: Oxford University Press, 1980. 13–96.

Clampitt, Amy. *Archaic Figure.* New York: Alfred A. Knopf, 1987.

_____. *The Collected Poems of Amy Clampitt*. New York: Alfred A. Knopf, 1998.

_____. *The Kingfisher*. New York: Alfred A. Knopf, 1983.

_____. *Predecessors, Et Cetera*. Ann Arbor: The University of Michigan Press, 1991.

_____. *A Silence Opens*. New York: Alfred A. Knopf, 1994.

_____. *Westward*. New York: Alfred A. Knopf, 1990.

_____. *What the Light Was Like*. New York: Alfred A. Knopf, 1985.

Clark, Kenneth. *Civilisation: A Personal View*. 1969; rpt. London: John Murray, 2005.

Colwell, Anne. *Inscrutable Houses: Metaphors of the Body in the Poems of Elizabeth Bishop*. London: The University of Alabama Press, 1997.

Conforti, Joseph A. *Saints and Strangers: New England in British North America*. Baltimore: The Johns Hopkins University Press, 2006.

Connelly, Joan Breton. *Portrait of a Priestess: Women and Ritual in Ancient Greece*. Princeton: Princeton University Press, 2007.

Costello, Bonnie. *Elizabeth Bishop: Questions of Mastery*. Cambridge: Harvard University Press, 1991.

Cressy, David. *Coming Over: Migration and Communication Between England and New England in the Seventeenth Century*. New York: Cambridge University Press, 1987.

Darwin, Charles. *The Voyage of the Beagle*. Intro. Walter Sullivan. 1836; rpt. London: Penguin, 1988.

Defoe, Daniel. *Robinson Crusoe*. Intro. Angus Ross. 1719; rpt. London: Penguin, 1985.

Deloria, Vine. *God Is Red: A Native View of Religion*. 1973; rpt. Golden, Co.: Fulcrum, 2003.

Dennett, Daniel C. *Darwin's Dangerous Idea: Evolution and the Meanings of Life*. New York: Touchstone, 1995.

Desai, Anita. "'Feng Sui' or Spirit of Place." In *A Sense of Place: Essays in Post-Colonial Literatures*. Ed. Britta Olinder. Goteborg: Gothenburg University, 1984.

Dillard, Annie. *Pilgrim at Tinker Creek*. New York: Harper & Row, 1974.

Dorst, Jean. *Before Nature Dies*. Trans. Constance D. Sherman. 1965; rpt. Boston: Houghton Mifflin, 1970.

Dudley, Thomas. "Letter to the Countess of Lincoln." *Chronicles of the First Planters*. Boston: Little & Brown, 1846. 301–343.

Eliade, Mircea. *Myth and Reality*. Trans. Willard R. Trask. New York: Harper & Row, 1963.

Eliot, T.S. *Collected Poems: 1909–1963*. London: Faber, 1963.

_____. "The Metaphysical Poets." *Seventeenth-Century Prose and Poetry*. Second Edition. Ed. F.J. Warnke and A.M. Witherspoon. New York: Harcourt Brace Jovanovich, 1982.

Fanon, Frantz. *The Wretched of the Earth*. Preface Jean-Paul Sartre. Trans. Constance Farrington. 1961; rpt. New York: Grove Press, 1963.

Fender, Stephen. *Sea Changes: British Emigration & American Literature*. Cambridge: Cambridge University Press, 1992.

Frost, Robert. *The Poetry of Robert Frost*. Ed. Edward Connery Lathem. New York: Henry Holt, 1975.

Frye, Northrop. *Words with Power: Being a Second Study of the Bible and Literature*. New York: Harcourt Brace Jovanovich, 1990.

Geddes, Gordon E. *Welcome Joy: Death in Puritan New England*. 1976; rpt. Ann Arbor: UMI Research Press, 1981.

Gimbutas, Marija. *The Language of the Goddess*. Foreword Joseph Campbell. San Francisco: Harper, 1991.

Goldensohn, Lorrie. *Elizabeth Bishop: The Biography of a Poetry*. New York: Columbia University Press, 1992.

Gore, Al. *An Inconvenient Truth*. Emmaus, PA.: Rodale, 2006.

Graves, Robert. *The White Goddess: A Historical Grammar of Poetic Myth*. 1948; rpt. London: Faber, 1961.

The Harvard University Hymn Book. Cambridge, Mass.: Harvard University Press, 1964.

Bibliography

Haeussler, Armin. *The Story of Our Hymns: The Handbook to the Hymnal of the Evangelical and Reformed Church.* St. Louis: Eden Publishing House, 1952.

Harrison, Robert Pogue. *Forests: The Shadow of Civilization.* Chicago: The University of Chicago Press, 1992.

Harrison, Victoria. *Elizabeth Bishop's Poetics of Intimacy.* Cambridge: Cambridge University Press, 1993.

Heaney, Seamus. *The Government of the Tongue: The 1986 T.S. Eliot Memorial Lectures and Other Critical Writings.* London: Faber & Faber, 1988.

Herzog, Werner, dir. *Grizzly Man: A True Story of a Life Gone Wild.* DVD. Lions Gate Films, 2005.

Hillman, James. *A Blue Fire: Selected Writings.* Ed. Thomas Moore. 1989; rpt. New York: HarperPerennial, 1991.

Horowitz, David. *The First Frontier: The Indian Wars & America's Origins: 1607–1776.* New York: Simon & Schuster, 1978.

Huxley, Aldous. "Wordsworth in the Tropics." *Collected Essays.* Toronto: Clarke, Irwin & Company, 1960.

Jewett, Sarah Orne. "A White Heron." *The Norton Anthology of American Literature, Vol. C, 1865–1914.* Seventh ed. Eds. J.C. Reesman and A. Krupat. New York: Norton, 2007.

Johnson, Samuel. *Samuel Johnson's Dictionary: Selections from the 1755 Work That Defined the English Language.* Ed. Jack Lynch. Delay Beach: Levenger Press, 2004.

Jonson, Ben. "On My First Son." *Seventeenth-Century Prose and Poetry.* Second Edition. Ed. F.J. Warnke and A.M. Witherspoon. New York: Harcourt Brace Jovanovich, 1982.

Kalstone, David. *Becoming a Poet: Elizabeth Bishop with Marianne Moore and Robert Lowell.* New York: Farrar Straus and Giroux, 1989.

Kammen, Michael. *People of Paradox: An Inquiry Concerning the Origins of American Civilization.* 1972; rpt. New York: Oxford University Press, 1980.

Kirby, Ken, prod. *Savagery and the American Indian: The Wilderness.* Videotape. BBC Television, 1991.

Leed, Eric J. *The Mind of the Traveler: From Gilgamesh to Global Tourism.* New York: Basic Books, 1991.

Light, Andrew. "Boyz in the Woods: Urban Wilderness in American Cinema." *The Nature of Cities: Ecocriticism and Urban Environments.* Ed. Michael Bennett and David W. Teague. Tucson: University of Arizona Press, 1999. 137–156.

Livingston, John A. *Rogue Primate: An Exploration of Human Domestication.* Toronto: Key Porter, 1994.

Lombardi, Marilyn May. *The Body and the Song: Elizabeth Bishop's Poetics.* Carbondale: Southern Illinois University Press, 1995.

_____, Ed. *Elizabeth Bishop: The Geography of Gender.* Charlottesville: University Press of Virginia, 1993.

Longenbach, James. "Answer to a Question." *The Yale Review.* Vol. 86, No. 1, January 1998.

Lopez, Barry. *Arctic Dreams: Imagination and Desire in a Northern Landscape.* 1986; rpt. New York: Bantam, 1989.

Lovelock, James. *Gaia: A New Look at Life on Earth.* 1979; rpt. Oxford: Oxford University Press, 2000.

_____. *The Revenge of Gaia.* London: Penguin, 2006.

MacKendrick, Paul and Howe, Herbert M., eds. "Introduction." Selections from Thucydides' *History. Classics in Translation, Vol. 1.* Madison: University of Wisconsin Press, 1952.

Mann, Charles C. "America, Found & Lost." *National Geographic.* Vol. 211, No. 5, May 2007, 32–55.

Martin, Wendy. *An American Tryptich: Anne Bradstreet, Emily Dickinson, Adrienne Rich.* London: University of North Carolina Press, 1984.

Marx, Leo. *The Machine in the Garden: Technology and the Pastoral Ideal in America*. London: Oxford University Press, 1964.

Mather, Cotton. *Magnalia Christi Americana; or, The Ecclesiastical History of New England*. New York: Russell & Russell, 1967.

_____. *The Wonders of the Invisible World*. The Norton Anthology of American Literature. 3rd Ed. Vol. 1. Ed. Nina Baym *et al*. New York: Norton, 1989. 217–222.

Matthiessen, Peter. *The Cloud Forest: A Chronicle of the South American Wilderness*. New York: Ballantine, 1961.

Mawer, Randall R. "'Farewel Dear Babe': Bradstreet's Elegy for Elizabeth." *Critical Essays on Anne Bradstreet*. Ed. Pattie Cowell and Ann Stanford. Boston: G.K. Hall, 1983. 205–218.

McCabe, Susan. *Elizabeth Bishop: Her Poetics of Loss*. University Park: The Pennsylvania State University Press, 1994.

McClatchy, J.D. "Amy Clampitt: The Mirroring Marryings." *White Paper on Contemporary American Poetry*. Columbia University Press, 1989.

McElrath, Jr., Joseph R., and Allan P. Robb. Introduction. *The Complete Works of Anne Bradstreet*. Boston: Twayne, 1981.

McKibben, Bill. *The End of Nature*. New York: Random House, 1989.

Merchant, Carolyn. 1980; rpt. *The Death of Nature: Women, Ecology and the Scientific Revolution*. San Francisco: HarperCollins, 1989.

_____. *Reinventing Eden: The Fate of Nature in Western Culture*. New York: Routledge, 2003.

Merrill, James. *From the First Nine: Poems 1946–1976*. New York: Atheneum, 1981.

_____. *Recitative*. Ed. J.D. McClatchy. San Francisco: North Point Press, 1986.

Miller, Perry, Ed. *The American Puritans: Their Prose and Poetry*. Garden City: Doubleday, 1956.

Millier, Brett C. *Elizabeth Bishop: Life and the Memory of It*. Berkeley: University of California Press, 1995.

Montaigne, Michel De. "On the Cannibals." *Four Essays*. Trans. M.A. Screech. London: Penguin, 1995.

Monteiro, George, Ed. *Conversations with Elizabeth Bishop*. Jackson: University Press of Mississippi, 1996.

Morris, Timothy. *Becoming Canonical in American Poetry*. Champaign, IL: University of Illinois Press, 1995.

Morrison, Blake. "The Cross-Country Poet." *The New Republic*. Vol. 203, No. 1, July 2, 1990, 29–32.

Morrisroe, Patricia. "The Prime of Amy Clampitt." *New York*. Vol. 17, No. 41, October 15, 1984, 44–8.

Nash, Roderick. *The Rights of Nature: A History of Environmental Ethics*. Madison: The University of Wisconsin Press, 1989.

_____. *Wilderness and the American Mind*. Revised ed. 1967; rpt. New Haven: Yale University Press, 1974.

Neumann, Erich. *The Great Mother: An Analysis of the Archetype*. Trans. Ralph Manheim. 1955; rpt. Princeton: Princeton University Press, 1991.

Oelschlaeger, Max. *The Idea of Wilderness: From Prehistory to the Age of Ecology*. New Haven: Yale University Press, 1991.

Oser, Lee. "Almost a Golden World: Sidney, Spenser, and Puritan Conflict in Bradstreet's 'Contemplations.'" *Renascence*. 52.3 (Spring 2000), 187–202.

Ovid. *Metamorphoses*. Trans. Charles Martin. New York: Norton, 2004.

Pascal, Blaise. *Pensées: Notes on Religion and Other Subjects*. Trans. John Warrington. London: J.M. Dent & Sons, 1960.

Paulin, Tom. *Minotaur: Poetry and the Nation State*. London: Faber, 1992.

Perkins, David. *A History of Modern Poetry: Modernism and After*. Cambridge: Harvard University Press, 1987.

Picchi, Debra. *The Bakairí Indians of Brazil: Politics, Ecology, and Change.* Prospect Heights: Waveland Press, 2000.

Piercy, Josephine K. *Anne Bradstreet.* New York: Twayne Publishers, 1965.

Pollack, Sidney, dir. *Jeremiah Johnson.* DVD. Warner Bros., 1972.

Ponting, Clive. *A Green History of the World.* London: Sinclair-Stevenson, 1991.

Popescu, Petru. *Amazon Beaming.* New York: Viking Penguin, 1991.

Prest, Wilfrid. *Albion Ascendant: English History 1660–1815.* Oxford: Oxford University Press, 1998.

Pynchon, Thomas. *V.* New York: Harper & Row, 1961.

Quinones, Ricardo. *The Changes of Cain: Violence and the Lost Brother in Cain and Abel Literature.* Princeton: Princeton University Press, 1991.

Ratzinger, Joseph Cardinal. *Seek That Which is Above: Meditations through the Year.* Trans. Graham Harrison. San Francisco: Ignatius Press, 1986.

Rees, Ennis, trans. *The Odyssey of Homer.* New York: Modern Library, 1960.

Requa, Kenneth A. "Anne Bradstreet's Poetic Voices." *Critical Essays on Anne Bradstreet.* Ed. Pattie Cowell and Ann Stanford. Boston: G.K. Hall, 1983. 150–166.

Richardson, Robert D., Jr. "The Puritan Poetry of Anne Bradstreet." *Critical Essays on Anne Bradstreet.* Ed. Pattie Cowell and Ann Stanford. Boston: G.K. Hall, 1983. 101–115. See also *Texas Studies in Literature and Language.* Vol. 9, 1970, 79–96.

Rieu, E.V., trans. *The Odyssey.* London: Penguin, 1946.

Rosenfeld, Alvin H. "Anne Bradstreet's 'Contemplations': Patterns of Form and Meaning." *Critical Essays on Anne Bradstreet.* Ed. Pattie Cowell and Ann Stanford. Boston: G.K. Hall, 1983. 123–136. See also *The New England Quarterly.* Vol. 43, 1967, 317–331.

Rosenmeier, Rosamond. *Anne Bradstreet Revisited.* Boston: Twayne, 1991.

Rosenthal, Elizabeth. "Vatican Penance: Forgive Us Our Carbon Output." *The New York Times.* September 17, 2007.

Rotella, Guy. *Reading and Writing Nature: The Poetry of Robert Frost, Wallace Stevens, Marianne Moore, and Elizabeth Bishop.* Boston: Northeastern University Press, 1991.

Samuels, Peggy. "Imagining Distance: Spanish Explorers in America." *Early American Literature.* Vol. 25, No. 3, 1990, 233–252.

Salter, Mary-Jo. Foreword. *The Collected Poems of Amy Clampitt.* New York: Knopf, 1998.

Schama, Simon. *Landscape and Memory.* Toronto: Random House, 1995.

Scheick, William J. "Tombless Virtue and Hidden Text: New England Puritan Funeral Elegies." *Puritan Poets and Poetics: Seventeenth-Century American Poetry and Practice.* Ed. Peter White. London: The Pennsylvania State University Press, 1985.

Schwartz, Lloyd, and Sybil P. Estess, Eds. *Elizabeth Bishop and Her Art.* Ann Arbor: The University of Michigan Press, 1983.

Schweninger, Lee. *John Winthrop.* Boston: Twayne, 1990.

Shakespeare, William. *The Tempest.* Ed. Northrop Frye. London: Pelican, 1978.

Shepard, Paul. *Nature and Madness.* San Francisco: Sierra Club Books, 1982.

_____. "*From* The Others: How Animals Made Us Human." *This Sacred Earth: Religion, Nature, Environment.* Second ed. Ed. Roger S. Gottlieb. New York: Routledge, 2004. 505–508.

Singer, Peter. *Animal Liberation.* Second ed. 1975; rpt. New York: New York Review, 1990.

_____. *One World: The Ethics of Globalization.* Second ed. New Haven: Yale University Press, 2002.

Smith, Anthony. *Explorers of the Amazon.* Chicago: University of Chicago Press, 1990.

Stanford, Ann. "Ann Bradstreet as a Meditative Writer." *Critical Essays on Anne Bradstreet.* Ed. Pattie Cowell and Ann Stanford. Boston: G.K. Hall, 1983. 89–96.

_____. "Anne Bradstreet: Dogmatist and Rebel." *Critical Essays on Anne Bradstreet.* Ed. Pattie Cowell and Ann Stanford. Boston: G.K. Hall, 1983. 76–88. See also *Puritan*

New England: Essays on Religion, Society, and Culture. Ed. Alden T. Vaughan and Francis J. Bremer. New York: St. Martin's Press, 1977. 287–298.

_____. "Anne Bradstreet's Emblematic Garden." *Critical Essays on Anne Bradstreet.* Ed. Pattie Cowell and Ann Stanford. Boston: G.K. Hall, 1983. 238–253.

_____. *Anne Bradstreet: The Worldly Puritan.* New York: Burt Franklin, 1974.

Stannard, David E. *The Puritan Way of Death.* London: Oxford University Press, 1977.

Steiner, Rudolf. *Bees.* Trans. Thomas Braatz. Gt. Barrington, MA.: Anthroposophic Press, 1998.

Stevens, Wallace. *The Collected Poems.* New York: Vintage, 1990.

Sweet, Timothy. *American Georgics: Economy and Environment in Early American Literature.* Philadelphia: University of Pennsylvania Press, 2002.

Thoreau, Henry David. *Walden and Other Writings.* Intro. Joseph Wood Krutch. New York: Bantam, 1962.

Tichi, Cecilia. *New World, New Earth: Environmental Reform in American Literature from the Puritans through Whitman.* New Haven: Yale University Press, 1979.

Travisano, Thomas J. *Elizabeth Bishop: Her Artistic Development.* Charlottesville: University Press of Virginia, 1988.

Turner, Frederick Jackson. *The Frontier in American History.* 1920; rpt. New York: Holt, Rinehart and Winston, 1962.

Vendler, Helen. "Imagination Pressing Back." *The New Yorker.* Vol. LXVII, NO. 16, June 10, 1991, 103–11.

Virgil. *The Aeneid.* Trans. W.F. Jackson Knight. London: Penguin, 1959.

Walker, Cheryl. "Anne Bradstreet: A Woman Poet." *Critical Essays on Anne Bradstreet.* Ed. Pattie Cowell and Ann Stanford. Boston: G.K. Hall, 1983. 254–261.

_____. *God and Elizabeth Bishop.* New York: Palgrave MacMillan, 2005.

_____. "In the Margin: The Image of Women in Early Puritan Poetry." *Puritan Poets and Poetics: Seventeenth-Century American Poetry and Practice.* Ed. Peter White. London: The Pennsylvania State University Press, 1985.

Watson, Lyall. *Dark Nature: A Natural History of Evil.* London: Hodder and Stoughton, 1995.

Watts, Alan W. *Nature, Man and Woman.* 1958; rpt. New York: Vintage, 1970.

Weil, Simone. *Waiting on God.* Trans. Emma Cranford. 1951; rpt. London: Collins, 1971.

Weis, Tony. *The Global Food Economy: The Battle for the Future of Farming.* London: Zed, 2007.

White, Elizabeth Wade. *Anne Bradstreet: The Tenth Muse.* New York: Oxford University Press, 1971.

White, Lynn. "The Historical Roots of Our Ecological Crisis." *This Sacred Earth: Religion, Nature, Environment.* Second ed. Ed. Roger S. Gottlieb. New York: Routledge, 2004. 192–201.

Winthrop, John. *Winthrop Papers, 1623–1630.* Vol. II. Ed. Stewart Mitchell. 1931; rpt. New York: Russell & Russell, 1968.

Williams, Raymond. *Culture and Materialism.* 1980; rpt. London: Verso, 2005.

Wilson, Edward O. *Consilience: The Unity of Knowledge.* New York: Vintage, 1998.

_____. *The Creation: An Appeal to Save Life on Earth.* New York: Norton, 2006.

_____. *The Future of Life.* New York: Vintage, 2002.

_____. "Manifest Ecology." *The Atlantic* November 2007: 30.

_____. "Problems Without Borders." *Vanity Fair* May 2007: 164–166.

Wordsworth, William. *Selected Poems and Prefaces.* Ed. Jack Stillinger. Boston: Houghton Mifflin, 1965.

Wright, Ronald. *Stolen Continents: The "New World" Through Indian Eyes Since 1492.* Toronto: Penguin, 1992.

Yeats, W.B. *Collected Poems.* London: MacMillan, 1982.

Bibliography

Ziff, Larzer. *Puritanism in America: New Culture in a New World*. New York: Viking, 1973.

Zuckerman, Michael. "Identity in British America." *Colonial Identity in the Atlantic World, 1500–1800*. Ed. Nicholas Canny and Anthony Pagden. Princeton: Princeton University Press, 1987. 115–159.

Index

217

Index

Index

Index